SPARKNOTES®

WORKOUT in SPANISH

SPARK PUBLISHING

Contributing writer: Rebecca Ortman
Illustrations by Christina Berg Renzi.

SPARKNOTES is a registered trademark of SparkNotes LLC.

Spark Publishing
A Division of Barnes & Noble
120 Fifth Avenue
New York, NY 10011
www.sparknotes.com

ISBN-13: 978-1-4114-9680-4
ISBN-10: 1-4114-9680-9

Library of Congress Cataloging-in-Publication Data

Workout in Spanish: Practice for the tricky rules of Spanish grammar / Illustrations by Christina Renzi.
    p. cm.—(Workout in)
 ISBN-13: 978-1-4114-9680-4 (pbk.)
 ISBN-10: 1-4114-9680-9 (pbk.)
 1. Spanish language—Grammar—Problems, exercises, etc. 2. Spanish language—Self-instruction. 3. Spanish language—Textbooks for foreign speakers—English. I. Renzi, Christina.

PC4112.5.W67 2007
468.2'421—dc22

2007028607

Please submit changes or report errors to www.sparknotes.com/errors.

Printed and bound in Canada

10 9 8 7 6 5 4 3 2 1

A Note from SparkNotes

There's a saying that goes, *if you can speak three languages, you're trilingual; if you can speak two languages, you're bilingual; and if you speak only one language, you're American.* If you're a student who dreams of bilingual fluency—or who just dreams of passing that Spanish final exam—you've come to the right place.

We've designed the *Workout In* series to be the hammer that helps you nail down your studies. The 100 workouts you're holding in your hands cover all of the trickiest grammar rules. Whether you're taking your first course in a language, moving from a beginner to an intermediate level, or coming back for a little refresher course, these bite-size lessons and power-packed exercises will give you the help you need.

This book is organized by subject, some of which include Nouns, Verbs, Adjectives, and Adverbs. Sample sentences show you how to apply these rules, and English translations and bolded text help you zero in on the words being discussed. The following features make it easy to navigate around trouble spots that are likely to cost you points on a test:

→ *¡Atención!* **boxes** provide tips and strategies to solidify your learning and alert you to potential pitfalls.

→ *La Excepción* **boxes** call out exceptions to the rules.

→ *Lenguaje en Práctica* **boxes** explain some of the quirkier rules or point out where a rule may differ from colloquial usage.

This format makes it easy for you to get the information you need most. But reading a bunch of rules on grammar will get you only so far. The key to learning any language is practice—and you'll get lots of practice with this book. To go with all the rules and fancy features, each workout includes several sets of exercises in a variety of formats, from fill-ins, translations, and matching questions to crossword puzzles, writing prompts, and personal profiles.

We've also included a glossary of irregular and special usage words, as well as a handy reference for general grammar terms (just in case you don't know your preterite from your past participle). So dig in. Whether you thumb through and find help in the areas you need it most or read it cover to cover, this book will give you what you need to get to the next level.

Contents

Special Verbs

Other

An Introduction to Spanish

More than 400 million people worldwide speak Spanish today. It's the predominant language in twenty countries, and many people across the globe learn Spanish as a second language. In fact, Spanish is the third most commonly spoken language after English and Chinese. According to the most recent U.S. Census, people of Hispanic origin constitute the largest racial or ethnic minority in the United States: about 14 percent of the total population. The number of Hispanics in the United States is expected to continue rising, making Spanish a very useful language to learn.

Spanish is a Romance language, as are French, Italian, Portuguese, and Romanian. The shared origin of these languages leads to many similarities in both sound and structure. The Romance languages originated from Vulgar Latin, the common language of the Roman Empire (not to be confused with Classical Latin, the language of the Roman elite). As regional languages were constantly evolving and changing (due primarily to contact with different language groups, such as Arabic or Germanic), Vulgar Latin morphed into several distinct languages. An early version of what we now know as Spanish was created when Vulgar Latin mixed with the Celtiberian language, a hybrid of the Iberian and Celtic languages spoken on the Iberian Peninsula.

In the year 1200, various regional dialects of Spanish existed. In response to this linguistic chaos, King Alfonso X of Spain decided to standardize Spanish across the peninsula. He chose the Castilian dialect as the official language of all governmental documents. In 1492, monarchs Isabella of Castile and Ferdinand of Aragon went one step further by making Castilian the official dialect of the entire kingdom. The Castilian dialect, which became standard in Spain's school systems and writing, is the language that we know as Spanish today. Nevertheless, other dialects still exist in Spain, including Catalan, Basque, and Galician.

Modern Spanish varies from region to region across the globe. The Spanish spoken in Madrid is slightly different from that spoken in Mexico City, Lima, or New York, just as the English spoken in London differs from that spoken in Sydney or Chicago. Accents are the most noticeable difference, but the meaning of some words and expressions varies as well. For example, in Puerto Rico, the word for bus is *guagua*, while in Ecuador, the word is for bus is *autobus*. (Interestingly enough, in Ecuador, *guagua* is an informal way of saying *baby,* originating from the indigenous Inca language, Quechua.) Still, most structures and vocabulary are identical from Spanish-speaking country to country, so differences might result in only slight misunderstandings. A good grasp of the basics allows you to converse with Spanish speakers across the world.

English and Spanish are both Indo-European languages (a family of hundreds of related languages in Europe and part of Asia). They belong, however, to separate branches of this broad group of languages: English belongs to the Germanic branch, and Spanish to the Italic. While the two language groups were developing into an early form of English and Latin (and later Spanish), speakers of both languages came into substantial contact with each other, due to trade, battle, and colonization. Consequently, many Latin words worked their way into the English language, accounting for similarities in words found in English and Romance languages such as Spanish.

Today, especially with the influence of technology, many English words are working their way into everyday Spanish (for example, *hacer clic* means *to click* and *internet* means *Internet*). Additionally, a hybrid referred to as Spanglish, in which Spanish speakers blend English and Spanish, is prevalent in areas with large Hispanic American populations, such as New York City and Miami. As with pure Spanish, Spanglish varies from region to region. New York City Spanglish is different from Los Angeles Spanglish, and both differ from Miami Spanglish.

Several types of emerging Spanglish dialects exist. In the most common variation, called code switching, a person speaks in a mixture of Spanish and English. For example, a code switching Spanglish speaker might say *Vamos a la library* (Let's go to the library) or *No estoy listo because I have to shower* (I'm not ready because I have to shower). In other variations, English words are pronounced and spelled in a Spanish style and used in place of Spanish words. For example, "Spanglish" speakers may say *lonche* rather than *almuerzo* (lunch), or *vacumear* instead of *pasar la aspiradora* (to vacuum). In another type of Spanglish, speakers use English syntax when speaking Spanish. For example, they might put the adjective before the noun, rather than after it, saying *Es una bonita muchacha* rather than *Es una muchacha bonita* (She's a pretty girl).

This intermingling of words and cultures shows no sign of abating. It's exciting to think about how the Spanish language will grow and transform in the future.

Spanish punctuation is very similar to English punctuation, with some notable exceptions.

Question marks (*signos de interrogación*) and exclamation marks (*signos de exclamación*) are used at both the beginning and end of a sentence. They are inverted when they appear at the beginning of a sentence.

¿Cuándo empieza el concierto de Maná?
When does the Maná concert start?

¡Estoy tan cansada!
I'm so tired!

La Excepción

If a question or exclamation within a sentence is merely a short part of it, then the punctuation marks frame only the emphasized question or exclamation.

Penélope Cruz es española, ¿verdad?
Penélope Cruz is Spanish, right?

Si estás listo, ¡vámonos!
If you're ready, let's go!

Periods (*puntos*) rather than commas are used to separate digits.

1.100 hormigas   →   1,100 ants

1.200.021 mosquitos   →   1,200,021 mosquitos

Commas (*comas*) rather than periods are used to indicate decimals.

1.342,30 dólares   →   1,342.30 dollars

In Spanish, the series comma—the one that separates the second-to-last item in a list and the Spanish forms of *and*—is not used.

*Estudio francés, química, **física y biología.***
I study French, chemistry, physics, and biology.

When writing dialogue, em dashes are used instead of quotation marks to indicate spoken words. Guillemet (French quotes) are also used for dialogue, but em dashes are preferred. Guillemet are more commonly used for quoted material that is not necessarily dialogue.

—¿Quieres salir a comer? —preguntó Manuel.
"Do you want to eat out?" asked Manuel.

«La verdad es que no tengo mucha hambre.»
"The truth is, I'm not very hungry."

Exercise 1

Rewrite the following figures using Spanish punctuation.

1. 4.5% _____

2. $3,041.10 _____

3. 1.02% _____

4. 2,501,034.03 _____

5. 99.98 _____

Exercise 2

Write out the following currency amounts in numbers.

1. two thousand forty Peruvian nuevo soles

_____

2. one hundred Mexican pesos and ten centavos

_____

3. thirteen hundred seven hundred twelve Venezuelan bolívares and eleven centavos

_____

4. four thousand seven hundred eighty three euros and four centavos

_____

5. seventy eight thousand four hundred fourteen Guatemalan quetzales and fifty five centavos

_____

Exercise 3

Add punctuation marks to the following exchanges. Be careful: The meaning will change depending on how you punctuate the conversations.

1. Julieta: me amas Romeo

Romeo: no puedo vivir sin ti

2. Señor Suárez: tienes un dólar

Señor Espinosa: no tengo 25 centavos

3. Aurelio: quieres ir a la discoteca

Elisa: no me parece mala idea

4. Mamá: no estás feliz Jaimito

Jaimito: no estoy feliz

5. Maristela: me quieres dejar

Juan: si no me quieres…

Exercise 4

Guillermo needs to borrow some money from Hernán. Insert the correct punctuation for the following dialogue.

Hernán me prestas dinero preguntó Guillermo

Para qué lo quieres contestó Hernán

Pues tengo una deuda dijo Guillermo

Y cuánto necesitas hermano

Necesito 1100 pesos

Tanto exclamó Hernán Estás loco Qué tipo de deuda es

Una deuda a mi novia Ayer salimos a comer fuimos al teatro y después a bailar

Soy tan bobo que me olvidé la billetera Y ahora Rosa espera el reembolso

1

2 Writing Elements *Accents*

Accent marks follow very specific and easy-to-memorize rules that native Spanish speakers are taught beginning in elementary school.

A *palabra aguda* is a word that is stressed on its final syllable. If a word is a *palabra aguda* that ends in *-n, -s,* or a vowel, an accent mark is placed on the final vowel.

| volcán | (vol-CAHN) | volcano |
| mamá | (mah-MAH) | mom |

A *palabra llana* (also referred to as *grave*) is a word that is stressed on its second-to-last syllable. If a word is a *palabra llana* that doesn't end in *-n, -s,* or a vowel, an accent mark is placed on the second-to-last vowel.

| fácil | (FAH-ceel) | easy |
| álbum | (AHL-boom) | album |

A *palabra esdrújula* has the stress on any syllable that comes before the second-to-last syllable. If a word is a *palabra esdrújula,* it always carries an accent on the stressed vowel.

| matemática | (mah-teh-MAH-tee-cah) | math |
| pájaro | (PAH-jah-roh) | bird |

Lenguaje en Práctica

Accent marks in Spanish, unlike in French, for example, do not change the sound of the vowels they accompany.

Exercise 1

Sort the following words into three bins: *palabras agudas, palabras llanas, palabras esdrújulas.* Use a dictionary, if necessary.

| computadora | película | biblioteca |
| canción | profesor | periódico |

Plabras Agudas	Plabras Lianas	Plabras Esdrújulas

Exercise 2

Determine whether the following words carry accents. Add them where necessary.

1. piscina
2. futbol
3. electronico
4. universidad
5. algodon
6. musica
7. silla
8. colchon
9. pantalla
10. portatil

Exercise 3

Match the clues in column A to the answers in column B.

	A		B
_____ **1.**	This *palabra* always carries an accent mark on the stressed vowel.		a. lápiz
_____ **2.**	This word carries an accent because it is a *palabra llana* and it doesn't end in *-n, -s*, or a vowel.		b. natación
_____ **3.**	This *palabra* has the stress on the last syllable.		c. esdrújula
_____ **4.**	This word carries an accent because it's a *palabra aguda* and it ends in *-n*.		d. llana
_____ **5.**	This *palabra* carries an accent if it ends in *-m*.		e. aguda

Exercise 4

Add accents where necessary.

Fatima Lopez tiene 28 años y vive en Queens, New York. Nacio en Mexico pero ha vivido en los Estados Unidos por quince años. Fatima enseña ingles a inmigrantes hispanos. A Fatima le gusta ayudar a la gente hispana. —Yo tambien tuve que aprender el ingles —dice—. Todos necesitamos un poco de apoyo.

Fatima tiene dos hermanos. Jose vive en Asuncion, Paraguay y Ramon vive en Puebla, Mexico. Fatima extraña a sus hermanos. —Quisiera vivir juntos como cuando eramos pequeños —dice—. Es dificil. Algun dia, si Dios quiere, viviremos, por lo menos, en el mismo pais.

2

Nouns *Gender*

All Spanish nouns have a gender: masculine or feminine. There is no set rule for determining noun gender: Each word must be learned separately. However, there are two indicators that help determine whether a noun is masculine or feminine: its ending and its meaning.

Endings for most nouns can be used to determine gender.

Masculine	Feminine
-o (el númer**o**)	-a (la tiz**a**)
-l (el barri**l**)	-ad (la libert**ad**)
-r (el sabo**r**)	-ción (la condi**ción**)
-aje (el person**aje**)	-sión (la deci**sión**)
	-umbre (la cost**umbre**)
	-ud (la sal**ud**)

Nouns that refer to males are always masculine.

el rey	the king
el toro	the bull

Nouns that refer to females are always feminine.

la actriz	the actress
la vaca	the cow

¡Atención!

Many masculine nouns that end in -o change to -a to form the feminine.

el tí**o** / la tí**a**	the aunt / the uncle
el hij**o** / la hij**a**	the son / the daughter

Exercise 1

Are the following words masculine or feminine? Sort them into the two bins below.

sabor	carrera
vaca	barril
camino	actriz
rey	libertad

Masculine	Feminine

Exercise 2

Change the nouns in boldface from masculine to feminine and vice versa. Be sure to change the article as well as the noun.

1. Mi **tío** vive en Nicaragua.

_____

2. **El rey** vive en un gran castillo.

_____

3. Mi **madre** está en casa.

_____

4. **La señora** Méndez es **profesora** de matemáticas.

_____

5. **La mujer** es **actriz**.

_____

Exercise 3

Provide nouns that fit each of the following rules.

1. Most nouns that end in *-o* are masculine:

_____

2. Most nouns that end in *-l* are masculine:

_____

3. Most nouns that end in *-aje* are masculine:

_____

4. If a noun refers to a male, it will be masculine:

_____

5. Most nouns that end in *-a* are feminine:

_____

6. Most nouns that end in *-ad* are feminine:

_____

7. Most nouns that end in *-ción* are feminine:

_____

8. If a noun refers to a female, it will be feminine:

_____

Exercise 4

Fill in the blanks in the letter below with the correct words. Be sure to match nouns with the correct article.

broma	ducha
novia	toalla
situación	baño
papel	consejo
mañana	hombre

Querida Daniela,

Te escribo porque necesito un (**1.**)_____ . ¡Estoy

en una (**2.**)_____ muy desagradable y no sé qué

hacer!

Esta (**3.**)_____ me levanté temprano. Fui al

(**4.**)_____ y me tomé una (**5.**)_____ bien

caliente. Pero cuando quise secarme no había ni siquiera

una (**6.**)_____. Miré alrededor del baño y ¡había

desaparecido también el (**7.**)_____ higiénico!

¿Podría haber sido mi (**8.**)_____? Pues anoche

nos peleamos. ¿Sería una (**9.**)_____? Soy un

(**10.**)_____ muy orgulloso…¡No puedo dejarle

ganar! Daniela, ¡ayúdame a engañarle a ella…!

Francisco

3

Not all Spanish nouns have straightfoward gender.

Nouns that end in *-ista* refer to people, and can be masculine or feminine depending on whether the person is male or female.

*el / la art**ista**,* the artist   *el / la pian**ista**,* the pianist

*el / la tur**ista**,* the tourist   *el / la dent**ista**,* the dentist

Nouns that end in *-e* also can be either feminine or masculine.

*el / la estudiant**e**,* the student
*el / la client**e**,* the client

Although nouns that end in *-l* are generally masculine, a few are feminine.

*la capita**l**,* the capital city   *la pie**l**,* the skin
*la mie**l**,* the honey   *la sa**l**,* the salt

Some nouns change meaning with a change in gender.

el cólera, cholera (M)
la cólera, anger (F)

el papa, pope (M)
la papa, potato (F)

el cura, priest (M)
la cura, cure (F)

el consonante, rhyming word (M)
la consonante, consonant (F)

el orden, arrangement (M)
la orden, order, command (F)

el capital, money (M)
la capital, capital city (F)

Exercise 1

Sort the following words into two bins based on their gender.

poema   mapa
idioma   papá
miel   capital
foto   mano

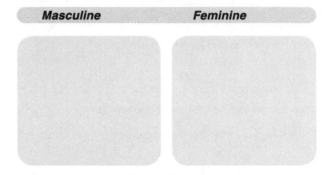

Masculine	Feminine

Exercise 2

Circle the masculine words and underline the feminine words. Then indicate how each deviates from the normal gender indicators.

1. día

_____

2. radio

_____

3. sal

_____

4. planeta

_____

5. moto

_____

6. piel

_____

Exercise 3

Match the clues in column A to the answers in column B.

	A		B
_____ **1.**	This is what cures a sickness or malady		a. la papa
_____ **2.**	This is a deadly disease spread in contaminated water or food		b. la cura
_____ **3.**	You might eat this with steak		c. el cura
_____ **4.**	This holy man lives in the Vatican		d. la cólera
_____ **5.**	This man gives sermons at your local church		e. el cólera
_____ **6.**	This is great anger		f. el papa

Exercise 4

Change the gender of the following nouns, making masculine nouns feminine and vice versa.

1. la artista _____

2. el client _____

3. el cura _____

4. la consonante _____

5. el capital _____

6. la tía _____

7. la hija _____

8. la conductora _____

9. el chico _____

10. la turista _____

Nouns *Number*

In English, the plural is generally formed by adding an *-s* to the end of a noun. Spanish nouns follow different rules according to their endings.

If a noun ends in a vowel, the plural is formed by adding *-s*.

el gat**o** → los gato**s**	the cat / the cats
la plum**a** → las pluma**s**	the pen / the pens

¡Atención!

The masculine singular definite article *el* becomes the plural *los*. The feminine singular definite article *la* becomes the plural *las*.

If a noun ends in a consonant, the plural is formed by adding -es. For nouns that end in -z, the -z is changed to a -c before adding -es.

el relo**j**→	los reloj**es**
	the watch / the watches
la actri**z** →	las actri**ces**
	the actress / the actresses

Singular nouns that end in -es do not change in the plural.

el miércol**es** → los miércol**es**
Wednesday / Wednesdays

When referring to a group that includes both masculine and feminine nouns, the masculine plural ending is used.

cuatro profesor**as** (four professors, f) + **un** profesor (a professor, m)
= *cinco profesor**es*** (five professors)

Exercise 1

Complete the crossword puzzle with Spanish plural forms suggested in the clues below.

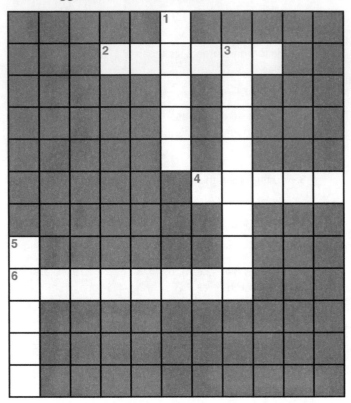

Across
2. Plural of Thursday (*jueves*)
4. Plural of law (*ley*)
6. Plural of actress (*actriz*)

Down
1. Plural of fish (*pez*)
3. Plural of exam (*examen*)
5. Plural of house (*casa*)

Exercise 2

Change the singular words to plural and the plural words to singular.

1. moneda: _____   **6.** conductores: _____

2. lápices: _____   **7.** computadoras: _____

3. mono: _____   **8.** actriz: _____

4. hermanas: _____   **9.** leopardo: _____

5. país: _____   **10.** nacionalidades: _____

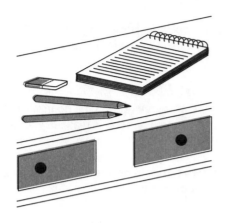

3. Hay dos _____ , un _____ y

un _____ en el escritorio.

Exercise 3

Complete the sentences based on what you see in the drawings.

1. Tengo tres _____ en mi mochila.

4. Hay cuatro _____ en el tren.

2. Hay tres _____ en la vitrina.

5

Articles *Definite Articles*

Definite articles point out something specific. Their English equivalent is *the,* as in *the desk* or *the dog.*

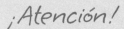

¡Atención!

Learning the article along with the noun will help you remember whether the noun is masculine or feminine.

Definite articles agree in gender and number with the nouns they accompany.

	Singular	Plural
Masculine	*el*	*los*
Feminine	*la*	*las*

La Excepción

When the definite article comes before a feminine noun that begins with *a-* or *ha-*, the singular masculine article is used. This is done to avoid the awkward double "a" sound. The noun is still considered feminine.

el agua (**the** water) → *las* aguas (**the** waters)
NOT: *la* agua

el águila (**the** eagle) → *las* águilas (**the** eagles)
NOT: *la* águila

When referring to a group that includes both masculine and feminine nouns, the masculine plural definite article is used.

las niñas (**the** girls)

el niño (**the** boy)
} *los* niños (**the** children)

When paired with the prepositions *a* (to) and *de* (of), the masculine singular definite articles form a contraction.

a + el → *al* (**to the**)
de + el → *del* (**of the**)

*Vamos **al** parque.*
Let's go **to the** park.

*La gorra es **del** señor.*
The hat is **the** man's.
(Literally, the hat is of the man.)

Exercise 1

Supply both the singular and plural definite articles for each set of words.

1. _____ diario: _____ diarios

2. _____ profesora: _____ profesoras

3. _____ bolígrafo: _____ bolígrafos

4. _____ águila: _____ águilas

5. _____ cuaderno: _____ cuadernos

6. _____ escuela: _____ escuelas

Exercise 2

Match the nouns in column A to their definite articles in column B.

A	B
_____ **1.** estudiante	a. las
_____ **2.** agua	b. los
_____ **3.** palabras	c. la
_____ **4.** nacionalidad	d. el
_____ **5.** reyes	e. el or la

Exercise 3

Correct the errors in the following sentences. Note: Some of the sentences do not have errors.

1. El casa de Laura es blanca.

   _____

   _____

2. Mañana vamos a el restaurante nuevo.

   _____

   _____

3. Los niños juegan en la plaza.

   _____

4. Las águilas comen ratones.

   _____

   _____

5. La agua está sucia.

   _____

   _____

6. Es la carro de el vecino.

   _____

   _____

Exercise 4

Imagine you're organizing a surprise birthday party for your friend. Make a list of items you need. Be sure you include the correct definite articles.

_____

_____

_____

_____

_____

_____

_____

_____

_____

_____

_____

_____

_____

_____

_____

_____

_____

_____

_____

_____

7 Articles *Indefinite Articles*

The indefinite articles *un*, *una*, *unos*, and *unas* are equivalent to the English *a*, *an*, and *some*. The indefinite article refers to something in a general sense. For example, in *a desk*, *a* refers to any desk, not a specific one.

Definite articles agree in gender and number with the nouns they accompany.

	Singular	Plural
Masculine	*un*	*unos*
Feminine	*una*	*unas*

La Excepción

When the indefinite article comes before a feminine word that begins with *a-* or *ha-*, the singular masculine article is used. This is done to avoid the awkward double "a" sound. The noun is still considered feminine.

un *agua* (**a** water) → **unas** *aguas* (**some** waters)

NOT: **una** *agua*

un *hacha* (**an** axe) → **unas** *hachas* (**some** axes)

NOT: **una** *hacha*

Use the masculine plural indefinite article when referring to a group that includes both masculine and feminine nouns.

unas *niñas* (some girls)
un *niño* (a boy)
} **unos** *niños* (**some** children)

The singular masculine form can also refer to the number one.

un *cuaderno* (**a** notebook / **one** notebook)

Exercise 1

Imagine you're at the library. The librarian is helping you find some resources for a history paper. Tell her what you need. Fill in the blanks with the correct indefinite articles.

1. _____ libros sobre la Segunda Guerra Mundial

2. _____ revista americana de junio de 1941

3. _____ artículo del periódico inglés durante la guerra

4. _____ fotos de Alemania en los años 40

5. _____ entrevista con un soldado italiano

Exercise 2

Fill in the blanks with the correct indefinite article.

Hoy fui con mi clase de biología a (**1.**)_____ museo muy interesante. Vimos los esqueletos de (**2.**)_____ dinosaurios de hace millones de años. ¡Había (**3.**)_____ dinosaurio que medía cerca de catorce metros de altura!

Luego fuimos al salón de insectos. Observamos (**4.**)_____ mariposas de todos los colores del espectro.

Vimos también (**5.**)_____ especie de bicho prehistórico que se parece mucho a la cucaracha de hoy en día.

Exercise 3

Imagine you're walking through a mall (*centro comercial*). Use the following construction to describe what you see: *hay* + indefinite article + *en* + definite article + noun. Write five sentences.

_____

_____

_____

_____

_____

_____

_____

_____

_____

_____

Exercise 4

Translate the following sentences into Spanish using the correct articles.

1. There's a girl in my class. _____

_____

2. I see some kids outside. _____

_____

_____

3. It's a literature course. _____

_____

_____

4. They are some of Pancho's [female] friends. _____

_____

_____

5. Do you want a pear or some bananas? _____

_____

_____

8 Adjectives *Gender and Number Agreement*

Adjectives modify, or describe, nouns. Adjectives must agree in gender and number with the nouns they modify.

Masculine adjectives usually end in *-o* and feminine adjectives usually end in *-a*.

el libr**o** viej**o**	the old book
la cas**a** viej**a**	the old house

Some adjectives don't end in *-a* or *-o*. These adjectives can generally modify either feminine or masculine nouns.

la tarea fáci**l**	the easy homework
el ejercicio fáci**l**	the easy exercise

Masculine adjectives that end in *-or* can be made feminine by adding *-a*.

un hombre hablad**or**	a talkative man
una mujer hablad**ora**	a talkative woman
un hombre trabajad**or**	a hardworking man
una mujer trabajad**ora**	a hardworking woman

If a noun is plural, its accompanying adjective should also be plural. To form the plural of an adjective that ends in a vowel, add *-s* to the end.

los libro**s** viej**os**	the old books
las casa**s** viej**as**	the old houses

To form the plural of an adjective that ends in a consonant, add *-es* to the end.

los hombres jóven**es**	the young man
las mujeres jóven**es**	the young woman

To form the plural of an adjective that ends in *-z*, change *-z* to *-c* and add *-es*.

el niño feli**z**	the happy boy
los niños feli**ces**	the happy boys

¡Atención!

Use the masculine plural ending to modify a group that includes both masculine and female nouns.

las niñ**as** travies**as**
(the mischievous girls)

los niñ**os** travies**os**
(the mischievous boys)

} **los** niñ**os** travies**os** (the mischievous children)

Exercise 1

Complete the crossword puzzle with the correct forms of the adjectives.

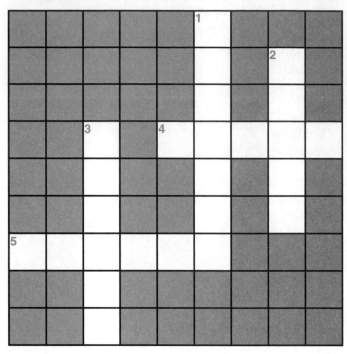

Across

4. unas muchachas _____ (*lindo*)

5. un estudiante _____ (*joven*)

Down

1. unos leones _____ (*feroz*)

2. una mesa _____ (*viejo*)

3. unos libros _____ (*bueno*)

Exercise 2

Choose the correct adjective to complete each sentence.

1. Mis clases están muy _____ este semestre.
   a. aburridos
   b. aburridas
   c. aburrida

2. ¡La señora Méndez es muy _____!
   a. antipática
   b. antipático
   c. antipáticas

3. Las gemelas son _____.
   a. rubios
   b. rubias
   c. rubio

4. ¡Qué _____ es tu novio!
   a. guapa
   b. guapos
   c. guapo

5. Plácido Domingo es _____.
   a. bajo y gorda
   b. bajos y gordos
   c. bajo y gordo

Exercise 3

Use your own adjectives to describe the following people. Use the following construction: person/s + es/son + adjective. Make sure your adjectives agree in number and gender with the nouns they modify.

1. Shakira _____

_____

_____

_____

2. Mis amigas _____

_____

_____

_____

3. Antonio Banderas _____

_____

_____

_____

4. Mis padres _____

_____

_____

_____

5. Enrique Iglesias _____

_____

_____

_____

Exercise 4

Imagine you meet someone interesting in a chat room. He or she only speaks Spanish. Luckily, this gives you an opportunity to practice. The person asks you to describe yourself. How do you do it? Write five sentences that describe your physical looks. Make sure the adjectives agree in number and gender with the nouns they modify.

1. _____

_____

2. _____

_____

3. _____

_____

4. _____

_____

5. _____

_____

8

Demonstrative adjectives distinguish one group of items from another, and are equivalent to the English *this, that, these,* and *those.*

¡Atención!

As with all adjectives, demonstratives must agree in number and gender with the nouns they describe.

Demonstrative adjectives change depending on the location of the object that the speaker is talking about. *Este (esta)* is used to refer to something that is close to the speaker.

Singular	
este libro	**this** book
esta pluma	**this** pen

Plural	
estos libros	**these** books
estas plumas	**these** pens

*¿Quieres **este** libro, o **estas** plumas?*
Do you want **this** book or **these** pens?

Ese *(esa)* is used to refer to something that is close to the listener.

Singular	
ese libro	**that** book
esa pluma	**that** pen

Plural	
esos libros	**those** books
esas plumas	**those** pens

*¿Quieres **esa** camisa, o **esos** pantalones?*
Do you want **that** shirt or **those** pants?

Aquel *(aquella)* is used to refer to something that is far from both the speaker and listener.

Singular	
aquel libro	**that** book
aquella pluma	**that** pen

Plural	
aquellos libros	**those** books
aquellas plumas	**those** pens

*¿Ves **aquel** pájaro? ¿Ves **aquellos** patos?*
Can you see **that** bird? Can you see **those** ducks?

Exercise 1

Insert the correct demonstrative adjective for the objects and locations described below.

1. An eraser sitting in front of you:

_____ *borrador*

2. A dictionary on a bookshelf at the other end of the room:

_____ *diccionario*

3. A pencil sitting on the desk next to yours:

_____ *lápiz*

4. Two pens in your hand: _____

plumas

5. Some maps on the wall furthest from you:

_____ *mapas*

6. A calculator in your lab partner's hand:

_____ *calculadora*

Exercise 2

Match the demonstrative adjectives in column A to their Spanish equivalents in column B. Use the context clues provided, and watch for gender and number agreement.

A   **B**

_____1. **that** student (at the other end of the library)   a. aquella

_____2. **these** compact disks (in my hand)   b. estos

_____3. **that** computer (that we saw in the store)   c. esta

_____4. **this** lesson (that we're doing right now)   d. esos

_____5. **those** papers (right over there)   e. aquel

Exercise 3

Complete the dialogue with the correct demonstrative adjectives. Pay close attention to the clues.

Vendedor: (**1.**) _____ discos compactos aquí cuestan 200 pesos. (**2.**) _____ en su mano cuesta 100.

Mirta: ¿Y por qué cuestan más (**3.**) _____?

Vendedor: Porque (**4.**) _____ fue importado desde los Estados Unidos.

Mirta: ¿Y (**5.**) _____ ahí, en la vitrina?

Vendedor: Pués (**6.**) _____ cuestan solo 50 pesos. ¡Son pirateados!

Possessive adjectives indicate possession, ownership, or relationship.

Possessive adjectives agree in gender and number with the nouns possessed, not with the possessors. These are the short forms.

Singular Nouns		
my	mi libro/mochila	my book/backpack
your (sing.)	tu libro/mochila	your book/backpack
his/her/ its/your (sing. formal)	su libro/mochila	his/her/ its/your book/backpack
our	nuestro libro nuestra mochila	our book/backpack
your (pl.)	vuestro libro vuestra mochila	your book/backpack
their/your (pl. formal)	su libro/mochila	their/your book/backpack

Plural Nouns		
my	mis libros/mochilas	my books backpacks
your (sing.)	tus libros/mochilas	your books backpacks
his/her/ its/your (sing. formal)	sus libros/mochilas	his/her/its/ your books/backpacks
our	nuestros libros nuestras mochilas	our books/backpacks
your (pl.)	vuestros libros vuestras mochilas	your books/backpacks
their/your (pl. formal)	sus libros/mochilas	their/your books/backpacks

Possessive adjectives can be placed either before or after the nouns they modify in sentences. If possessive adjectives are placed before the nouns, they should be in short form.

Mi carro es viejo.
No tengo mis libros hoy.

My car is old.
I don't have **my** books today.

When the possessive adjective comes after the noun, a long possessive adjective is used. The long possessive adjective is similar to *of*...in English.

Singular Nouns		Plural Nouns	
of mine	mío/mía	of mine	míos/mías
of yours	tuyo/tuya	of yours	tuyos/tuyas
of his, hers, its, yours (formal)	suyo/suya	of his, hers, its, yours (formal)	suyos/suyas
of ours	nuestro/ nuestra	of ours	nuestros/ nuestras
of yours (pl.)	vuestra/ vuestro	of yours (pl.)	vuestras/ vuestros
of theirs, yours (pl., formal)	suyo/suya	of theirs, yours (pl., formal)	suyos/suyas

Es una amiga mía.   She is a friend **of mine.**

There is little or no difference between the long and short forms of possessive adjectives. Use depends strictly on whether the possessive adjective is placed before or after the noun.

Es mi pluma.
It's **my** pen.

Es una pluma mía.
It's a pen **of mine.**

¡Atención!
Short possessive adjectives are more common in everyday speech. Long possessive adjectives are more common in literature.

Exercise 1

Match the phrases in column A to their Spanish translations in column B.

A	B
_____ **1.** my pencil	a. sus discos
_____ **2.** my pencils	b. tus cuadernos
_____ **3.** his discs	c. sus cuadernos
_____ **4.** her disc	d. mis lápices
_____ **5.** your notebooks	e. su disco
_____ **6.** their notebooks	f. mi lápiz

Exercise 2

Circle the nouns that these possessive adjectives can modify in their current form.

1. suyo: problema, primos, familia, dinero

2. tus: hijos, profesores, guitarra, oficina

3. nuestra: tía, animal, ventana, carro

4. vuestro: computadora, música, disco compacto, idea

5. mío: televisión, bolígrafo, residencia, madre

Exercise 3

Turn the short possessive adjectives into long ones, and the long possessive adjectives into short ones. It won't be a simple switch: You'll have to change the order of the words.

1. su computadora

_____

2. las llaves mías

_____

3. tu cámara

_____

4. el carro nuestro

_____

5. mi televisión

_____

6. la casa nuestra

_____

10

11 Adjectives *Placement*

In English, adjectives can come before or after the nouns they modify (as in *the new computer*), or after the noun in the case of *to be* phrases (as in *the computer is new*). In Spanish, placement depends on the actual adjective being used.

Descriptive adjectives, such as *guapo*, *hermosa*, or *delgada*, usually come after the nouns they describe.

*una actor **guapo***	a **good-looking** actor
*una actriz **hermosa***	a **beautiful** actress

Adjectives that indicate a number or quantity usually go before the nouns they describe.

***algunos** actores guapos*	**some** good-looking actors
***muchas** actrices hermosa*	**many** beautiful actresses

Demonstrative and possessive adjectives go before the nouns they describe.

***esta** clase aburrida*	**this** boring class
***nuestro** libro nuevo*	**our** new book

¡Atención!

Some adjectives change meaning depending on where they're placed in a sentence. *Gran* and *grande* are two examples.

*un **gran** evento* (a **great** event)
*un evento **grande*** (a **big** event)

Other common examples include:

*un **viejo** amigo* (a **longtime** friend)
*un amigo **viejo*** (an **elderly** friend)

*una **pobre** mujer* (a **pitiful** woman)
*una mujer **pobre*** (a woman **with no money**)

*el **único** álbum* (the **only** album)
*el álbum **único*** (the **unique** album)

Exercise 1

Unscramble the following sentences. Pay attention to adjective placement, gender, and number.

1. perro / este / travieso / es

_____

_____

2. una / simpática / vi / chica

_____

_____

3. son / mis / pesados / libros

_____

_____

4. estudiantes / difícil / inteligentes / los / examen / el / pasan

_____

_____

5. es / Salma Hayek / una / talentosa / actriz

_____

_____

Exercise 2

Correct the errors in the following sentences.
Note: Some of the sentences do not have errors.

1. Esta canción es buena.

_____

_____

2. Me gustan las rojas manzanas.

_____

_____

3. Mi mamá lee románticas novelas.

_____

_____

4. Compré un café dulce.

_____

_____

5. Mis estudiosos amigos sacan buenas notas.

_____

_____

Exercise 3

Match the English phrases in column A to their Spanish equivalents in column B. Keep in mind the placement of the adjectives.

A	B
_____ **1.** a great woman	a. un amigo viejo
_____ **2.** a large woman	b. un pobre niño
_____ **3.** a longtime friend	c. la camisa única
_____ **4.** an elderly friend	d. un niño pobre
_____ **5.** a pitiful boy	e. un viejo amigo
_____ **6.** a boy who has no money	f. una mujer grande
_____ **7.** the unique shirt	g. la única camisa
_____ **8.** the one and only shirt	h. una gran mujer

11

A pronoun replaces a noun in a sentence. A subject pronoun replaces a noun that is the subject of a sentence.

Andrew likes hamburgers. **He** likes hamburgers.

¡Atención!

Subject pronouns are not used as often in Spanish as in English. In Spanish, the subject of the sentence is usually clear based on the verb conjugation.

Subject pronouns identify the subject of the verb that they precede.

Singular		Plural	
yo	I	nosotros	we (M)
		nosotras	we (F)
tú	you	vosotros	you (pl. M)
usted	you (formal)	vosotras	you (pl. F)
		ustedes	you (pl., formal)
él	he	ellos	they (M)
ella	she	ellas	they (F)

Yo hablo español.	**I** speak Spanish.
Tú eres mi amigo.	**You** are my friend.
Ella es mi compañera de clase.	**She** is my classmate.
Usted es muy alto.	**You** are very tall.
Nosotros somos hermanos.	**We** are brothers.
Vosotros sois de España.	**You** are from Spain.
Ellas son de Bolivia.	**They** are from Bolivia.

¡Atención!

Note that there is no Spanish equivalent for the English *it*.

Lenguaje en Práctica

The *vosotros* form, while common in Spain, is not used in Latin America. In Latin American countries, the more formal *ustedes* is used in all situations.

Spanish has four subject pronouns that translate in English as you. These subject pronouns have specific uses.

Subject Pronoun	Use to Address...
tú	someone informally, such as a friend or younger person
usted	someone formally, such as a teacher, stranger, professional, or significantly older person
ustedes	1. two or more people formally or informally in Latin America 2. two or more people formally in Spain
vosotros/vosotras	two or more people informally in Spain

¡Atención!

Nosotros, vosotros, and *ellos* can refer to either a group of men or a group of men and women. *Nosotras, vosotras,* and *ellas* can refer only to a group of women.

Lenguaje en Práctica

The rules governing which pronouns to use to address people can vary enormously from country to country. To be safe, most people err on the side of formality (*usted/ustedes*). When in doubt, ask the person how he or she wants to be addressed.

Exercise 1

Fill in the table with the correct subject pronouns.

Person	Singular	Plural
I/we		Feminine: _____
	_____	Masculine: _____
you	Informal: _____	Feminine: _____
	Formal: _____	Masculine: _____
		Gender neutral: _____
he/she/they	Feminine: _____	Feminine: _____
	Masculine: _____	Masculine: _____

Exercise 2

Complete the equations with the correct subject pronouns.

1. *he* = _____

2. *I* = _____

3. *she* = _____

4. *you*, singular, informal = _____

5. *us*, feminine = _____

6. *you*, singular, formal = _____

7. *they*, masculine = _____

8. *you*, plural, masculine = _____

Exercise 3

Match the descriptions in column A to the appropriate subject pronoun in column B.

Use this subject pronoun to...

A	B
_____**1.** ...address two or more people informally in Latin America	a. vosotras
_____**2.** ...address a stranger on the bus	b. tú
_____**3.** ...refer to your two brothers	c. usted
_____**4.** ...address two or more of your girlfriends in Spain	d. ellos
_____**5.** ...address your younger brother	e. ustedes

Exercise 4

Would you use *tú* or *usted* with the following people? Sort the people into the appropriate bins.

your professor   your younger cousin
the bus driver   your father
a classmate   your elderly neighbor

Tú	*Usted*

12

Pronouns *Possessive Pronouns*

Possessive pronouns express something that is possessed. They replace a noun that is followed by a possessive adjective.

A possessive pronoun agrees in number and in gender with the noun it replaces.

	Masculine		Feminine	
	Singular	Plural	Singular	Plural
mine	*mío*	*míos*	*mía*	*mías*
yours	*tuyo*	*tuyos*	*tuya*	*tuyas*
his/hers/its/ yours (formal)	*suyo*	*suyos*	*suya*	*suyas*
ours	*nuestro*	*nuestros*	*nuestra*	*nuestras*
yours (informal)	*vuestra*	*vuestras*	*vuestra*	*vuestras*
theirs/yours (formal)	*suyo*	*suyos*	*suya*	*suyas*

*Aquí está mi **computadora**. ¿Dónde está la **tuya**?*
Here's my **computer.** Where's **yours**?

¡Atención!

Possessive pronouns have the same form as long possessive adjectives. The difference between the two forms is very subtle and can confuse the native speaker and second language learner alike. When you study possessive pronouns, remember that an adjective *modifies* a noun while a pronoun *replaces* a noun.

*Estas son las **películas tuyas**.* (noun+possessive adjective)
These are your movies.

*Estas son las **tuyas**.* (possessive pronoun)
These are yours.

In the first example, the adjective *tuyas* modifies the noun *películas*. In the second example, the noun *películas* has been replaced by *tuyas*.

Exercise 1

Select the correct possessive pronouns for the English nouns given.

1. her book:
   a. la suya
   b. el nuestro
   c. el suyo

2. our television:
   a. la nuestra
   b. el nuestro
   c. los nuestros

3. their keyboards:
   a. las suyas
   b. los suyos
   c. el suyo

4. your (plural) calendars:
   a. el tuyo
   b. los vuestros
   c. la míos

5. my computer:
   a. la mía
   b. las mías
   c. el mío

Exercise 2

Match the English possessive pronouns in column A to the Spanish equivalents in column B.

	A	B
_____	**1.** ours (plural, masculine)	a. mío
_____	**2.** yours (plural, feminine, formal)	b. suyo
_____	**3.** his (plural)	c. vuestras
_____	**4.** mine (singular, masculine)	d. tuyo
_____	**5.** yours (plural, feminine, informal, Spain)	e. nuestros
_____	**6.** yours (singular, masculine, informal)	f. suyas

Exercise 3

Fill in the blanks with the correct possessive pronoun.

1. A Julio le encanta su iPod nuevo pero a ti no te gusta el

_____.

2. Mi carro es un Toyota. ¿Señor Costa, de qué marca es el

_____?

3. Claudia olvidó sus llaves en el dormitorio. Por suerte no

nos olvidamos las _____.

4. El gato de Olivia es siamés. Yo también tengo un gato. El

_____ es persiano.

5. Mi pintor favorito es El Greco. Rosa y Jaime, ¿quién es el

_____?

13

27

The direct object of a sentence indicates who or what is receiving the direct action of the verb. A direct object pronoun replaces a direct objects noun in a sentence.

Direct object pronouns agree in gender and number with the nouns they replace.

Singular		Plural	
me	*me*	us	*nos*
you	*te*	you	*os*
him, it (M), you (formal)	*lo*	them (M), you (formal)	*los*
her, it (F), you (formal)	*la*	them (F), you (formal)	*las*

Direct object pronouns are ususally placed before the verb.

*Compro la **manzana**. **La** compro.*
I buy **the apple.** I buy **it.**

***Te** veo.*	I see **you.**
*José **la** ve.*	José sees **her.**
***Los** conozco bién.*	I know **them** well.
***Os** entiendo.*	I understand **you.**

¡Atención!

The personal *a* is used when the direct object is a person. The presence of the personal *a* following a verb can be used to identify the direct object in a sentence.

*Mauricio ve **a Federico**. Mauricio **lo** ve.*
Mauricio sees **Federico.** Mauricio sees **him.**

In negative sentences, the direct object pronoun comes between the verb and *no*.

*Maribel tiene **la llave**. Maribel **la** tiene.*
Maribel has **the key.** Maribel has **it.**

*Maribel no tiene **la llave**. Maribel no **la** tiene.*
Maribel doesn't have **the key.** She doesn't have **it.**

¡Atención!

Direct object pronouns may also be attached to the end of an infinitive.

Quiso **tomarla.**
*She wanted to **drink it.***

Exercise 1

Match the direct object pronouns in column A to their Spanish equivalents in column B.

A	B
_____ **1.** me	a. nos
_____ **2.** you (second person, plural, Spain)	b. los
_____ **3.** them (masculine)	c. me
_____ **4.** her	d. os
_____ **5.** us	e. la

Exercise 2

Correct the errors in the following sentences. Note: Some of the sentences do not have errors.

1. Teodoro escribe unas cartas postales. Teodoro las escribe.

_____

_____

_____

2. Alexandra escucha el CD de Jennifer López. Alexandra las escucha.

_____

_____

3. Lupe y Daniel miran el partido de la Copa Mundial. Lupe y Daniel las miran.

_____

_____

_____

4. Antonio lee las revistas. Antonio las lee.

_____

_____

_____

5. Vosotras estudiáis las lecciones. Vosotras los estudiáis.

_____

_____

_____

3. ¿Necesitas la calculadora, Paco?

_____

_____

_____

4. ¿Puedes oírme?

_____

_____

_____

5. ¿Cuándo van a ver la película?

_____

_____

_____

Exercise 3

Answer the following questions. In your answer, replace the noun with a direct object pronoun.

1. Iris, ¿tienes los discos compactos?

_____

_____

_____

2. ¿Dónde compraste los libros?

_____

_____

_____

14

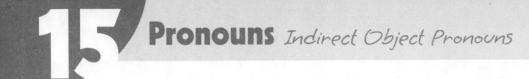

Pronouns *Indirect Object Pronouns*

The indirect object pronouns identify the indirect object of a sentence: who or what benefits from (or is harmed by) the action of the verb.

Indirect object pronouns take the place of both the preposition (*to* or *for*) and the indirect object noun. The indirect object pronoun agrees in number with the indirect object.

Singular		Plural	
to/for me	*me*	to/for us	*nos*
to/for you	*te*	to/for you	*os*
to/for him/ her/it/you (formal)	*le*	to/for them/ you (formal)	*les*

¡Atención!

The indirect object pronouns *le* and *les* are used for both masculine and feminine indirect objects.

An indirect object pronoun is usually placed in front of the verb. Unlike English speakers, Spanish speakers often keep the indirect object to clarify to whom the pronoun refers.

> Yo *le* escribo una carta *a Susana.*
> I write a letter **to Susana.**

> Tú *les* prestas dinero *a Martín y a Ramiro.*
> You lend money **to Martín and Ramiro.**

As in English, if the indirect object is understood, the indirect object noun can be dropped to avoid redundancy. In this case, only the indirect object pronoun is used in the sentence.

> Yo *le* escribo una carta.   I write a letter **to her.**
> Tú *les* prestas dinero.   You lend money **to them.**

¡Atención!

The prepositions *a* or *para* can be used to identify the indirect object of a sentence in Spanish. However, don't confuse the preposition *a* with the personal *a*, which is used with the direct object of a sentence.

*Le traigo una torta **a mi abuela.***
(preposition + indirect object)
I bring a pie **to my grandmother.**

*Mauricio ve **a Federico**.*
(personal *a* + direct object)
Mauricio sees **Federico.**

When the preposition *a* (to) precedes the third person indirect object (he, she, or it), the indirect object pronoun (*le* or *les*) is used along with the indirect object.

> *Le* doy una muñeca *a mi hermana.* (indirect object)
> I give a doll **to my sister.**

When *para* (for) precedes the indirect object, do not include the indirect object pronoun.

> *Compro una mesa **para la cocina.*** (indirect object)
> I buy a table **for the kitchen.**

¡Atención!

Indirect object pronouns may also be attached to the end of an infinitive.

dar (to give)
*Voy a **darle** un regalo.*
I'm going to give a presen **to her.**

Exercise 1

Answer true or false to the following statements about indirect object pronouns.

1. _____ To locate the indirect object of a sentence, look for the prepositions *a* and *para*.

2. _____ When *para* precedes the indirect object, include the indirect object *le* or *les*. For example: *Le hago una torta para mi hermana.*

3. _____ The indirect object pronoun *le* can replace the formal direct object *usted*.

4. _____ The third person singular indirect object pronoun is the same as the third person singular direct object pronoun.

5. _____ You can drop the indirect object noun if it's understood from context. For example: *Arturo le regala un peluche.* (You already know that *le* refers to Arturo's girlfriend.)

Exercise 2

Use the cues in parentheses to provide the appropriate indirect object pronoun for the sentence.

1. Juan _____ regala un álbum de fotos. (*to his parents*)

2. La niña _____ canta en español. (*to us*)

3. La profesora _____ enseña los verbos. (*to me*)

4. Nosotras _____ compramos una camiseta roja. (*for her*)

5. Yo _____ doy mi opinión solamente. (*to you, informal*)

Exercise 3

Use the prompts below to write three sentences about what your aunt bought for people. Use indirect object pronouns.

1. mis hermanos / diez discos compactos

   _____

   _____

2. yo / unos aretes de plata

   _____

   _____

3. su hija / una muñeca de porcelana

   _____

   _____

Exercise 4

Indicate whether each sentence requires the direct object pronoun or the indirect object pronoun.

A. direct object pronoun   **B. indirect object pronoun**

1. Irina compra unas arepas de maíz en el restaurante colombiano. Irina _____ compra.

2. Doy la regla a mi compañero. _____ doy la regla.

3. Mauricio ve a su hermana en el centro comercial. Mauricio _____ ve.

4. Mando un regalo a mis abuelos. _____ mando un regalo.

5. Mi papá tiene el dinero para la cena. Mi papá _____ tiene.

Exercise 5

Imagine you are being interviewed for a local Hispanic newspaper. Answer the following questions using indirect object pronouns.

Periodista: ¿A quién escribes mensajes electrónicos?

Respuesta: (**1.**) _____

_____

Periodista: ¿A quién mandas cartas postales?

Respuesta: (**2.**) _____

_____

Periodista: ¿A quién prestas tu computadora?

Respuesta: (**3.**) _____

_____

Periodista: ¿A quién comprarías un disco de Luis Miguel?

Respuesta: (**4.**) _____

_____

Periodista: ¿A quién regalarías un obsequio muy caro?

Respuesta: (**5.**) _____

_____

15

A verb may take both a direct object pronoun (*lo, la, los,* or *las*) and an indirect object pronoun (*me, te, le, se, nos, os,* or *les*). This combination is called a *double object pronoun.*

When both a direct and an indirect object pronoun appear in a sentence, the indirect object pronoun always comes first. Both pronouns precede the noun.

> *Compro un regalo y* **te** (indirect object pronoun) **lo** (direct object pronoun) *doy.*
> I buy a gift and I give **it to you.**

The direct object pronouns *le* and *les* change to *se* when followed by indirect object pronouns *lo, la, los,* or *las.*

Le *vendo la mochila.*	I sell **him/her** the backpack.
Se la *vendo.*	I sell **it to him/her.**
Les *compro los lápices.*	I buy **them** the pencils.
Se los *compro.*	I buy **them for them.**

Double object pronouns may also be attached to the end of an infinitive. In this case, an accent is always added to the stressed vowel of the infinitive.

Te lo *quiero comprar.*	I want to buy **it for you.**
Quiero **comprártelo.**	I want **to buy it for you.**

Exercise 1

Rewrite the following sentences and replace the phrases in boldface with pronouns.

1. Jaime me regaló **un anillo de oro.**

   _____

   _____

2. Tu padre te dio **un abrazo.**

   _____

   _____

3. Ustedes le prestaron **la computadora.**

   _____

   _____

4. Ellas te piden **más agua.**

   _____

   _____

5. El camarero nos sirve **los platos.**

   _____

   _____

Exercise 2

Reorder the words below to form complete sentences.

1. los / vendí / se

_____

_____

2. traemos / las / te

_____

_____

3. leertela / quiero

_____

_____

4. ¿guardáis / las / nos?

_____

_____

5. cantó / os / la

_____

_____

Exercise 3

Translate the following sentences into Spanish using double object pronouns.

1. He took an apple and gave it to me.

_____

_____

_____

2. Marisela sent the magazine to her brother.

_____

_____

_____

3. I want to lend them my car.

_____

_____

_____

4. Are you going to give it to us?

_____

_____

_____

5. I bought it and showed it to them.

_____

_____

_____

16

In addition to direct and indirect object pronouns, Spanish also uses prepositional object pronouns.

A preposition requires an object; a prepositional object pronoun replaces a noun that follows a preposition.

Las notas (noun) *son para* (preposition) ***Mercedes*** (noun).
The notes are for **Mercedes.**

Las notas (noun) *son para* (preposition) ***ella*** (prepositional object pronoun).
The notes are for **her.**

Prepositional object pronouns agree in number and gender with the objects they replace.

Singular		Plural	
mí	me	*nosotros*	we (M)
		nosotras	we (F)
ti	you	*vosotros*	you (pl. M)
		vosotras	you (pl. F)
usted	you (formal)	*ustedes*	you (pl., formal)
él	he	*ellas*	they (F)
ella	she	*ellos*	they (M)

¡Atención!

Except for *mí* and *ti*, the prepositional object pronouns are the same as the subject pronouns.

The preposition *con* (with) combines with *mí* and *ti* to form *conmigo* and *contigo*.

*¿Quieres ir al cine **conmigo**?*
Do you want to go to the movies **with me?**

La Excepción

The subject pronouns *yo* and *tú* (not the prepositional object pronoun) are used after the propositions *entre* (between, among), *excepto* (except for), and *según* (according to).

***Entre tú** y **yo**, ¡Ana está embarazada!*
Between you and **me,** Ana is pregnant!

Exercise 1

Complete the crossword puzzle with prepositional object pronouns. Use the clues.

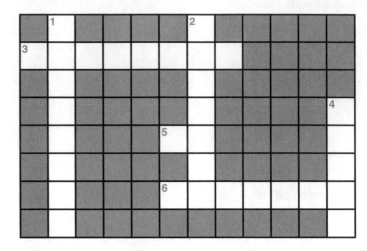

Across

3. First person, plural, masculine
5. First person, singular
6. Second person, singular, plus preposition *with*

Down

1. Second person, plural, masculine, Spain
2. First person, singular, plus preposition *with*
4. Third person, plural, masculine

Exercise 2

Use the cues to complete the sentences in column A with the correct prepositional object pronoun phrases in column B.

	A	B
_____	**1.** Este reloj es _____. (*for you,* singular, familiar)	a. conmigo
_____	**2.** Me gusta salir _____. (*with you,* plural, masculine, informal, Spain)	b. para ti
_____	**3.** ¿Vienes_____? (*with me*)	c. con ella
_____	**4.** Anoche la pasé muy bien _____ (*with her*)	d. para ustedes
_____	**5.** Compré las flores _____. (*for you,* plural, formal)	e. con vosotros

Exercise 3

Answer the following questions in complete sentences using the prepositional object pronoun.

1. ¿Quién está al lado de Dolores?

_____

_____

_____

2. ¿Quién está al lado de Juan Carlos?

_____

_____

_____

3. ¿Quién está delante de Raúl?

_____

_____

_____

4. ¿Con quiénes está cenando Andrea?

_____

_____

_____

5. ¿Con quiénes están cenando Raúl y Juan Carlos?

_____

_____

_____

17

Relative pronouns link two sentences that share a common element.

que	that, which, who
quien/quienes	who, whom, that
lo que	what, that which

*Conozco a una **mujer**. La **mujer** habla tres idiomas.*
I know a **woman**. The **woman** speaks three languages.

*Conozco a una mujer **que** habla tres idiomas.*
I know a woman **who** speaks three languages.

Que can refer to people or things. Unlike its equivalent in English (that), it cannot be ommited from the sentence.

*Ésta es la guitarra **que** compré.*
This is the guitar **(that)** I bought.

Quien, and the plural *quienes,* can refer only to people. *Quien* is most commonly used after prepositions like *a* and *de*.

*Rebeca es la chica **de quien** te hablé.*
Rebeca is the girl **whom** I told you about.

*Kati y Anita, **quienes** son de Quito, viajaron a Miami.*
Kati and Anita, **who** are from Quito, traveled to Miami.

Lo que, unlike *que* and *quien,* does not refer to a specific noun. *Lo que* refers to an idea or a situation.

Lo que necesito es estudiar más.
What I need is to study more.

Exercise 1

Fill in the blanks with the correct relative pronoun.

1. Este apartamento tiene todo_____

necesitamos.

2. Los señores_____ viste en el patio son mis

vecinos.

3. ¿Dónde están las flores_____ compré para

mi abuela?

4. _____ me gusta es bailar.

5. El chico a_____ regalé el iPod es mi

hermano.

Exercise 2

Make logical sentences by matching column A with column B.

A	B
_____ **1.** La mujer…	a. …lo que necesitas para el viaje.
_____ **2.** El abogado,…	b. …que compramos en Madrid?
_____ **3.** No trajiste…	c. …quien se llama Sergio, es muy bueno.
_____ **4.** ¿Le gusta el regalo…	d. …con quien bailé se llama Rosa.
_____ **5.** Son las chicas…	e. …de quienes nos hablaron.

Exercise 3

The following sentences have a common element. Link the two sentences using a relative pronoun.

1. Fuimos a la nueva librería. La librería está cerca de la escuela.

   _____

   _____

   _____

2. Delia tiene un hermano mayor. Su hermano estudia en la Universidad Central.

   _____

   _____

   _____

3. El vendedor de relojes nos ayudó. Estaba muy informado.

   _____

   _____

   _____

4. Fui a una doctora chilena. La doctora se llamaba Zorayda Preto.

   _____

   _____

   _____

5. Cristina es muy inteligente. Cristina estudia matemáticas.

   _____

   _____

   _____

18

19 Adverbs Using -mente

Adverbs are used to modify, or describe, the verbs they accompany. There are several kinds of adverbs in Spanish. The easiest adverbs are those that end in *-mente,* the Spanish equivalent of *-ly* in English.

To form a *-mente* adverb, add *-mente* to the feminine form of the adjective.

Masculine Adjective	Feminine Adjective	Adverb
lento (slow) →	*lenta* →	*lentamente* (slowly)

¡Atención!

When the masculine and feminine forms of an adjective are the same, add *-mente* to the base form of the adjective.

Adjective		+ *-mente*
alegre (happy)	→	*alegremente* (happily)

Adverbs that end in *-mente* follow the verbs they modify.

Aida baila **maravillosamente.**
Aida dances **wonderfully.**

When multiple *-mente* adverbs are used in a series, drop the ending for all but the last one.

La profesora habla **clara** *y* **lentamente.**
The teacher speaks **clearly** and **slowly.**

¡Atención!

If an adjective has an accent, the accent remains in the adverb form.

fácil, fácilmente (easy, easily)

Exercise 1

Convert the following adjectives into adverbs.

1. sencillo _____

2. difícil _____

3. rápido _____

4. energético _____

5. sensible _____

Exercise 2

Rewrite the following sentences correctly. Note: Some of the sentences do not have errors.

1. Facilmente llego a la universidad en autobús.

_____

_____

_____

2. Es necesario que la clase empieze inmediatamente.

_____

_____

_____

3. Cuando veo la television, mi hermano constantemente cambia el canal.

_____

_____

_____

4. María está confundida totalmente.

_____

_____

_____

5. Les espero pacientemente en la esquina.

_____

_____

_____

Exercise 3

Think about your best friend. First write down three adjectives that describe him or her. Next turn the adjectives into adverbs and use the adverbs in three sentences to describe that person.

_____

_____

_____

1. _____

_____

_____

2. _____

_____

_____

3. _____

_____

_____

19

20 Adverbs *Adverbs of Manner and Place*

There are adverbs that do not end in *-mente*. These adverbs are easiest to learn if you think of them as answers to certain questions.

Some adverbs answer the question *how* (¿*Cómo?*). These adverbs are known as *adverbs of manner*.

| ¿Cómo cocinas? | How do you cook? |
| Cocino **bien.** | I cook **well.** |

¡Atención!

The adverb *bien* (well) is often confused with the adjective *bueno* (good).

Other common adverbs of manner include the following:

así	like that
claramente	clearly
de pronto	suddenly
mal	badly
bien	well
menos	less
más	more
mejor	better
peor	worse

Some adverbs answer the question *where* (¿*Dónde?*). These adverbs are known as *adverbs of place*.

| ¿Dónde está la escuela? | Where is the school? |
| La escuela está **cerca.** | The school is **close.** |

Other common adverbs of place include the following:

abajo	below
acá	over here
adelante	in front
adentro	inside
aquí	here
allá	over there
arriba	above
debajo	underneath
delante	in front
detrás	behind
encima	on top
lejos	far

Exercise 1

The following word pool has five hidden ¿*Dónde?* adverbs. Can you find them?

a	d	e	l	a	n	t	e	u	p	l	h	l	k	a	a
p	d	é	o	a	r	r	i	b	a	e	d	m	i	o	q
a	v	a	d	r	f	s	i	l	w	j	p	é	h	d	u
s	w	b	n	x	p	z	q	b	g	o	i	p	a	j	í
d	e	t	r	á	s	r	l	n	e	s	r	m	b	p	i

Exercise 2

Imagine that your classmate Gabriela contradicts everything you say. Use the correct adverbs to write Gabriela's response to the following statements.

1. Tú haces la tarea *rápidamente*.

   _____

   _____

   _____

2. Ahora el profesor nos da *más* exámenes.

   _____

   _____

   _____

3. Yo estudio *menos* que Julio.

   _____

   _____

   _____

4. Esta clase es *mejor* que la otra.

   _____

   _____

   _____

5. El profesor enseña *bien*.

   _____

   _____

   _____

Exercise 3

Fill in the blanks by choosing the correct adverb from the list below.

mal	aquí	debajo
así	lejos	

1. Mamá, ¿dónde está el gato? Está _____

   del sofá.

2. ¿Cómo te sientes? Me siento muy _____.

3. ¿Dónde estacionaste el carro? Lo estacioné

   _____ de aquí.

4. Paula, ¿cómo haces ese ejercicio? Lo hago

   _____.

5. ¿Dónde estás, Sarita? ¡Estoy _____!

20

Some adverbs answer the question *when (¿Cuándo?).* **These adverbs are known as** *adverbs of time.*

¿Cuándo vas al aeropuerto?
When are you going to the airport?

*Voy **pronto** al aeropuerto.*
I'm going to the airport **soon.**

Other common adverbs of time include the following:

ahora	now
hoy	today
anoche	last night
ayer	yesterday
mañana	tomorrow
de día	during the day
de noche	at night
a la una (a las dos, etc.)	at one o'clock (at two, etc.)
a veces	sometimes
antes	before
después	after
entonces	then
luego	later
mientras	during
nunca	never
siempre	late
tarde	always
temprano	early
todavía	still
ya	already

Some adverbs answer the question *how much (¿Cuánto?).* **These adverbs are known as** *adverbs of quantity.*

¿Cuánto cuesta la televisión?
How much does television cost?

*¡Cuesta **demasiado**!*
It costs **too much**!

Other common adverbs of quantity include the following:

algo	a bit, rather
apenas	barely
bastante	a lot
casi	almost
cuanto	as much
más	more
medio	half
menos	less
mucho	a lot
muy	very
nada	not at all
poco	a little
sólo	only
tanto	so much

Exercise 1

The following word pool has five hidden ¿Cuánto? adverbs. Can you find them?

p	d	e	z	q	v	b	e	u	p	l	h	l	p	a	n
o	m	é	b	a	s	t	a	n	t	e	d	l	i	o	a
c	v	u	d	r	f	s	í	l	z	w	p	é	h	d	d
o	w	b	y	x	p	z	q	a	p	m	u	c	h	o	a
d	o	h	s	e	o	r	l	n	e	s	r	m	r	p	i

Exercise 2

How often do you do the following activities? Write complete sentences using the adverbs of time.

Actividades

1. mirar la televisión
2. dormir en el tren
3. leer un libro
4. sacar la basura
5. lavar los platos

Oraciones Completas

1._____

_____

2._____

_____

3._____

_____

4._____

_____

5._____

_____

Exercise 3

Translate the following paragraph into Spanish. Be sure to use the correct adverbs.

I like to relax on the weekend. On Saturday I never wake up before eleven or twelve. I shower, and then I eat lunch. Sometimes I watch TV. If there's nothing on TV, I'll read a book or magazine. At night, there's not much to do in my apartment. I prefer to go out with my friends. We almost always go to the same discotheque. It's called "Blues." I really like dancing. I come home very early the next morning, and my routine begins again on Sunday!

_____

_____

_____

_____

_____

_____

_____

_____

_____

_____

_____

_____

_____

_____

21

An adjective modifies the noun it accompanies. An adverb modifies the verb. Some words can be either adverbs or adjectives, depending on their function in the sentence.

As an adjective, *mucho* means *a lot of, much*. As an adverb, *mucho* means *very much*.

*Comen **mucho** pan.*	They eat **a lot of** bread.
*Duermen **mucho**.*	They sleep **a lot**.

¡Atención!

Be careful not to confuse *mucho* (a lot) and *muy*. *Mucho* is an adjective; *muy* is an adverb.

When used as adjectives, these words change their form to agree in gender and number with the nouns they modify. Adverbs do not change their form.

*Comen **muchos** panecitos.*	They eat **a lot of** rolls.
*Julieta tiene **mucha** ropa.*	Julieta has **a lot of** clothes.

Some other common words that can function as both adjectives and adverbs include the following:

poco	a little
bastante	a lot
mal	bad

*Tengo **bastantes** amigos.* (adjective)
I have **a lot of** friends.

*El gato duerme **bastante**.* (adverb)
The cat sleeps **a lot**.

The adjectives *alto* and *bajo* change meaning depending on whether they are used as adverbs or adjectives.

*Es un hombre **bajo**.*
He's a **short** man.

*Antonieta, habla **bajo** por favor.*
Antonieta, please speak **quietly**.

*El edificio es **alto**.*
The building is **tall**.

*Es una mujer **altamente** moral.*
She's a **very** moral woman.

Exercise 1

Which of the following sentences contain adjectives? Which contain adverbs? Underline the adjectives and circle the adverbs.

1. Tengo pocos amigos.

2. Me gusta mucho la música *reggaetón*.

3. El verano pasado fuimos a bastantes fiestas.

4. Mi primo viaja de vez en cuando a Perú.

5. Juegan mal al tenis.

Exercise 2

Translate the following sentences into Spanish.

1. My aunt is a tall woman.

_____

_____

_____

2. You speak very loudly, Marta.

_____

_____

_____

3. Today I washed a lot of clothes.

_____

_____

_____

4. Juan, my neighbor, is a short man.

_____

_____

_____

5. I eat very little these days.

_____

_____

_____

Exercise 3

Imagine your pet keeps a journal. Use five sentences to describe what it may write about a typical day. Use each of the following words.

mucho (adverb), _poco_ (adjective), _bastante_ (adverb), _mal_ (adjective)

1. _____

_____

_____

2. _____

_____

_____

3. _____

_____

4. _____

_____

_____

5. _____

_____

_____

22

23 Comparisons *Equality*

Comparisons of equality compare two or more items that are equal. In Spanish, specific constructions are used to make comparisons of equality.

To compare equal items using adjectives and adverbs, use the construction *tan* + adjective + *como* or *tan* + adverb + *como*.

*La comida en la universidad es **tan buena como** en casa.*
The food at the university is **as good as** it is at home.

*María habla **tan bien como** tú.*
María speaks **as well as** you do.

To compare equal items using singular nouns, use the construction *tanto/a* + singular noun + *como*.

*Sandra tiene **tanto dinero como** Ana.*
Sandra has **as much money as** Ana does.

*Tú comes **tanta comida como** mi padre.*
You eat **as much food as** my father does.

To compare equal items using plural nouns, use the construction *tantos/as* + plural noun + *como*.

*Ustedes prueban **tantos platos como** nosotros.*
You try **as many dishes as** we do.

*Yo tengo **tantas amigas como** mi hermana.*
I have **as many friends as** my sister does.

¡Atención!

Tanto will change form to agree with the gender of the noun. *Tanto(s)* is used with a masculine noun and *tanta(s)* is used with a feminine noun.

To compare equal items using verbs, use the construction verb + *tanto como*.

*Yo **duermo tanto como** mi tía.*
I **sleep as much as** my aunt does.

Exercise 1

Translate the following sentences about Ernesto into Spanish.

1. Ernesto is as smart as a university professor.

2. Ernesto's house is as big mine.

3. Ernesto has as many children as Jorge does.

4. Ernesto's son sleeps as much as his daughter does.

5. Ernesto reads as many books as his wife does.

Exercise 2

Write comparisons of equality with the words provided. Make sure you use the proper constructions.

1. caliente

_____

_____

_____

2. cantar

_____

_____

_____

3. mal

_____

_____

_____

4. bonita

_____

_____

_____

5. habltaclones

_____

_____

_____

Exercise 3

From whom did you inherit your traits? Compare yourself to a family member. Write three sentences. Use comparisons of equality.

1. _____

_____

_____

2. _____

_____

_____

3. _____

_____

_____

23

Más is equivalent to *more* and *menos* is equivalent to *less*. Both generally combine with *que* (than) to indicate *more than* and *less than* in comparisons of inequality.

To compare unequal items using adjective and adverbs, use the construction *más/menos* + adjective/adverb + *que*.

*El elefante es **más grande que** el caballo.*
The elephant is **bigger than** the horse.

*Me acuesto **más tarde que** tú.*
I go to bed **later than** you do.

*La biología es **menos interesante que** la química.*
Biology is **less interesting than** chemistry.

*Mi hermano corre **menos rápidamente que** Alfredo.*
My brother runs **less quickly than** Alfredo does.

To compare unequal items using nouns, use the construction *más/menos* + noun + *que*.

*Teresa tiene **más discos compactos que** Zoila.*
Teresa has **more compact discs than** Zoila does.

*Yo compro **menos camisas que** Roberto.*
I buy **fewer shirts than** Roberto does.

To compare unequal items using verbs, use the construction verb + *más/menos que*.

*Mi abuelo **duerme más que** mi abuela.*
My grandfather **sleeps more than** my grandmother does.

*El bebé de Marta **llora menos que** el bebé de Adelia.*
Marta's baby **cries less than** Adelia's baby does.

La Excepción
De replaces *que* when comparing numbers of items.

*Tengo **más de veinte** libros.*
I have **more than twenty** books.

*Hay **menos de diez** estudiantes en la clase.*
There are **fewer than ten** students in the class.

Some adjectives and adverbs have irregular comparison forms. These words do not take *más* and *menos* when used to make comparisons of inequality.

Adjective		Comparative	
bueno/a	good	mejor	better
malo/a	bad	peor	worse
joven	young	menor	younger, minor
viejo/a	old	mayor	older, major

Adjective		Comparative	
bien	well	mejor	better
mal	badly	peor	worse
mucho	a lot	más	more
poco	a little	menos	less

*El café es **bueno**. El café es **mejor** que el té.*
Coffee is **good**. Coffee is **better** than tea.

*Gonzalo toca **bien** el clarinete. Toca el clarinete **mejor** que Nicolás.*
Gonzalo plays the clarinet **well**. He plays the clarinet **better than** Nicolás does.

¡Atención!
Though most adjectives change form to agree in gender and number with the nouns they modify, *mejor, peor, menor,* and *mayor* do not. They keep the same form with all nouns.

Exercise 1
Magdalena and Catalina are identical twins, but there are some differences between them. Fill in the blanks with the correct comparative term indicated by the cue in parentheses.

Magdalena y Catalina son gemelas. Son idénticas físicamente, pero en otras maneras son muy distintas.

Catalina mira (**1.**) _____ televisión que Magdalena. (*more*)

Magdalena es (**2.**) _____ popular que Catalina. (*less*)

Catalina no estudia (**3.**) _____ Magdalena. (*as much as*)

Magdalena tiene (**4.**) _____ amigas que Catalina. (*fewer*)

Catalina sale a bailar (**5.**) _____ que Magdalena. (*more*)

Exercise 2

Translate the following sentences into Spanish. Be sure to use the correct comparative.

1. The music of los Aterciopelados is better than the music of Fobia.

_____

_____

_____

2. This radio station is worse than that one.

_____

_____

_____

3. Los Héroes del Silencio play better live than Los Enanitos Verdes.

_____

_____

_____

4. The band members are younger than we are.

_____

_____

_____

5. Beto Cuevas's songs are less interesting than Andrea Echeverri's.

_____

_____

_____

Exercise 3

Read the following advertisement for Restaurante Pío Pío, and then answer the questions below.

El pollo del Restaurante Pío Pío es más rico que el pollo de otros restaurantes. Servimos ("we serve") el pollo al horno que también tiene menos grasa que el pollo en otros restaurantes. Además es menos caro. ¡Te esperamos en Pío Pío!

1. What is being compared in the advertisement?

_____

_____

2. Name three comparisons in the advertisement.

_____

_____

3. What words do the comparisons have in common?

_____

_____

24

25 Comparisons *Superlatives*

Superlatives express comparisons to the highest or lowest degree.

The construction **definite article + noun + *más* + adjective + *de*** expresses comparisons of the highest degree (the most, the best, the highest, and so on).

> *Iris es **la chica más guapa de** la clase.*
> Iris is **the best-looking girl** in the class.

The construction **definite article + noun + *menos* + adjective + *de*** expresses comparisons of the lowest degree (the least, the worst, the lowest, and so on).

> *Patricio es **el chico menos estudioso de** la clase.*
> Patricio is **the least studious boy** in the class.

¡Atención!

In superlative constructions, the preposition *de* is equivalent to the English *in* or *of*.

As with comparatives, some adjectives have irregular superlative forms.

Adjective		Superlative	
bueno/a	good	*el mejor*	best
malo/a	bad	*el peor*	worst
joven	young	*el menor*	youngest
viejo/a	old	*el mayor*	oldest

> *Isabel es **la mayor** de su familia.*
> Isabel is the oldest in her family.

> *Yo soy **el mejor** de la clase.*
> I'm the best in the class.

¡Atención!

As with comparisons, these irregular superlatives do not change form to agree with the nouns. However, the accompanying definite article always agrees in gender and number with the noun it accompanies.

The absolute superlative can be used to express an even higher degree of quality, equivalent to *extremely*, *exceptionally*, or *very*. To form the absolute superlative for adjectives and adverbs that end in a vowel, drop the final vowel and add *-ísimo/a*.

> *malo* (bad) → *mal-* → *malísimo/a* (very bad)

> *¡El libro es **malísimo**!*
> The book is **very bad**!

To form the absolute superlative for adjectives and adverbs that end in *-co*, *-go*, or *-zo*, drop the vowel, then make the following spelling changes.

> *c* → *qu* + *-ísimo/a*

> *rico* (rich) → *riquísimo* (very rich)

> *g* → *gu* + *-ísimo/a*

> *largo* (long) → *larguísimo* (very long)

> *z* → *c* + *-ísimo/a*

> *feliz* (happy) → *felicísimo* (very happy)

To form the absolute superlative for adjectives and adverbs that end in any other consonant, just add *-ísimo/a* to the end.

> *fácil* (easy) → *facilísimo/a* (very easy)

> *¡La lección es **facilísima**!*
> The lesson is **very easy**!

Exercise 1

Fill out the table with the correct irregular comparative and superlative forms.

Adjective	Comparative	Superlative
1. bueno		
2. malo		
3. joven		
4. viejo		

Exercise 2

Use the absolute superlatives of the adjectives in the sentences below.

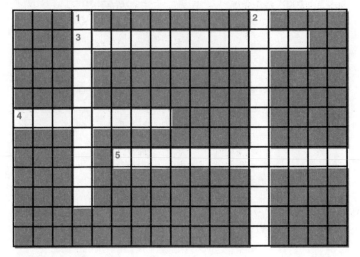

Across

3. La materia es muy aburrida.

Es _____ .

4. El profesor es muy malo.

Es _____ .

5. El aula de clase está muy caliente.

Está _____ .

Down

1. Esta clase es muy larga.

Es _____ .

2. El cálculo es muy difícil.

Es _____ .

Exercise 3

An out-of-town friend is coming to visit and needs your help in planning the trip. Answer her questions in Spanish using the absolute superlatives in complete sentences.

1. What is the most elegant restaurant in your city?

_____

_____

_____

2. Which is the least expensive hotel in your city?

_____

_____

_____

3. Which is the most beautiful tourist attraction of your city?

_____

_____

_____

4. Which is the least dangerous neighborhood of your city?

_____

_____

_____

25

51

Affirmative words, such as *someone* and *something*, refer to nonspecific people and things. Negative phrases and words, such as *no one* and *nothing*, refer to people and things that don't exist.

Spanish has several common affirmative and negative words.

Affirmative		Negative	
algo	something	*nada*	nothing, not anything
alguien	someone, anyone	*nadie*	no one, not anyone, nobody
cualquier, cualquiera	anybody, any	*nadie*	nobody, no one, not anything
alguno, alguna	some, someone, any	*ninguno, ninguna,*	no, no one, none, neither
algunos, algunas, unos	some, several, any	*ninguno*	nobody, no one, none, not any
alguna, vez, siempre	ever always	*nunca, jamás*	never
también	also, too	*tampoco*	not either, neither
o...o	either...or	*ni...ni*	neither...nor
sí	Yes	*no*	no, not

Double (and multiple) negatives in the same sentence are common, sometimes even required, in Spanish. If *no* or another negative word comes before the verb, negative words such as *nada* or *ninguno* must follow.

> ***No** quiero **nada**.*
> I **don't** want **anything**.

> ***No** hay **ninguna** razón para armar un escandalo.*
> There is **no** reason to make a scene.

If a negative word comes before the verb, the word *no* is not used in addition to the negative.

> ***Nunca** como ensalada.*   I **never** eat salad.

¡Atención!

If an object pronoun (*me, te, lo, la, le, nos, os, los, las,* or *les*) precedes the verb, the negative word precedes the object pronoun.

> *Yo no **lo** se.*   I don't know **it.**

A number of common expressions are formed using affirmative and negative words.

Affirmative Expressions		Negative Expressions	
en alguna parte	somewhere	*en ninguna parte*	nowhere
de alguna manera	somehow	*de ninguna manera*	in no way
alguna vez	ever	*ni siquiera*	not even
algunas veces	sometimes	*ya no*	no longer
		todavía no	not yet

> *El lápiz tiene que estar **en alguna parte**.*
> The pencil has to be **somewhere**.

> ***Ya no** sé hablar inglés.*
> I **no longer** know how to speak English.

¡Atención!

The conjunctions *pero* and *sino* both mean *but* and often accompany negative and affirmative words. However, they are used differently. *Pero* means *however*. *Sino* is used after a negative statement to express a contrast, as in *but rather* or *on the contrary*.

> *No soy norteamericano, **pero** hablo inglés.*
> I'm not American; **however,** I speak English.

> *Los libros no son viejos **sino** nuevos.*
> The books are not old **but rather** new.

Pero links two complete sentences. For the word *pero* to be used, there must be a conjugated verb on each side of it. *Sino* may link a sentence to a word or phrase.

> *Tengo hambre, **pero** no quiero comer.*
> I'm hungry, **but** I don't want to eat.

> *No tengo un gato, **sino** tres.*
> I don't have one cat, **but rather** three.

52

Exercise 1

Match the affirmative words in column A to their negative equivalents in column B.

	A		B
_____	**1.** También	a.	nada
_____	**2.** Alguna	b.	nadie
_____	**3.** Algo	c.	nunca
_____	**4.** Cualquier	d.	tampoco
_____	**5.** Siempre	e.	ninguna

Exercise 2

Which sentences below require *sino*? Which require *pero*? Fill in the correct answer.

Mi apartamento es pequeño (**1.**) _____

muy cómodo. Tengo todo lo que necesito: un dormitorio, una

sala, una cocina y, por supuesto, ¡un baño! El apartamento

no es feo (**2.**) _____ bonito. La renta

es muy alta, (**3.**) _____ la ubicación

es estupenda. Vivo a dos cuadras de la universidad. No me

voy a mudar, (**4.**) _____ quedarme

aquí un año más.

Exercise 3

Juan is the exact opposite of David. Rewrite the following paragraph to describe Juan. Replace the affirmative words with negative words, and vice versa.

David se viste siempre de negro. Jamás viene a clase, porque siempre se levanta tarde. Siempre se enoja con sus amigos. Por eso nunca mantiene sus amistades.

_____

_____

_____

_____

_____

_____

_____

_____

_____

_____

_____

26

Alguien and *nadie* always refer to people, and are always in the singular. When *alguien* or *nadie* are the direct object of a verb, the personal *a* must be used before them.

> *¿Conoces **a alguien*** (direct object) *aquí?*
> Do you know **anyone** here?

> *No conozco **a nadie*** (direct object) *aquí.*
> I don't know **anyone** here.

When *alguien* or *nadie* are the subject of the sentence, the personal *a* is not required.

> ***Alguien*** (subject) *te llama.*
> **Someone** is calling you.

> ***Nadie*** (subject) *está en casa.*
> **No one's** home.

Alguno and *ninguno* refer to objects or people. When *alguno* and *ninguno* come in front of a masculine singular noun, they are shortened to *algún* and *ningún*.

> *¿Hay **algún** libro aquí?*
> Are there **any** books here?

> *No hay **ningún** libro aquí.*
> There are **no** books here.

Use the personal *a* when *alguno* or *ninguno* refer to a person and are the direct objects of a verb.

> *¿Conoces **a algún** profesor* (direct object)*?*
> Do you know any **teachers**?

> *No conozco **a ningún** profesor* (direct object).
> I don't know any **teachers.**

> *Veo **a algunas** niñas en el parque* (direct object).
> I see some **girls** at the park.

También expresses agreement with an affirmative statement.

> *Quiero ir.*
> I want to go.

> *Yo quiero ir **también.***
> I want to go **too.**

Tampoco expresses agreement with a negative statement.

> *No quiero ir.*
> I don't want to go.

> *Yo no quiero ir **tampoco.***
> I **don't** want to go **either.**

¡Atención!

The word *no* forces the use of the negative *tampoco* rather than the affirmative *también*. Because the use of double negatives is not allowed in English, *no... tampoco* is translated as "not...either."

Exercise 1

Use the clues to complete the crossword puzzle.

Across

2. This affirmative word refers to people only.
5. This negative word does not require the personal *a* when it is the subject of a sentence.

Down
1. This word expresses agreement with a negative statement.
3. This negative word requires the personal *a* when it refers to a person and is the direct object of a verb.
4. This word expresses agreement with a negative statement.

Exercise 2

Translate the following sentences into Spanish using negative and affirmative words.

1. I know someone in Barcelona.

_____

_____

_____

2. Someone in Mexico City sent me a package.

_____

_____

_____

3. Although it's winter, I see some ducks on the lake.

_____

_____

_____

4. I haven't spoken to anyone this morning.

_____

_____

_____

5. Roberto didn't like this book. He didn't like that one either.

_____

_____

_____

Exercise 3

Answer the following questions in Spanish. Use the cues to determine if the answers should be negative or affirmative.

1. ¿Con quién sales los fines de semana? (negative)

_____

_____

_____

2. ¿Has consultado a algún médico acerca de tu tos? (negative)

_____

_____

_____

3. ¿Viste a alguien en la biblioteca? (affirmative)

_____

_____

_____

4. ¿Quién te llama por teléfono? (affirmative)

_____

_____

_____

5. ¿Tienes algún lápiz que me puedas prestar? (negative)

_____

_____

_____

Prepositions & Conjunctions *Prepositions*

Prepositions express the relationship between things in terms of time or place. They answer the questions *where* and *when*.

Common prepositions in Spanish include the following:

a	at, to	*excepto*	except
ante	before	*hacia*	toward
bajo	under	*hasta*	to, up to, as far as, until
con	with	*para*	for
contra	against	*por*	for
de	of, from	*según*	according to
desde	from, since	*sin*	without
durante	during	*sobre*	on, over, about, on top of
en	in, into, on, at	*tras*	after
entre	between, among		

¡Atención!

Prepositions cannot stand alone in a sentence. They must be followed by a noun, pronoun, or verb in the infinitive.

*Salgo **con** Ana.* (noun)
I go out with **Ana.**

*Vamos **con** ellos.* (pronoun)
Let's go with **them.**

Hace todo **excepto** cocinar. (infinitve verb)
*He does everything **except** cook.*

Prepositions can be grouped with adverbs or other prepositions to form a single prepositional expression, called a compound preposition. Some common compound prepositions include the following:

además de	in addition to, besides
antes de	before
cerca de	near, close to
debajo de	under, beneath
delante de	in front of, before
dentro de	inside, within
después de	after
detrás de	after, behind
encima de	on, on top of, over
enfrente de	in front of, opposite

frente a	in front of, opposite
fuera de	outside of, beyond
lejos de	far from
por delante de	in front of

*Ella está **delante de** mí.*
She is **in front of** me.

*Vivo **cerca de** la escuela.*
I live **close to** school.

*Las llaves están **encima de** la mesa.*
The keys are **on top of** the table.

Prepositions appear in several common phrases.

a causa de	because of
acerca de	about, concerning
al lado de	next to, beside
en vez de	instead of
frente a	across from, opposite to

*Las tijeras están **al lado del** lápiz.*
The scissors are **next to** the pencil.

*Quiero hablar con la profesora **acerca de** mi nota.*
I want to talk to my teacher **about** my grade.

Exercise 1

Match the Spanish prepositions in column A with their English equivalents in column B.

A	B
_____ **1.** bajo	a. since
_____ **2.** con	b. until
_____ **3.** para	c. on top of
_____ **4.** durante	d. between
_____ **5.** hasta	e. with
_____ **6.** sobre	f. without
_____ **7.** entre	g. against
_____ **8.** desde	h. for
_____ **9.** sin	i. during
_____ **10.** contra	j. under

Exercise 2

Use the following compound prepositions to compose sentences expressing where the car is: *delante de, debajo de, encima de, dentro de, lejos de.*

5._____

_____

1._____

_____

2._____

_____

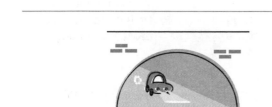

3._____

_____

4._____

_____

Exercise 3

Choose the preposition that best completes the sentences below.

1. El bolígrafo está_____ la mesa.
   a. detrás de   b. encima de

2. El pizarrón está_____ los estudiantes.
   a. delante de   b. con

3. El estudiante lleva los libros_____ la mochila.
   a. en   b. debajo de

4. El profesor escribe_____ una tiza.
   a. encima de   b. con

5. La silla está_____ la mesa.
   a. detrás de   b. fuera de

Exercise 4

Read the following descriptions of several Latin American countries. What countries are being described? Use a map if you need to.

1. Este país está al norte de Argentina. Está cerca de Chile, pero lejos de Venezuela. Está entre Perú y Brasil. ¿Cuál país es?

_____

2. Este país está cerca de Panamá. Está al norte de Ecuador pero al sur de Venezuela. ¿Cuál país es?

_____

The prepositions *para* and *por* can both be translated in English as *for*. However, they have a variety of different uses in Spanish, depending on the context.

The preposition *para* is used in the following situations:

to indicate a particular use for which something is intended	*Las piernas son **para** caminar.* Legs are **for** walking.
to show the destination or direction to which something or someone is headed	*El regalo es **para** mi padre.* The gift is **for** my father. *Salió **para** Mexico.* He went **to** Mexico.
to express the purpose of something, with an infinitive	***Para** comer, necesito un tenedor.* **To** eat, I need a fork.
to indicate a time or date in the future	*La entrada es **para** el concierto del domingo.* The ticket is **for** Sunday's concert.
to make comparisons, similar to *considering that*	***Para** ser extranjero, habla bien el español.* **For** a foreigner, he speaks Spanish well.
to express a purpose or a goal	*Estudia **para** ser médico.* He studies **to** be a doctor.

The preposition *por* is used in the following situations:

to indicate duration	*¿Me puedes prestar el carro **por** dos días?* Will you lend me the car **for** two days?
to indicate movement through, by, or along something, after a verb of motion	*El gato pasa **por** la ventana.* The cat goes **through** the open window.
to indicate the means by which something is communicated	*Te llamo **por** teléfono.* I call you **on** the phone.
to indicate the means of an errand, after the verbs *ir* (to go), *mandar* (to send), *enviar* (to mail), *volver* (to return), *regresar* (to come back), *preguntar* (to ask for)	*Te mando el paquete **por** avión.* I will send you the package **by** airmail.
to indicate the reason for an action	*Estoy en la universidad **por** mis padres.* I'm in the university **for the sake of** my parents.
to indicate a substitution, as in *instead of*, *for the sake of*, or *on behalf of*	*Yo corro **por** Manuel.* I'm running **in place of** Manuel.
to indicate an exchange of one thing for another	*Te doy diez dólares **por** la chaqueta.* I'll give you ten dollars **for** the jacket.
to indicate a unit of measurement, as in *per* or *by the*	*El carro va a ochenta kilómetros **por** hora.* The car is going at eighty kilometers **per** hour.
to introduce the agent in a passive construction	*México fue conquistado **por** Cortés.* Mexico was conquered **by** Cortés.

Exercise 1

Correct the errors in the following sentences. Note: Some of the sentences do not have errors.

1. Mando un mensaje a Arturo por correo electrónico.

_____

_____

2. La mantequilla es por el pan.

_____

_____

3. La caja es para los lápices.

_____

_____

4. No fui a ver la película para miedo.

_____

_____

5. Por verano hace demasiado frío.

_____

_____

Exercise 2

Choose the preposition that matches the given uses.

A. por   **B. para**

_____ **1.** Indicates a deadline.

....

_____ **2.** Indicates the recipient of something.

....

_____ **3.** Indicates the means by which something is done, that is, by telephone.

....

_____ **4.** Indicates a destination.

....

_____ **5.** Indicates the duration of an action.

....

_____ **6.** Indicates the motive for an action.

Exercise 3

Choose one element from each column to make three sentences. Add *por* or *para* where necessary.

fui	a la biblioteca	carro	estudiar
fuimos	a la playa	comprar	tomar sol
fueron	al supermercado	fruta	mi mamá
		estudiar	

1. _____

_____

2. _____

_____

3. _____

_____

Exercise 4

Translate the following paragraph into Spanish using *por* and *para*.

The Cobos family left for Perú yesterday. They went by plane, although they plan to travel throughout the country by car. They're going to stay for two months. It's going to be an extraordinary experience for the whole family.

_____

_____

_____

_____

_____

_____

_____

29

In almost all situations, *con* translates as *with*; however, *con* is more versatile than its English equivalent. The preposition *sin* generally means *without*.

The preposition *con* is used in the following situations:

to express accompaniment	*Voy **con** ellos al cine.* I'm going **with** them to the movies.
to indicate adherence, possession, or content	*El hombre **con** la guitarra se llama Pablo.* The man **with** the guitar is named Pablo.
to indicate that a tool or instrument performs an action, followed by a noun	*Hay que abrirlo **con** un abrelatas.* It has to be opened **with** a can opener.
followed by a noun in an adverbial expression	*Los visito **con** frecuencia.* I visit **with** them frequently.

Con is also used in the common expressions *con tal de que* (provided that) and *con respecto a* (regarding).

*Puedes escuchar música, **con tal de que** no me molestes.*
You can listen to music, **provided that** you don't bother me.

*No sé qué hacer **con respecto a** mi hermana.*
I don't know what to do **regarding** my sister.

Con often follows certain verbs to form other common expressions.

casarse con to get married to	*Alexandra **se casó con** un muchacho muy agradable.* Alexandra **married** a very pleasant guy.
contar con to count on	*Hermano, puedes **contar conmigo**.* Brother, you can **count on** me.
encariñarse con to become attached to	*Cecilia se **encariñó con** el cachorro.* Cecilia became **attached to** the puppy.

encontrarse con to meet up with	***Me encontré con** mi amiga en el centro.* I **met up with** my friend downtown.
enojarse con to get angry with	*Mi madre **se enojó conmigo** cuando rompí el plato.* My mother **got angry with** me when I broke the dish.
quedarse con to keep	*Francisco **se quedó con** mi calculadora.* Francisco **kept** my calculator.
soñar con to dream about	*Anoche **soñé con** mi profesora de biología.* Last night I **dreamed about** my biology professor.

***Sin* generally means *without*.**

*El ladrón me dejó **sin** dinero.*
The thief left me **without** any money.

***Sin* is not generally followed by an indefinite article, unless the object indicated by *sin* is followed by an adjective.**

*Esta mañana mi esposo me dejó **sin** carro.*
This morning my husband left me **without** a car.

*Esta mañana mi esposo me dejó **sin el** carro **rojo**.*
This morning my husband left me **without the red** car.

***Sin* can also be used to indicate an action that was not completed or performed. In these instances, *sin* is followed by the infinitive form of a verb.**

*El edificio estaba **sin terminar**.*
The building **wasn't finished**.

Exercise 1

Use context to determine if the blank should be filled with *con* or *sin*.

1. Mi madre nos mandó al supermercado. Nos dio 100 pesos.

   Nos mandó _____ dinero.

2. Graciela nos acompañó.

   Fuimos _____ Graciela.

3. Se nos olvidó comprar huevos.

   Regresamos _____ huevos.

4. Mi madre se enojó _____ nosotros.

5. Mi madre no puede hacer la tortilla sin huevos.

   ¡Nos quedamos _____ comer!

Exercise 2

Complete the *con* phrases below with ideas of your own.

1. A veces me enojo con... _____

   _____

2. De noche sueño con... _____

   _____

3. Los fines de semana me encuentro con... _____

   _____

4. Quiero casarme con... _____

   _____

5. Generalmente me encariño con..._____

   _____

Exercise 3

Translate the following dialogue into Spanish.

"Yesenia, come to the park with us," said Nela. "We're taking our bicycles."
"I don't know, girls. My bike is broken. I have to fix it."
"You can fix it with a screwdriver, I'm sure!" said Susana.
"We're going to meet up with that guy with a dog."
"Ah, I dream about him! I'll go provided that he's there!"

_____

_____

_____

_____

_____

_____

_____

_____

_____

_____

_____

_____

_____

_____

_____

_____

_____

_____

_____

30

The preposition *a* appears frequently in Spanish and has a number of uses. *A* is used to identify people who and things that act or are acted upon. *A* is also used to indicate movement, position, and duration.

The preposition *a* is used in the following situations:

to introduce an indirect object	*Le doy la manzana al caballo.* I give the apple **to the** horse.
to show movement toward something or someplace	*Vamos a la cabaña.* We're going **to** the cabin.
to indicate the time at which something happens	*El concierto es a las ocho.* The concert is **at** eight o'clock.
to show distance	*La escuela está a una cuadra.* The school is one block away.
when alguien, nadie, alguno, and ninguno are used as direct objects referring to people (personal *a*)	*No veo a nadie.* I don't see **anyone.**
to introduce a noun as a direct object referring to a person. (personal *a*)	*Veo a mi hermana.* I see my sister.
to express a command	*¡Al carro!* **To the** car!
to show simultaneous actions, when used in the construction al + infinitive	*Al entrar,* vi a Pedro. **Upon entering,** I saw Pedro.

¡Atención!
The preposition *a* combines with the definite article *el* to form *al*.

A is also used in a number of common expressions.

a causa de   because of

No fuimos al partido de fútbol a causa de la lluvia.
We didn't go to the soccer game **because of** the rain.

a la vez   at the same time

No puedo hacer dos cosas a la vez.
I can't do two things **at a time.**

al menos   at least

Nos quedan al menos tres días.
We have **at least** three days left.

a lo mejor   probably

¿Quién canta? A lo mejor es mi vecina.
Who's singing? It's **probably** my neighbor.

a mano   by hand

Lo escribí a mano.
I wrote it **by hand.**

a pie   by foot

Fui a tu casa a pie.
I went to your house **by foot.**

The preposition *a* often accompanies certain verbs to form other common expressions. These expressions are always followed by another verb in the infinitive.

aprender a + infinitive to learn to	*Aprendo a tocar el piano.* I **learn how to** play the piano.
ayudar a + infinitive to help	*Le ayudo a mi madre a preparar la cena.* I **help** my mother prepare dinner.
comenzar/empezar a + infinitive to begin to	Comienza *a llover.* It **starts to** rain.
enseñar a + infinitive to show how to	*Te enseño a dibujar.* I'll **teach** you to draw.
invitar a + infinitive to invite to	*Le invito a ir al cine.* I **invite** him/her to go to the movies.

Exercise 1

Form sentences using the preposition *a* in the following situations.

1. To say where you're going for your next vacation.

_____

_____

2. To say how far you are from the closest coffee shop.

_____

_____

3. To say what you'd like to learn to do someday.

_____

_____

4. To say whom you like to help.

_____

_____

5. To say whom you see every day.

_____

_____

Exercise 2

Complete the sentences below with the most appropriate expression from the choices given.

a causa de
a la vez
al menos
a lo mejor
a mano

1. No tengo una computadora. Voy a tener que escribir el

ensayo _____.

2. ¿Dónde está mi teléfono celular? _____

está en tu mochila.

3. Puedo escribir y esuchar música _____.

4. _____ mi dolor de cabeza, no voy a

clase.

5. Te quedan _____ treinta minutos

para terminar el examen.

Exercise 3

Juan took a trip. Translate the following paragraph about his journey into Spanish.

Juan was going to Cuenca for business. He got on the bus and sat next to an attractive girl. When they arrived in the city, Juan was hungry. He invited the girl to eat with him. He helped her get off the bus. They went to a restaurant that was two blocks away from the bus station. Then they visited the city on foot. At 5:00, Juan had to go back to the station. Because of an attractive girl, Juan forgot about his meeting!

_____

_____

_____

_____

_____

_____

_____

_____

_____

_____

_____

Prepositions & Conjunctions *De and En*

As with the preposition *a, de* and *en* are used frequently in Spanish and show direction, position, and motion. They can also be used to describe other qualities of an item.

The preposition *de* is used in the following situations:

to show possession	*La camisa es **de** Marta.* The shirt is Marta**'s.**
to indicate origin	*Soy **de** Río de la Plata.* I'm **from** Río de la Plata.
to identify the material that something is made of	*El plato es **de** plástico.* The plate is made **of** plastic.
to describe a physical characteristic	*La señora **de** los ojos azules es mi madre.* The woman **with** blue eyes is my mother.

***De* is also used in a number of common expressions.**

de esta manera like this, in this manner	*Mira, se hace **de esta manera.*** *Look, you do it **like this.***
de nuevo again	*Mi abuela se cayó **de nuevo** en la escalera.* My grandmother fell on the staircase **again.**
de pie on someone's feet	*Estoy cansadísimo. He estado **de pie** toda la mañana.* I'm really tired. I've been **on** my **feet** all morning.
de repente suddenly	***De repente** el perro empezó a ladrar.* **Suddenly** the dog started barking.
de veras truly	***De veras** que no sé dónde está mi hermano.* I **truly** don't know where my brother is.

The preposition *en* is used in the following situations:

to describe where something is located	*La clase de español está **en** la Sala B.* Spanish class is **in** Room B.
to say *inside of* or *in*	*La leche está **en** la nevera.* The milk is **in** the refrigerator.
to say *on* or *on top of*	*La lámpara está **en** la mesa.* The lamp is **on** the table.
with time expressions, when a specific day of the week is not mentioned	*Tendremos el dinero **en** dos días.* We'll have the money **in** two days.
to express participation in an event	*¿Estuviste **en** la boda?* Were you **at** the wedding?
to express method of travel	*Voy a Granada **en** tren.* I'm going to Granada **by** train.

***En* is used in a number of common expressions.**

en cambio on the other hand	*Yo no hablaba su idioma.* ***En cambio ellos** hablaban el mío.* I didn't speak their language. They, **on the other hand,** spoke mine.
en cuanto a in regard to	***En cuanto a** la música clásica, no soy experto.* **In regards** to classical music, I'm no expert.
en seguida right away	*Te atiendo **en seguida.*** I'll help you **right away.**
en vez de instead of	*Voy a comprar estas zanahorias **en vez de** esas.* I'm going to buy these carrots **instead of** those.

The prepositions *de* and *en* accompany certain verbs to form a number of other common expressions. Some of these expressions are followed by another verb in the infinitive.

acabar de + infinitive to have just done something	**Acabo de comer.** I **just ate.**
dejar de + infinitive to stop	Quiero **dejar** de fumar. I want **to stop smoking.**
depender de depend on	Todavía **dependo de** mis padres. I still **depend on** my parents.
disfrutar de to enjoy	**Disfrutamos del** silencio. We **enjoy the** silence.
pensar de to think of or about	¿Qué **piensas del** libro? What **do you think about** the book?
terminar de + infinitive to finish	**Termino de lavar** los platos. I **finish washing** the dishes.
tratar de + infinitive to try to	**Trata de ayudarme.** He/She **tries to help me.**
consentir en + infinitive to consent to	No **consintió en vender** la casa. He didn't **consent to selling** the house.
consistir en to consist of	¿**En** qué **consiste** el plan? What does the plan **consist of**?
especializarse en to specialize in	Mi hijo **se especializa en** ingeniería. My son **specializes in** engineering.
fijarse en to focus on	**Fíjate en** tu manera de hablar. **Focus on** your way of speaking.
insistir en + infinitive insist on	**Insistimos en ir** a la playa. We **insisted on going to** the beach.
pensar en to think of	Todos los días **pienso en** mi difunto abuelo. I **think of** my late grandfather every day.

Exercise 1

Choose which preposition is indicated by each rule.

A. de   **B. en**

_____ **1.** Indicates possession.

_____ **2.** Indicates where something is located.

_____ **3.** Expresses a method of travel.

_____ **4.** Indicates a material that something is made of.

_____ **5.** Is used with time expressions

_____ **6.** Indicates origin.

Exercise 2

The paragraph below tells a little bit about your friend Julio. Choose between *de* or *en* to fill in the blanks.

El muchacho (**1.**) _____ pelo largo es mi amigo Julio. Es

(**2.**) _____ Perú pero ha vivido (**3.**) _____ Venezuela casi toda

su vida. Julio vive (**4.**) _____ un apartamento con su novia,

Frances. Julio y Frances se acaban (**5.**) _____ comprometer.

Se van a casar (**6.**) _____ mayo. Voy a estar (**7.**) _____ la

boda. (**8.**) _____ repente ¡me quiero casar yo también!

Exercise 3

Imagine that you're the family pet. Write three sentences describing your living situation using the expressions below.

depender de, consistir en, disfrutar de, fijarse en, tratar de

1. _____

2. _____

3. _____

When the direct object of a verb is a person, the preposition *a* must proceed it. This is refered to as the personal *a*, and its only function is to signal that the person that follows is the direct object of the verb, rather than the subject.

Levanté la mesa. (direct object, thing)
I picked up the table.

*Levanté **al** bebé.* (direct object, person)
I picked up the baby.

The personal *a* is also used before the direct object of a verb if the direct object is a pronoun refering to a person, geograhic name (not preceded by the definite artcle), or domestic animal or pet.

*Oigo **a alguien** en el corredor.*
I hear **someone** in the hall.

*No encontré **a nadie** en la oficina.*
I didn't find **anyone** in the office.

*¿Conociste **a alguno** de los amigos de Adriana?*
Did you meet **any** of Adriana's friends?

*No conozco **a ningún** Señor Ramos.*
I don't know **any** Mr. Ramos.

*¿Llamaste a tus primos? Llamé **a uno** de ellos.*
Did you call your cousins? I called **one of them.**

*Extraño mucho **a Bolivia.***
I really miss **Bolivia.**

*Encontré **a mi gato** debajo del sillón.*
I found **my cat** under the couch.

The personal *a* is used before the interrogative words *¿quién?* and *¿quiénes?* (who?), when they are direct objects.

*¿**A quién** esperas?*
Whom are you waiting for?

Exercise 1

Indicate whether the word in boldface in each sentence is the personal *a* or the preposition *a*.

1. Hoy fuimos **al** zoológico.

   _____

2. Invitamos **a** mi amiga, pero ella no nos pudo acompañar.

   _____

3. Vimos muchos animales, inclusive un mono que se acercó **a** mi hermanita.

   _____

4. Mi hermanita se espantó, entonces levanté **a** la niña en mis brazos.

   _____

5. Mi hermanita me dijo: ¡La próxima vez traigo **a** mi perro, Campeón! ¡Él me protegerá!

   _____

Exercise 2

Rewrite the following sentences correctly.
Note: Some of the sentences do not have errors.

1. ¿Viste alguien en el pasillo?

_____

_____

2. Fui a comprar un disco compacto.

_____

_____

3. No quiero discutir a nada con él.

_____

_____

4. Manuel, ¿a quién esperas?

_____

_____

5. Extraño mucho a mi país.

_____

_____

6. Tengo a una amiga peruana.

_____

_____

Exercise 3

Fill in the blanks with *a*, if necessary. Note: Some of the blanks should remain empty.

Tengo (**1.**) _____ vecinos muy desconsiderados. Anoche, por

ejemplo, oí (**2.**) _____ la niña que lloraba toda la noche sin

cesar. Y en el jardín, el gato, Figaro, llamaba (**3.**) _____ su

novia. ¡Miauuu! El hijo de la familia, Rafael, tocaba (**4.**) _____

su música rock a todo volumen. La música despertó hasta

(**5.**) _____ mi abuela sorda. Pensé en llamar (**6.**) _____ la

policía pero decidí hablar con el señor de la casa. Cuando

llegué a la casa no encontré (**7.**) _____ nadie, ni escuché

(**8.**) _____ ningún ruido. ¡Que raro! ¿Me estaba

enloqueciendo? O, se escondieron todos?

Coordinating conjunctions join words, clauses, or sentences that have equivalent functions.

*Ramón **y** Mariana estudian juntos todos los martes.*
Ramón **and** Mariana study together every Tuesday.

*Voy al doctor **porque** me siento muy enfermo.*
I'm going to the doctor **because** I feel really sick.

There are a number of common coordinating conjunctions in Spanish.

o or	*¿Quieres una hamburguesa **o** un perro caliente?* Do you want a hamburger **or** a hotdog?
y and	*Leo el libro **y** tomo notas.* I read the book **and** I take notes.
pero but	*Quisiera ir al concierto **pero** tengo demasiadas tareas.* I'd like to go to the concert **but** I have too much homework.
entonces so, then	*Rompe el sello, **entonces** abre el paquete.* Break the seal, **then** open the package.
sino but rather	*No soy costarricense **sino** guatemalteca.* I'm not Costa Rican **but rather** Guatemalan.
aunque although	*Voy a clase **aunque** no me sienta bien.* I'm going to class **although** I don't feel well.
porque because	*Estas cansado **porque** trabajas tanto.* You're tired **because** you work so much.

The conjuction y becomes e when it precedes a word that begins with the long "i" sound (typically i- or hi-).

*Nina y Lola son madre **e** hija.*
Nina and Lola are mother **and** daughter.

La Excepción

The conjunction *y* does not change to *e* when it precedes words with a *y* sound (as in *hielo*), even if the word starts with *hi-*.

*Este té contiene flores **y** hierbas aromáticas.*
This tea is made of flowers **and** aromatic herbs.

The conjunction o becomes u when it precedes a word that begins with o- or ho-.

*¿Fue ayer **u** hoy que me hablaste de Sara?*
Was it today **or** yesterday that you told me about Sara?

¡Atención!

When *o* joins two numbers, it takes an accent mark to become *ó*. The accent mark distinguishes *o* as a conjunction, rather than the number zero.

*Necesito 100 **ó** 150 pesos.*
I need 100 **or** 150 pesos.

A number of common phrases use coordinating conjunctions.

o...o	either...or
no...ni	neither...nor
a pesar de	in spite of
no obstante	nevertheless
sin embargo	nevertheless

***O** haces tus tareas, **o** no sales con tus amigas.*
Either you do your homework, **or** you're not going out with your friends.

*Voy al parque **a pesar de** la lluvia.*
I'm going to the park **in spite of** the rain.

Exercise 1

Match the Spanish conjunctions in column A to their English equivalents in column B.

	A		B
_____	**1.** e		a. but
_____	**2.** u		b. but rather
_____	**3.** pero		c. so
_____	**4.** aunque		d. and
_____	**5.** sino		e. although
_____	**6.** entonces		f. or

Exercise 2

Below is dialogue you'd likely find in a Spanish soap opera. Complete the exchange between Jaime and Rosa by adding the correct coordinating conjunction phrases.

—Jaime, (**1.**) _____ te vas tú, _____

me voy yo. No podemos continuar así.

—Rosa, corazón mío, pero te amo tanto

(**2.**) _____ que seas tan cruel.

—(**3.**) _____ soy cruel, ¡ _____

soy tu corazón! Esto se acabó.

—Rosa mía, no me dejes. Arruinaste mi futuro

_____ Me aislaste de mi familia _____

Estoy en bancarrota _____ y yo te amo

(**4.**) _____. Te ruego…¡no me dejes sólo!

—Adiós, Jaime.

Exercise 3

Use the most appropriate coordinating conjunction to join the sentence pairs below.

1. ¿Quieres un jugo? ¿Quieres una cola?

_____

_____

2. No es doctora. Es abogada.

_____

_____

3. Mi mamá hace un postre con helado. Mi mamá hace un postre con higos en almíbar.

_____

_____

4. No había nadie en el baño. Entré.

_____

_____

5. Me gusta la música cubana. Tiene un buen ritmo.

_____

_____

Most Spanish numbers are simple to memorize and use. Some numbers, however, change form depending on the nouns they precede.

The number *one* in Spanish changes depending on the noun it modifies. *Un* is used before singular masculine nouns. *Una* is used before singular feminine nouns.

un hombre	**one** man
una manzana	**one** apple

¡Atención!

Uno means *one* when counting.

uno, *dos, tres...*
one, two, three...

The number *twenty-one* also changes depending on the noun it modifies. *Veintiún* is used before masculine nouns. *Veintiuna* is used before feminine nouns.

21 murciélagos = **veintiún** *murciélagos*
twenty-one bats

21 rosas = **veintiuna** *rosas*
twenty-one roses

Starting with the number *thirty-one*, Spanish numbers are written as three separate words. When *one* is part of a compound number, *uno* becomes *un* before a masculine noun and *una* before a feminine noun.

treinta y **una** *sillas*
thirty-**one** chairs

sesenta y **un** *perros*
sixty-**one** dogs

With the exception of *uno,* the numbers up to 199 do not agree in gender. When the numbers 200 through 900 modify a noun, they agree in gender.

*quinient**os** alumn**os***	500 pupils
*trescient**as** niñ**as***	300 girls

The Spanish words for hundred, thousand, and million follow a specialized set of rules. *Ciento* (one hundred) becomes *cien* when it precedes numbers larger than itself.

***cien** mil semillas*	**one hundred** thousand seeds
***ciento** veinte semillas*	**one hundred** and twenty seeds

***Mil* (a thousand, one thousand) is almost always used in the singular, regardless of the number of thousands it represents.**

***dos mil** canciones*	**two thousand** songs

La Excepción

Mil stands alone to indicate one thousand. It is not preceded by *un*.

***mil** centavos*	**one thousand** cents

***Un millón* (a million, one million) is used in both the singular and the plural. When *millón* precedes a noun, it is accompanied by *de*.**

un millón de dólares	**one million** dollars
dos millones de habitantes	**two million** inhabitants

¡Atención!

Mil millones means *a billion* in Spanish. *Un billón* actually means *a trillion*.

Exercise 1

Complete the crossword puzzle by spelling out the cardinal numbers indicated by the clues.

Across

3. 600 platos
4. 1.000 tenedores
5. 1 mesa

Down

1. 21 cucharas
2. cuchillos

Exercise 2

Solve the simple arithmetic problems. Write out the numbers.

1. 1.000 + 200 = _____ páginas

2. 50 – 9 = _____ bolígrafos

3 500.000 + 500.000 = _____ palabras

4. 300 + 24 = _____ escuelas

5. 12 – 11 = _____ profesor

Exercise 3

How much do you think the following items cost, in dólares (dollars)? Write out the numbers in Spanish.

1. un BMW nuevo

_____

2. una casa en tu ciudad

_____

3. un reloj Rolex de oro

_____

4. un viaje en crucero al Caribe

_____

5. un apartamento penthouse en Nueva York

_____

35

36 Numbers *Ordinal Numbers*

Ordinal numbers are the adjective form of cardinal numbers. The ordinal numbers through ten are as follows:

Cardinal Number		Ordinal Number	
uno	one	primero	first
dos	two	segundo	second
tres	three	tercero	third
cuatro	four	cuarto	fourth
cinco	five	quinto	fifth
seis	six	sexto	sexto
siete	seven	séptimo	seventh
ocho	eight	octavo	eight
nueve	nine	noveno	ninth
diez	ten	décimo	tenth

As with other adjectives, ordinal numbers agree in gender and number with the nouns they modify.

el **cuarto** hijo	the **fourth** son
la **cuarta** lección	the **fourth** lesson
las **primeras** gotas de lluvia	the **first drops** of rain
los **primeros** días	the **first days**

As with the adjective *bueno* (*buen*), the ordinals *primero* and *tercero* drop the -o before masculine singular nouns.

el **primer** beso	the **first** kiss
el **tercer** mes	the **third** month

Ordinal numbers usually precede the nouns they modify.

la **sexta** vez	the **sixth** time
el **décimo** aniversario	the **tenth** anniversary

La Excepción

If an ordinal number refers to royalty, a street, or a pope, it comes after the noun.

Juan Pablo **Segundo** (II)	John Paul **the Second**
Alfonso **Octavo** (XIII)	Alfonso **the Eighth**

When using both a cardinal and an ordinal number, the cardinal number comes first.

*Tengo que leer los dos **primeros** capítulos para el martes.*
I need to read the **first two** chapters for Tuesday.

¡Atención!

Ordinal numbers can also stand alone as nouns.

*Fue el **tercero** en irse de la fiesta.*
He was the **third one** to leave the party.

¡Atención!

As in English, ordinal numbers are abbreviated by adding the last syllable, in superscript, to the number.

| primero | 1ro |
| segundo | 2do |

Unlike in English, Spanish ordinals can also be abbreviated also simply by adding the last letter.

| tercero | 3o |
| décimo | 10o |

Lenguaje en Práctica

In many Latin American countries, it is common to name a second-born son *Segundo*. However, parents do not generally name first-born sons *Primero*, or third-born sons *Tercero*.

For numbers after ten, it's common to use the cardinal number rather than the ordinal number. These ordinal numbers are used only in extremely formal situations.

| la calle **treinta y cinco** | **thirty-fifth** street |
| el siglo **dieciocho** | the **eighteenth** century |

undécimo (11th)	quincuagésimo (50th)
duodécimo (12th)	sexagésimo (60th)
decimotecero (13th)	septuagésimo (70th)
decimocuarto (14th)	octogésimo (80th)
decimoquinto (15th)	nonagésimo (90th)
decimosexto (16th)	centésimo (100th)
decimocéptimo (17th)	ducentésimo (200th)
decimoctavo (18th)	tricentésimo (300th)
decimonoveno (19th)	cuadringentésimo (400th)
vigésimo (20th)	quingentésimo (500th)
vigésimo primero (21st)	sexcentésimo (600th)
vigésimo segundo (22nd)	septingentésimo (700th)
vigésimo tercero (23rd)	octigentésimo (800th)
vigésimo cuarto (24th)	noningentésimo (900th)
trigésimo (30th)	milésimo (1,000th)
cuadragésimo (40th)	dosmilésimo (2,000th)

Exercise 1

Answer the following questions.

1. ¿Cuál es la primera letra del alfabeto?

   _____

2. ¿Cuál es la tercera letra del alfabeto?

   _____

3. ¿Cuál es la quinta letra del alfabeto?

   _____

4. ¿Cuál es la séptima letra del alfabeto?

   _____

5. ¿Cuál es la novena letra del alfabeto?

   _____

Exercise 2

Use ordinal numbers to label the floors of the apartment building.

1. _____ piso   4. _____ piso

2. _____ piso   5. _____ piso

3. _____ piso

Exercise 3

Armando is arguing with his brother about channel surfing. Translate their dialogue into Spanish using the correct cardinal and ordinal numbers.

"Armando, it's the fourth channel you've put on! Please don't change the channel!"
"No, it's the third. First I was watching that comedy on Univision, then I was watching the show about Pope Pius the Seventh."
"And then you were watching the second episode of *Betty la Fea*. And now you're watching this documentary on the Spanish king, Phillip the Fourth. That's four. You need to learn to add!"

_____

_____

_____

_____

_____

_____

_____

_____

_____

_____

_____

_____

_____

_____

_____

_____

36

As in English, Spanish uses the verb *estar* (to be) to tell time. Spanish, however, uses the singular (*es*) for the hour of one, and the plural (*son*) for the hours two and above. The definite article also changes from singular (*la*) to plural (*las*).

¿Qué hora **es**?	What time **is it**?
Es la una.	It **is** one o'clock.
Son las dos.	It **is** two o'clock.

The conjunction *y* (and) is used to express the minutes.

Es la una **y cinco**.	It's one-**oh-five**.
Son las cuatro **y quince**.	It's four **fifteen**.

¡Atención!

Son las dos means *it's two o'clock*, while *a las dos* means *at two o'clock*.

There are a number of common time expressions in Spanish.

a... at	*a las diez y media* **at** ten thirty
en punto sharp	*a las seis en punto* at six **sharp**
de la mañana in the morning	*a las nueve de la mañana* at nine **in the morning**
de la tarde in the afternoon	*a las cinco de la tarde* at five **in the afternoon**
de la noche in the evening	*a las diez de la noche* at ten **in the evening**
y media half-past	*a las cuatro y media* at **half-past** four
y cuarto quarter past	*a las once y cuarto* at **quarter past** eleven
y media and a half	*a las siete y media* at seven **thirty** (literally, seven **and a half**)
y cuarto and a quarter	*a las cuatro y cuarto* at four **fifteen** (literally, four **and a quarter**)
mediodía midday	*a mediodía* at **midday** (noon)

medianoche midnight	*a medianoche* at **midnight**

After the half-hour, the minutes can be subtracted from the next hour to express the time, in the same way that *to* or *of* the hour are used in English.

Son las nueve **menos veinte**.	It's nine **minus twenty**. (literally)
Son las seis **menos quince**.	It's six **minus fifteen**. (literally)
Son las seis menos **cuarto**.	It's six **minus one quarter**. (literally)

Lenguaje en Práctica

In most Spanish-speaking countries, the twenty-four-hour clock is used for bus, train, and airplane schedules. In some countries, such as Argentina, this clock is also used more casually, to differentiate between A.M. and P.M. The same language rules apply to the twenty-four-hour clock as apply to the twelve-hour clock, except that speakers do not generally subtract minutes from the hour to come.

*El tren sale a las **trece y quince**.*
The train leaves at **thirteen fifteen**. (1:15 P.M.)

Exercise 1

Fill in the arms of the clocks below to indicate the following times.

1. las cinco menos diez
2. las doce y media
3. las trece y quince
4. las tres en punto
5. las veintitrés y quince

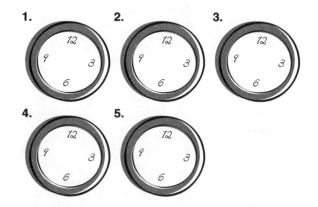

Exercise 2

Use complete sentences to answer the following questions about your daily routine.

1. ¿A qué hora te despiertas generalmente?

_____

_____

_____

2. ¿A qué hora llegas al trabajo/a la escuela?

_____

_____

_____

3. ¿A qué hora almuerzas?

_____

_____

_____

4. ¿A qué hora regresas a la casa?

_____

_____

_____

5. ¿A qué hora te vas a la cama?

_____

_____

_____

Exercise 3

Complete the sentences below with the correct time expression. You may need to consult a map showing time zones.

1. Cuando son las cinco de la mañana en Perú,

_____ en Argentina.

2. Cuando son las cuatro de la tarde en Ecuador,

_____ en México.

3. Cuando son las ocho de la mañana en España,

_____ en Puerto Rico.

4. Cuando son las nueve y cuarto de la noche en la República

Dominicana, _____ en Cuba.

5. Cuando son las dos de la tarde en Guatemala,

_____ en Venezuela.

37

All days of the week are masculine and begin with a lowercase letter.

el lunes	Monday
el martes	Tuesday
el miércoles	Wednesday
el jueves	Thursday
el viernes	Friday
el sábado	Saturday
el domingo	Sunday

Lenguaje en Práctica

Most Spanish-speaking countries consider Monday the first day of the week.

The singular definite article *el* + the day of the week is used when an activity occurs on a specific day. The plural definite article *los* + the day of the week is used when an activity occurs regularly.

El viernes voy a la biblioteca.
On **Friday** I'm going to the library.

Los viernes voy a la biblioteca.
On **Fridays** I go to the library.

La Excepción

All the days of the week use the same form for the plural as they do for the singular, with the exception of *el sábado* (*los sábados*) and *el domingo* (*los domingos*).

The months of the year are also masculine and begin with lowercase letters.

enero	January
febrero	February
marzo	March
abril	April
mayo	May
junio	June
julio	July
agosto	August
septiembre	September
octubre	October
noviembre	November
diciembre	December

The preposition *de* connects the day with the month, and the month with the year.

*Mis padres se mudaron al Ecuador el siete **de** agosto **de** 1973.*
My parents moved to Ecuador on August 7, 197**3**.

Lenguaje en Práctica

In Spanish, years are said aloud just as they are written out.

mil novecientos sesenta y tres
one thousand nine hundred sixty three (1963)

The days of the month are expressed by the cardinal numbers. The definite article *el* always precedes them.

*El Día de la Independencia es **el 24 de mayo**.*
Independence Day is **May 24.**

La Excepción

The first day of the month is always expressed by the ordinal number: *primero.*

*Nací el **primero** de mayo.*
I was born on May **first.**

La Excepción

The definite article is omitted when dating a letter.

14 de abril de 2006
April 14, 2006

Lenguaje en Práctica

In Spanish-speaking counties, the date is written with the day first, followed by the month, then the year. When the date is written in numeral form only, periods are used to separate the different elements.

| *el 30 de noviembre de 1970* | November 30, 1970 |
| *30.11.70* | 11/30/70 |

There are two common ways to ask about the date.

| *¿**Cuál es** la fecha?* | **What's** the date? |
| *Es **el once** de julio.* | It's July **11.** |

¿A cuántos estamos?   What's the date?
(Literally, **at how many** days are we?)

Estamos al once de julio.   It's July **11.** (Literally, we're at July 11.)

Exercise 1

Write complete sentences about the holidays below, including the full dates.

1. Día de San Valentín

_____

_____

_____

2. Día de los Muertos

_____

_____

_____

3. Día de la Raza

_____

_____

_____

4. Navidad

_____

_____

_____

5. Año Nuevo

_____

_____

_____

Exercise 2

Match the dates in column A to the Spanish equivalents in column B.

A	B
_____ **1.** May 1, 1976	a. 2.3.1920
_____ **2.** February 3, 1920	b. 12.11.2006
_____ **3.** November 12, 2001	c. 1.5.1976
_____ **4.** January 5, 1976	d. 3.2.1920
_____ **5.** March 2, 1920	e. 5.1.1976
_____ **6.** December 11, 2006	f. 11.12.2001

Exercise 3

When were the following people born? Write complete sentences using the full dates.

1. tu hermano/hermana _____

_____

_____

2. tu padre _____

_____

_____

3. tu abuelo _____

_____

_____

4. tu mejor amigo/amiga _____

_____

_____

5. tu primo _____

_____

_____

38

There are several ways to form a question in Spanish.

The subject and the verb can be inverted, (switched in placement), to form a question. Note that unlike in English, no equivalent of the verb *to do* is used to form questions in Spanish. This verb is implied.

Diego habla español.	Diego speaks Spanish.
¿Habla español Diego?	Does Diego speak Spanish?

¡Atención!

When inverting the subject and the verb, the word order will generally be: verb + rest of predicate (if any) + subject. However, Spanish is flexible: as long as the verb comes first, it generally doesn't matter which noun comes next.

*¿**Viaja** mucho Gustavo?*
Does Gustavo **travel** a lot?

*¿**Viaja** Gustavo mucho?*
Does Gustavo **travel** a lot?

Lenguaje en Práctica

Though it is not grammatically correct, some Spanish-speakers (notably, those in the Caribbean) do not always invert the subject and verb in a question, especially in *tú* questions with *¿Qué?* and *¿Quién?*

¿Qué tú quieres?	What do you want?
¿Quién tú eres?	Who are you?

Placing a remark, or tag, such as *sí* or *no,* at the end of a sentence can change it into a question.

*Diego habla español, ¿**no**?*	Diego speaks Spanish, **doesn't he**?

Some questions seek a specific piece of information. These questions begin with question words, or *palabras interrogativas*.

¿Qué? What?	*¿**Qué** quieres?* **What** do you want?
Which?	*¿**Qué** postre quieres?* **Which** dessert do you want?
¿Quién?/¿Quiénes? Who?/Who? (plural)	*¿**Quién** es?/¿**Quiénes** son?* **Who** is it?/**Who** are they?
¿Cuál? Which one?	*¿**Cuál** es tu libro?* **Which one** is your book?
¿Cuáles? Which ones?	*¿**Cuáles** son tus libros?* **Which ones** are your books?
¿Cuándo? When?	*¿**Cuándo** vamos al teatro?* **When are** we going to the theater?
¿Cuánto/a? How much?	*¿**Cuánta** leche quieres en tu café?* **How much** milk do you want in your coffee?
¿Cuántos/as? How many?	*¿**Cuántas** galletas quieres?* **How many** cookies do you want?
¿Dónde? Where?	*¿**Dónde** está el carro?* **Where** is the car?
¿Adónde? To where?	*¿**Adónde** vas?* **Where are** you going?
¿De dónde? From where?	*¿**De dónde** eres?* **Where** are you **from**?
¿Cómo? How?	*¿**Cómo** tomas el café?* **How** do you take your coffee?
¿Por qué? Why?	*¿**Por qué** estudias el español?* **Why** do you study Spanish?

¡Atención!

In Spanish, an accent mark is used to distinguish the interrogative words from their non-interrogative forms.

*¿**Dónde** está?*	**Where** is she?
*Está **donde** Lucía.*	She's **at** Lucia's.
*¿**Por qué** no vienes conmigo?*	**Why** aren't you coming with me?
***Porque** no quiero.*	**Because** I don't want to.

Exercise 1

Complete the crossword puzzle with the question words indicated in the clues below.

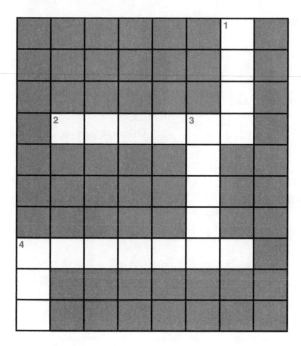

Across
2. When?
4. Who? (plural)

Down
1. How?
3. Where?
4. What?

Exercise 2

Form questions from the statements below. For an extra challenge, use mulitple interrogative forms for each item.

1. La banda se llama *Obsesión*.

_____

_____

2. Gabriela canta en la banda.

_____

_____

3. Rafael toca la guitarra.

_____

_____

4. A veces Aurelio toca la batería.

_____

_____

5. La banda viaja por todo el país.

_____

_____

Exercise 3

Use the interrogative words to form the questions that the following statements answer.

1. Es mi hermana, Katy.

_____

_____

2. Tiene 20 años.

_____

_____

3. Estudia en Salamanca, España.

_____

_____

4. Se llama Diego.

_____

_____

5. Es de Barcelona.

_____

_____

6. Regresa el lunes.

_____

_____

39

The distinctions between the interrogatives *¿qué?, ¿cuál?,* and *¿cómo?* can be confusing. Their usage depends on the words that follow them.

¿Qué? is used before both verbs and nouns. When *¿qué?* comes before a verb, it means *what*. When *¿qué?* comes before a noun, it means *which*.

¿Qué es ese ruido?	**What is** that noise?
¿Qué música prefieres?	**Which music** do you prefer?

¿Qué? is also used when asking for a definition or an explanation.

¿Qué significa vistazo?	**What does** *vistazo* **mean**?

¿Cuál? is used before a verb and before *de* + noun phrases to mean *which*.

¿Cuál escogiste?	**Which one** did you **choose**?
¿Cuál de las chaquetas es tuya?	**Which of** the jackets is yours?

¡Atención!

¿Cuál? cannot precede a noun on its own. *¿Qué?* is used to ask *which* in these instances.

¿Que chaqueta es tuya?	**Which jacket** is yours?

¿Cuál?/¿Cuáles? is also used when choosing among possibilities.

¿Cuál quiere, el jugo de papaya o el de maracuyá?
Which do you want, the papaya or maracuyá juice?

The interrogative word used to ask *how* depends on the words that follow it. **¿Cómo?** is used to ask *how* when a verb follows.

¿Cómo estás?	How **are you**?

In English, some questions that ask *how* are followed by an adjective or adverb, such as *how far* or *how fast*. In Spanish, these questions are formed using a preposition + *¿qué?*

How far is the store?	*¿A qué distancia queda el almacén?* **At what** distance is the store? (literally)
How big is your house?	*¿De qué tamaño es su casa?* **Of what** size is your house? (literally)
How often do you travel to Argentina?	*¿Con que frequencia viaja a Argentina?* **With what** frequency do you travel to Argentina? (literally)

Exercise 1

Match the rules in column A to the appropriate interrogative words in column B.

	A	B
____	**1.** It can come before a noun.	
____	**2.** It can come before a verb.	
____	**3.** It can come before *de* + noun phrase, but not a noun on its own.	a. ¿Qué?
____	**4.** It is used to choose among several options.	b. ¿Cuál?
____	**5.** It is used to request a definition.	c. ¿Qué? or ¿Cuál?
____	**6.** It means *which*.	

Exercise 2

Translate the following sentences into Spanish.

1. Which of the two cups is yours?

_____

_____

2. What did just ask for, sir?

_____

_____

_____

3. Which steak would you like?

_____

_____

4. What does *Chateaubriand* mean?

_____

_____

_____

5. Which would you like, the flan or the *crema catalana*?

_____

_____

_____

Exercise 3

Rewrite the following sentences correctly.
Note: Some of the sentences do not have errors.

1. Violeta, ¿cómo se llama tu profesor de historia?

_____

_____

_____

2. ¿Cómo interesante es su clase?

_____

_____

_____

3. ¿Cómo se porta con los estudiantes?

_____

_____

_____

4. ¿Cómo fáciles son las tareas?

_____

_____

_____

5. ¿Cómo larga es la clase?

_____

_____

_____

40

Verbs *Present Tense Regular Verbs*

To form the present tense of all regular *-ar, -er,* or *-ir* verbs, the first section of the word, or stem, remains the same, and the ending is conjugated to agree with the subject.

The present tense of an *-ar* verb with a singular subject drops the ending and adds *-o, -as,* and *-a.* The present tense of an *-ar* verb with a plural subject drops the ending and adds *-amos, -áis,* and *-an.*

	Singular	Plural
cantar (to sing)	yo cant**o** i sing	nosotros/as cant**amos** we sing
	tú cant**as** you sing	vosotros/as cant**áis** you sing
	él/ella cant**a** he/she/it sings usted cant**a** you (formal) sing	ellos/as cant**an** they sing ustedes cant**an** you (formal) sing

¡Atención!

A Spanish sentence can be made up of a single conjugated verb because the verb includes both the subject and the predicate. The subject of a verb can generally be determined simply by looking at the verb ending. The subject or subject pronoun is necessary only if there is ambiguity.

Canta. **He/She** sings.
Cantan. **They** sing.

The present tense of an *-er* verb with a singular subject drops the ending and adds *-o, -es,* and *-e.* The present tense of an *-er* verb with a plural subject drops the ending and adds *-emos, -éis,* and *-en.*

	Singular	Plural
comer (to eat)	yo com**o** I eat	nosotros/as com**emos** we eat
	tú com**es** you eat	vosotros/as com**éis** you eat
	él/ella com**e** he/she/it eats usted com**e** you (formal) eat	ellos/as com**en** they eat ustedes com**en** you (formal) eat

The present tense of an *-ir* verb with a singular subject drops the ending and adds *-o, -es,* and *-e.* The present tense of an *-ir* verb with a plural subject drops the ending and adds *-imos, -ís,* and *-en.*

	Singular	Plural
escribir (to write)	yo escrib**o** I write	nosotros/as escrib**imos** we write
	tú escrib**es** you write	vosotros/as escrib**ís** you write
	él/ella escrib**e** he/she/it writes usted escrib**e** you (formal) write	ellos/as escrib**en** they write ustedes escrib**en** you (formal) write

Exercise 1

Camila and Patricio are talking on the phone. Fill in the blanks with the correct present tense form of the verb in parentheses.

Camila: ¡Hola, Patricio!
Patricio: Hola, Camila. ¿Qué tal las clases?

Camila: Muy bien. (**1.**) _____ (tomar) cuatro

clases: inglés, biología, química y educación física.

—(**2.**) _____ (esperar) tomar una más, pero no

sé si tenga tiempo. Y tú, ¿cuántas clases (**3.**) _____

(tomar)?

Patricio: Uf…sólo dos. Pero son difíciles. Todas las noches

(**4.**) _____ (estudio) mucho.

Camila: ¿Cuáles son?

Patricio: Arte y un curso de cinematografía.

Camila: O sea, (**5.**) _____ (dibujar) y

(**6.**) _____ (mirar) la tele. ¡No me suena mal!

Exercise 2

Fill in the blank with the most appropriate verb from the options below. Conjugate the verb to agree with the subject.

escribir	vender
cree	comprender
aprender	leer

Mis padres van al trabajo todos los días de la semana. Ellos

(**1.**) _____ libros educativos en una librería.

Mi hermana y yo (**2.**) _____ mucho de

ellos. Por ejemplo, (**3.**) _____ que es más

importante estudiar que salir todas las noches con nuestros

amigos. Mi padre no (**4.**) _____ que es

necesario mirar mucho la televisión. Por eso, yo

(**5.**) _____ un libro o una revista antes de

acostarme. Mi hermana, en cambio, (**6.**) _____

mensajes electrónicos a sus amigas.

Exercise 3

The items below have to do with a quiet Sunday afternoon with the family. Form complete sentences by conjugating the verbs.

1. yo / comer / el desayuno

_____

2. tú / mirar / la / televisión

_____

_____

3. mi padre, Jaime / leer / el periódico

_____

_____

4. mi madre, Maite / abrir / las cartas

_____

_____

5. hoy / nosotros / recibir / una carta / de / Tía Roberta

_____

_____

6. ella / vivir / en / Costa Rica

_____

_____

41

In addition to regular -*ar*, -*er*, and -*ir* verbs, Spanish has stem-changing verbs. When stem-changing verbs are conjugated, the stressed vowel of their stem changes in all but the *nosotros/as* and *vosotros/as* forms. There are four types of stem-changing verbs: *e → ie*, *e → i*, *o → ue*, and *u → ue*.

For *e → ie* stem-changing verbs, the *e* changes to *ie* when conjugated.

	Singular	Plural
	*yo ci**e**rro* I close	*nosotros cerramos* we close
cerrar (to close)	*tú ci**e**rras* you close	*vosotros cerráis* you close
	*él/ella ci**e**rra* he/she/it closes *usted ci**e**rra* you (formal) close	*ellos/as ci**e**rran* they close *ustedes ci**e**rran* you (formal) close

Other common *e → ie* verbs include the following:

despertar	to awaken
empezar	to begin
pensar	to think
perder	to lose
defender	to defend
entender	to understand
querer	to want or love
sentir	to feel
mentir	to lie
divertir	to amuse
preferir	to prefer

¡Atención!

Pensar + infinitive expresses a plan to do something. *Pensar* + *en* means *to think about something or someone.*

¿Piensas ir a clase hoy?	Do you **think** you'll **go to** class today?
Pienso en *tí todos los días.*	I **think about** you every day.

For *e → i* stem-changing verbs, the *e* changes to *i* when conjugated.

	Singular	Plural
	*yo p**i**do* I ask	*nosotros pedimos* we ask
pedir (to request/ask)	*tú p**i**des* you ask	*vosotros pedís* you ask
	*él/ella p**i**de* he/she/it asks *usted p**i**de* you (formal) asks	*ellos/as p**i**den* they ask *ustedes p**i**den* you (formal) asks

Other common *e → i* verbs include the following:

repetir	to repeat
servir	to serve
vestir	to dress

For *o → ue* stem-changing verbs, the *o* changes to *ue* when conjugated.

contar	to count/tell

	Singular	Plural
	*yo c**ue**nto* I count	*nosotros contamos* we count
contar (to count/tell)	*tú c**ue**ntas* you count	*vosotros contáis* you count
	*él/ella c**ue**nta* he/she/it counts *usted c**ue**nta* you (formal) count	*ellos/as c**ue**ntan* they count *ustedes c**ue**ntan* you (formal) count

Other common *o → ue* verbs include the following:

almorzar	to have lunch
costar	to cost
recordar	to remember
volver	to return
devolver	to give back
llover	to rain
mover	to move

Jugar is the only *u → ue* stem-changing verb. **Jugar** is conjugated as follows:

Singular	Plural
*yo j**ue**go* I play	*nosotros jugamos* we play
*tú j**ue**gas* you play	*vosotros jugáis* you play
*él/ella j**ue**ga* he/she/it plays *usted j**ue**ga* you (formal) play	*ellos/as j**ue**gan* they play *ustedes j**ue**gan* you (formal) play

jugar (to play)

Exercise 1

Fill in the blank with the correct form of the verb.

1. pensar: *yo* _____

2. entender: *ella* _____

3. mentir: *nosotros* _____

4. repetir: *tú* _____

5. recordar: *vosotros* _____

6. mover: *ustedes* _____

Exercise 2

What are the people in the pictures doing? Describe each action with a complete sentence using the appropriate verb.

seguir   pensar   encontrar
jugar   dormir

1. El señor _____

2. Yo _____

3. Los niños _____

4. El bebé _____

5. Laura _____

42

Verbs *Present Tense Verbs with Irregular Yo Forms*

Some Spanish verbs are irregular in the first-person singular (*yo*) form of the present tense. These verbs follow the regular conjugation rules in all other forms.

The following verbs drop their endings and add -*go*:

hacer	to do, make
*yo ha**go***	I make

*Yo **hago** un pastel para el cumpleaños de mi hermana.*
I **am making** a cake for my sister's birthday.

poner	to put
*yo pon**go***	I put

*Yo **pongo** la carne en la refrigeradora.*
I **put** the meat in the refrigerator.

salir	to go out
*yo sal**go***	I go out

*Yo **salgo** con mis amigas cada viernes.*
I **go out** with my friends every Friday.

¡Atención!

The verb *hacer* is used to talk about the weather.

*¿Qué tiempo **hace**?*
What **is** the weather **like**?

***Hace** sol/calor/frio/viento.*
It's sunny/hot/cold/windy.

¡Atención!

Salir can be combined with prepositions to form certain common phrases. *Salir con* is used to say you're going out with someone. *Salir de* is used to say you're leaving a place. *Salir para* is used to refer to a destination.

*María **sale con** Francisco.*
María **is going out with** Francisco.

*Jaime **sale del** cine.*
Jaime **is leaving** the cinema.

*Mañana **salgo para** Puerto Rico.*
Tomorrow **I leave for** Puerto Rico.

Some -*go* verbs have both an irregular first-person singular conjugation and a stem change.

	Singular	Plural
decir (to say)	yo **digo** I say	nosotros decimos we say
	tú **dices** you say	vosotros decís you say
	él/ella **dice** he/she/it says usted **dice** you (formal) say	ellos/as **dicen** they say ustedes **dicen** you (formal) say
tener (to have)	yo **tengo** I have	nosotros tenemos we have
	tú **tienes** you have	vosotros tenéis you have
	él/ella **tiene** he/she/it has usted **tiene** you (formal) have	ellos/as **tienen** they have ustedes **tienen** you (formal) have
venir (to come)	yo **vengo** I come	nosotros venimos we come
	tú **vienes** you come	vosotros venís you come
	él/ella **viene** he/she/it comes usted **viene** you (formal) come	ellos/as **vienen** they come ustedes **vienen** you (formal) come

The following verbs drop their endings and add -*zco*:

conocer	to know
*yo cono**zco***	I know

parecer	to appear/to seem
*yo pare**zco***	I appear

The following verbs drop their endings and add -*oy*:

dar	to give
*yo d**oy***	I give

estar	to be
*yo **estoy***	I am

Exercise 1

Traer (to bring) is a *-go* verb. Fill in the table with the correct present tense forms of *traer*.

Person	Singular	Plural
1st	yo: (**1.**) _____	nosotros/as: (**6.**) _____
2nd	tú: (**2.**) _____	vosotros/as: (**7.**) _____
3rd	usted: (**3.**) _____	ellos: (**8.**) _____
	él: (**4.**) _____	ellas: (**9.**) _____
	ella: (**5.**) _____	ustedes: (**10.**) _____

Exercise 2

Fill in the blanks with the correctly conjugated verbs from the choices below.

traer   decir
poner   salir
dar

1. Yo _____ comida a la fiesta de Iris.

2. Yo _____ un disco nuevo en el

reproductor de CD.

3. Yo _____ a Iris un regalo muy bonito.

4. Yo le _____ que tenga un buen

cumpleaños.

5. Después de la fiesta, yo _____ con mi

novio, Gregorio.

Exercise 3

Read the description of Rosalba. Rewrite the description, putting yourself in Rosalba's place.

Rosalba es estudiante de arquitectura en la Universidad de Salamanca. Hace sus tareas por la tarde, y de noche sale con sus amigos. Rosalba lleva ropa bonita y se mantiene muy bien. ¡Pues está siempre en busca de un novio! Conoce a mucha gente pero nunca ha encontrado a su "media naranja." Supone que algún día le encontrará.

_____

_____

_____

_____

_____

_____

_____

_____

_____

_____

_____

_____

_____

_____

_____

_____

43

Regular verbs that end in *-uir*, *-iar*, and *-uar* change slightly when conjugated.

-uir verbs change spelling when conjugated in all forms except *nosotros/as* and *vosotros/as*. When conjugated, the *i* in -uir verbs becomes a *y*.

	Singular	Plural
incluir (to include)	yo inclu**y**o I include	nosotros incluimos we include
	tú inclu**y**es you include	vosotros incluís you include
	él/ella inclu**y**e he/she/it includes usted inclu**y**e you (formal) include	ellos/as inclu**y**en they include ustedes inclu**y**en you (formal) include

Other common verbs -uir verbs include the following:

destruir	to destroy
distribuir	to distruibute
huir	to flee
instruir	to instruct

When -iar verbs are conjugated, the *i* in the singular and third-person plural is stressed and takes an accent mark.

	Singular	Plural
enviar (to send)	yo env**í**o I send	nosotros enviamos we send
	tú env**í**as you send	vosotros enviáis you send
	él/ella env**í**a he/she/it sends usted env**í**a you send	ellos/as env**í**an they send ustedes env**í**an you send

Other common -iar verbs include the following:

confiar(en)	to trust (in)
guiar	to guide
criar	to bring up
espiar	to spy
vaciar	to empty

When -uar verbs are conjugated, the *u* in the singular and third-person plural is stressed and takes an accent mark.

	Singular	Plural
actuar (to act)	yo act**ú**o I act	nosotros actuamos we act
	tú act**ú**as you act	vosotros actuáis you act
	él/ella act**ú**a he/she/it acts usted act**ú**a you (formal) act	ellos/as act**ú**an they act ustedes act**ú**an you (formal) act

Other common -uir verbs include the following:

continuar	to continue
graduarse	to graduate
evaluar	to evaluate
insinuar	to hint

Exercise 1

Match the subject pronouns in column A to the correct conjunctions in column B.

A	B
_____ **1.** tú	a. guiáis
_____ **2.** nosotros	b. confían
_____ **3.** yo	c. se gradúa
_____ **4.** vosotros	d. destruyo
_____ **5.** ellos	e. actuamos
_____ **6.** él	f. distribuyes

Exercise 2

Use the elements below to create five logical sentences.

vosotros	graduarse	los documentos
ella	enviar	secretos
El señor Naula	confiar	los folletos
yo	distribuir	políticos
tú	destruir	en el doctor
		Espinosa
		el próximo mayo
		un carta de
		cumpleaños a
		Mónica

1. _____

_____

_____

_____

2. _____

_____

_____

_____

3. _____

_____

_____

_____

4. _____

_____

_____

_____

5. _____

_____

_____

_____

Exercise 3

Bernarda is struggling over an upcoming exam. Fill in the blanks in the dialogue below with the correct form of the verb in parentheses.

—Bernarda, ¿cuándo (**1.** *graduarse*) _____?

—En diciembre, pero tengo que pasar el examen de cálculo

primero. Va a ser muy dificil.

—No seas así. Si (**2.** *continuar*) _____

estudiando, te va a ir super bien.

—El profesor nos (**3.** *insinuar*) _____que

va a ser facil, pero no (**4.** *confiar*) _____en

él. ¡Quisiera saber que va a estar en el examen! Estoy tan

nerviosa. ¿Qué pasa si no me (**5.** *evaluar*) _____

justamente? ¡Voy a tener que repetir el año!

—No seas tonta. ¡Es cálculo! Hay una respuesta correcta y

una incorrecta!

The verb *to be* is one of the most important verbs in English. The same is true in Spanish. However, Spanish has two words that mean *to be*: *ser* and *estar*. Both are irregular verbs, and both have specific uses.

Ser is an irregular verb that expresses permanent characteristics.

	Singular	Plural
	yo **soy** I am	*nosotros* **somos** we are
ser (to be)	*tú* **eres** you are	*vosotros* **sois** you are
	él/ella **es** he/she/it is *usted* **es** you (formal) are	*ellos/as* **son** they are *ustedes* **son** you (formal) are

Ser is used in the following situations:

Rule	Example
to identify people and things	*José y Antonio* **son** *mis hermanos.* José and Antonio **are** my brothers.
to express possession, with *de*	*El lapíz* **es de** *Jaime.* The pencil **is** Jaime's.
to express origin or nationality, with *de*	*¿***Eres de** *Chile?* You **are from** Chile?
to tell time and date	**Son** *las tres y media.* It **is** three-thirty.
to indicate what something is made of	*El plato* **es** *de plástico.* The plate **is** plastic.
to identify where or when an event takes place	*La boda* **es** *en la Sala Grande.* The wedding **is** in the Grand Salon.

¡Atención!

You can think of the verb *ser* as generally equivalent to an equal (=) sign. *Ser* links two elements that are grammatically similar, such as two nouns, two infinitive verbs, or a pronoun and a noun.

Hoy (noun) **es** *martes* (noun).
Today **is** Tuesday.

Amar (infinitive) **es** *vivir* (infinitive).
To love **is** to live.

Yo (pronoun) **soy** *estudiante* (noun).
I **am** a student.

Estar has an irregular yo form and an accented á on most other forms.

	Singular	Plural
	yo **estoy** I am	*nosotros* estamos we are
estar (to be)	*tú* est**á**s you are	*vosotros* est**á**is you are
	él/ella est**á** he/she/it is *usted* est**á** you (formal) are	*ellos/as* est**á**n they are *ustedes* est**á**n you (formal) are

Estar often expresses incidental characteristics and is used in the following situations:

Rule	Example
to refer to location	*El libro* **está** *en la biblioteca.* The book **is** in the library.
to ask about health or state of being	*¿Cómo* **está** *tu mamá?* How **is** your mom?
to express physical states or conditions	**Estoy** *muy cansado.* I *am* very tired.
to refer to the weather	**Está** *nublado.* It **is** cloudy.
with the progressive tenses to indicate ongoing action	**Están** *comiendo en el comedor.* They **are** eating in the dining room.

¡Atención!

Estar is often used in prepositional phrases to indicate location.

*El libro **está encima de** la mesa.*
The book **is on top of** the table.

*La biblioteca **está lejos del** gimnasio.*
The library **is far from** the gym.

*El lápiz **está al lado del** papel.*
The pencil **is next to** the paper.

Exercise 1

Decide which of the situations below call for *ser* and which call for *estar*.

A. ser	B. estar

_____ **1.** To ask about health.

_____ **2.** To identify people and things.

_____ **3.** To express possession.

_____ **4.** To tell location.

_____ **5.** To express physical states.

_____ **6.** To say what something is made of.

Exercise 2

Choose between *son* and *están* to complete this paragraph about Enrique and Ana.

Enrique y Ana (**1.**)_____ mis primos argentinos.

(**2.**)_____ de Buenos Aires. (**3.**)_____ aquí

por un mes para visitar a nuestros abuelos. (**4.**)_____

muy simpáticos. (**5.**)_____ muy cansados por el

viaje pero (**6.**)_____ segura de que se animarán

después de descansar un poco.

Exercise 3

Imagine you're on a first date. Translate the following sentences into Spanish using the correct *to be* verb.

1. Hi! How are you?

_____

_____

2. I'm from Uruguay. Where are you from?

_____

_____

3. The restaurant is close to the library.

_____

_____

4. The concert is in the *Palacio de la Cumbia*.

_____

_____

5. It's midnight. Are you tired?

_____

_____

Exercise 4

You're writing a brief bio for your blog. Describe yourself using at least two sentences with *ser* and two sentences with *estar*.

_____

_____

_____

_____

_____

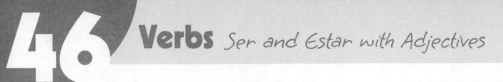

Ser and *estar* can both be used with descriptive adjectives.

Ser is used to express inherent qualities, or qualities that are unlikely to change. For example, *ser* is used with adjectives that describe nationality, size, or color.

Soy *ecuatoriana.*	I **am** Ecuadorian.
Las manzanas **son** *rojas.*	The apples **are** red.
La pelota **es** *redonda.*	The ball **is** round.

Ser is also used with adjectives that describe personal characteristics or qualities.

Miguel **es** *alto.*	Miguel **is** tall.
Mi hermana **es** *simpática.*	My sister **is** nice.

Estar is used with adjectives to describe qualities, or conditions, that are likely to change.

Estoy *cansado.*	**I'm** tired.
Mauricio **está** *nervioso.*	Mauricio **is** nervous.

¡Atención!

The meaning of a sentence can change depending on whether *ser* or *estar* is used. When *ser* is used, the accompanying adjective describes a permanent quality. When *estar* is used, the quality described is of the moment; it has changed from the past or will change in the future.

Las manzanas **son** *rojas.*
The apples **are** red.
Las manzanas **están** *rojas.*
The apples **are** red (right now).

*¡***Eres** *bella, Margarita!*
You **are** beautiful, Margarita!
*¡***Estás** *bella, Margarita!*
You **look** beautiful (at this moment), Margarita!

Some adjectives change meaning depending on whether *ser* or *estar* is used.

aburrido (boring, bored)	*Esa profesora* **es aburrida.** That professor **is boring.** *Esa profesora* **está aburrida.** That professor **is bored.**
bueno (good, tasty)	*La fruta* **es buena** *para la salud.* Fruit **is good** for your health. *La fruta* **está buena.** The fruit **is tasty.**
cómodo (comfortable object, comfortable person)	*La silla* **es cómoda.** The chair **is comfortable.** **Estoy cómodo.** I **am comfortable.**
rico (wealthy, tasty)	*Mi tío es* **rico.** My uncle **is wealthy.** *El pollo* **está rico.** The chicken **is good.**

Exercise 1

Decide whether *ser* or *estar* would be more appropriate in the statements below, and fill in the blank with the conjugated form.

1. Margarita_____ portuguesa.

2. Pancho, ¿_____ enamorado de Isabel?

3. ¡Qué altas_____ las niñas ahora!

4. Vosotros no_____ cansados; simplemente

   _____ perezosos.

5. Las monjas_____ muy humildes.

Exercise 2

Translate the following sentences into Spanish using the correct translation of *to be*.

1. Roberto won the lottery. Now Roberto is rich.
   This pea soup is really tasty.

   _____

   _____

   _____

2. Martín, your car is so comfortable.
   I'm going to stay here for a while. I'm comfortable.

   _____

   _____

   _____

3. I'm so bored! There's nothing to do...
   Javiera, your brother is so boring. How can you stand him?

   _____

   _____

   _____

Exercise 3

Describe each of the following people whom you know. Write one sentence with *ser* + adjective to describe a permanent quality, and one with *estar* + adjective to describe a temporary quality.

1. tu mejor amigo / a

   _____

   _____

2. tu abuelo / a

   _____

   _____

   _____

   _____

3. tu novio / a

   _____

   _____

   _____

4. tu profesor / a favorito / a

   _____

   _____

   _____

   _____

46

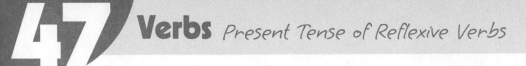

Reflexive verbs are used to indicate that the subject is doing something to or for himself/herself. In a sentence containing a reflexive verb, both the subject and object of the verb are the same person or thing.

A verb is made reflexive by adding the relative pronoun *se* to the end of the infinitive form.

lavar (to wash) + *-se*   *lavarse* (to wash oneself)
levantar (to raise, to lift) + *-se*   *levantarse* (to get oneself up)

acostarse	to go to bed
bañarse	to bathe
cepillarse	to brush
despedirse de	to say good-bye to
despertarse	to wake up
dormirse	to go to sleep
llamarse	to be called/named
peinarse	to comb one's hair
ponerse	to put on
preocuparse	to worry about
probarse	to try on
quedarse	to stay
quitarse	to take off
sentarse	to sit down
sentirse	to feel
vestirse	to get dressed

When conjugated, reflexive verbs always include the reflexive pronoun.

	Singular		Plural
me	myself	*nos*	ourselves
te	yourself	*os*	yourselves
se	himself/herself/ itself/yourself (formal)	*se*	themselves/ yourselves (formal)

Reflexive pronouns follow the same rules for placement as object pronouns. They usually appear before the conjugated verb.

*Yo **me lavo.***
I **wash myself.**

*Ellos **se visten.***
They **dress themselves.**

*Yo **me cepillo** los dientes.*
I **brush my** teeth.

¡Atención!

In Spanish, unlike in English, possessive adjectives (*mi*, *tu*, *su*, and so on) are not used with parts of the body. The definite article is used with the reflexive pronoun instead.

*María **se lava la** cara.*   María **washes her** face.

Some reflexive verbs have stem changes. Some common stem-changing reflexive verbs include the following:

o → ue	acostarse	*La niña se ac**ue**sta a las siete.* The girl goes to bed at seven.
e → i	despedirse de	*Me desp**i**do de mi abuela.* I say good-bye to my grandmother.
o → ue	dormirse	*Siempre me d**ue**rmo en el bus.* I always fall asleep on the bus.
o → ue	probarse	*La muchacha se pr**ue**ba el sombrero.* The girl tries on the hat.
e → ie	sentarse	*La mujer se s**ie**nta en la banca.* The woman sits on the bench.
e → ie	sentirse	*¿Te s**ie**ntes bien?* Do you feel all right?
e → i	vestirse	*El cura se v**i**ste de negro.* The priest wears black.

Exercise 1

Decide whether the statements below call for a reflexive or non-reflexive verb. Then complete the sentences with the correct form.

1. (despertarse, despertar)

El domingo Santiago _____ a las once

de la mañana.

Santiago _____ a su papá con su

música rock.

2. (ponerse, poner)

Yo _____ el agua a hervir.

Yo _____ las zapatillas antes de salir de

mi habitación.

3. (bañarse, baño)

Nosotros _____ antes de ir al trabajo.

Nosotros _____ al bebé con agua tibia.

Exercise 2

Use the phrases below to construct complete sentences. Conjugate the reflexive verbs for each.

1. mamá y papá/levantarse a las seis en punto

_____

_____

2. Ramona y yo / despertarse a las siete

_____

_____

3. yo / lavarse la cara y cepillarse los dientes

_____

_____

4. todos / sentarse a la mesa para desayunar

_____

_____

5. yo / ponerse la chaqueta antes de salir

_____

_____

Exercise 3

What's your morning routine? Fill out the schedule below using reflexive verbs in complete sentences to indicate what you do.

6:00 A.M. _____

_____

6:30 A.M. _____

_____

7:00 A.M. _____

_____

7:30 A.M. _____

_____

8:00 A.M. _____

_____

8:30 A.M. _____

_____

9:00 A.M. _____

_____

47

Some verbs take the reflexive construction even though they don't necessarily indicate an action done to or for oneself. These reflexive verbs have specific idiomatic meanings in Spanish.

acordarse de	to remember
arrepentirse de	to repent
atreverse a	to dare
burlarse de	to make fun of
irse	to go away
olvidarse de	to forget
parecerse a	to look like
quejarse	to complain
reírse	to laugh at
tratarse de	to be about

*¿**Te acuerdas** de Daniel?*
Do **you remember** Daniel?

*Los niños **se burlan** de la niña.*
The boys **make fun of** the girl.

Reflexive verbs are used to express a physical or mental change. In English, these changes would be expressed with the verb *to get* or *to become*.

asustarse	to get scared
cansarse	to get tired
casarse	to get married
desmayarse	to faint
enfadarse	to get angry
enojarse	to get angry
resfriarse	to catch a cold

*No puedo ver sangre, porque **me desmayo**.*
I can't see blood, because **I faint**.

*Rosa **se asusta** cuando ve un ratón.*
Rosa **gets scared** when she sees a mouse.

The reflexive verbs *hacerse, ponerse,* and *volverse* can all translate as *to become*, though each has a **specific application in Spanish. *Hacerse* suggests a conscious effort to become something, and is usually followed by a noun.**

*Para **hacerse abogado**, es necesario estudiar bastante.*
To become a lawyer, it is necessary to study a lot.

Ponerse expresses a physical, emotional, or mental change that one cannot necessarily control. *Ponerse* is followed by an adjective that must agree in gender and number with the subject.

Me pongo muy triste cuando te vas.*
I become very sad when you leave.

Volverse expresses a violent change. *Volverse* is also followed by an adjective that must agree in gender and number with the subject.

*Mi madre **se vuelve loca** cuando dejo mis zapatos en la entrada.*
My mom **goes crazy** when I leave my shoes in the entrance.

Exercise 1

Match the idiomatic reflexive verbs in column A to their meanings in column B.

A	B
_____ **1.** resfriarse	a. to get married
_____ **2.** atreverse a	b. to laugh
_____ **3.** casarse	c. to catch a cold
_____ **4.** asustarse de	d. to get angry
_____ **5.** enfadarse	e. to get scared
_____ **6.** reírse	f. to dare

Exercise 2

Translate the following sentences into Spanish using the correct form of the reflexive verb.

1. My mother becomes happy when I wash the dishes.

2. You drive us crazy when you sing, Dad!

3. Maite wants to become a doctor.

4. The dogs become depressed when we leave the house.

5. You want to become a priest, Miguel? Are you sure?

Exercise 3

Answer the following questions in Spanish using the reflexive verb.

1. ¿De qué te arrepientes?

2. ¿Qué te asusta?

3. ¿Cuándo fue la última vez que te resfriaste?

4. ¿De qué te quejas?

5. ¿A quién te pareces?

48

The third-person reflexive pronoun *se* has important uses beyond its use with reflexive verbs.

Se is used to make statements in which the person performing an action is not specified. In these statements, *se* accompanies the third-person singular (*él/ella/usted*) form of the verb and can be translated as *one*, *they*, *people*, or the general *you*.

> *Se come* bien en este restaurante.
> **One eats** well at this restaurant.

¡Atención!

The third-person plural (*ellos/ellas/ustedes*) of a verb can stand alone to make an impersonal statement.

> *Dicen* que el restaurante es bueno.
> **They say** that the restaurant is good.

> *Se dice* que el restaurante es bueno.
> **They say** that the restaurant is good.

The construction *se* + indirect object pronoun + verb + subject can express an action that has occurred unintentionally. In these cases, the use of *se* emphasizes that the action was accidental, or that the performer does not want to take responsibility.

> *Se me perdió* el libro.
> **My** book **got lost.**

¡Atención!

In *se* statements expressing unintentional actions, the verb must agree in number with the subject, not the object.

> *Se le **rompieron** las **gafas.*** His/her **sunglasses** got **broken.**

> *¿Se te **dañaron** los pantalones?* Were your **pants ruined?**

> *Se nos **olvidó** ir a la **fiesta.*** We **forgot** to go to **the party.**

To name the person performing the action, use the construction: *a* + noun + *se* or *a* + prepositional pronoun.

> *A Teodoro se* le cayó el libro.   **Teodoro** dropped his book.
> *A mí se* me perdió el lápiz.   **I** lost the pencil.

Exercise 1

Yolanda is very forgetful today. Match her lapses in memory in column A to their consequences in column B.

A	B
_____ **1.** Se le olvida cerrar la puerta de su casa.	a. El policía le da una multa.
_____ **2.** Se le olvida pagar la renta.	b. Se le quema la casa.
_____ **3.** Se le olvida llevar la licensia de conducir.	c. Se escapa el gato.
_____ **4.** Se le olvida apagar la estufa.	d. Se resfría.
_____ **5.** Se le olvida ponerse el abrigo.	e. El patrón de casa le va a echar a la calle.

Exercise 2

Below are some signs or ads you're likely to see as you go about your day. Translate each into Spanish using the impersonal *se*.

1. We Speak Spanish

_____

_____

2. Land Sold

_____

_____

3. Waiter Sought

_____

_____

4. Swimming Forbidden

_____

_____

5. Enter Through the Back Door

_____

_____

Exercise 3

Rewrite the following sentences by replacing the subject with the impersonal *se*.

1. Los sábados por la mañana nos vamos de compras al supermercado.

_____

_____

2. Los sábados por la noche me reúno con mis amigos.

_____

_____

3. Los domingos por la mañana descanso.

_____

_____

4. Los domingos por la noche hacemos las tareas.

_____

_____

5. Los domingos me acuesto temprano.

_____

_____

_____

49

The preterite tense can express a single action or event completed at a specific time in the past.

*Ayer **comí** dos caramelos.*
Yesterday I **ate** two candies.

*La señora **compró** flores para la sala.*
The woman **bought** flowers for the living room.

*Mi hermano **estuvo** varios meses en Montevideo.*
My brother **was** in Montevideo for several months.

*Mi hermana se **sintió** mal después de comer el pescado.*
My sister **felt** bad after eating the fish.

The preterite tense of a regular *-ar* verb is formed by dropping the infinitive ending, and then adding *-é*, *-aste*, and *-ó* for singular subjects and *-amos*, *-asteis*, and *-aron* for plural subjects.

	Singular	Plural
cantar (to sing)	yo cant**é** I sang	nosotros/as cant**amos** we sang
	tú cant**aste** you sang	vosotros/as cant**asteis** you sang
	él/ella cant**ó** he/she/it/sang	ellos/as cant**aron** they sang
	usted cant**ó** you (formal) sang	ustedes cant**aron** you (formal) sang

The preterite tense of a regular *-ir* or *-er* verb is formed by dropping the infinitive ending, then adding *-í*, *-iste*, and *-ió* for singular subjects and *-imos*, *-isteis*, and *-ieron* for plural subjects.

	Singular	Plural
comer (to eat)	yo com**í** I ate	nosotros/as com**imos** we ate
	tú com**iste** you ate	vosotros/as com**isteis** you ate
	él/ella com**ió** he/she/it ate	ellos/as com**ieron** they ate
	usted com**ió** you (formal) ate	ustedes com**ieron** you (formal) ate
escribir (to write)	yo escrib**í** I wrote	nosotros/as escrib**imos** we wrote
	tú escrib**iste** you wrote	vosotros/as escrib**isteis** you wrote
	él/ella escrib**ió** he/she/it wrote	ellos/as escrib**ieron** they wrote
	usted escrib**ió** you (formal) wrote	ustedes escrib**ieron** you (formal) wrote

Exercise 1

Fill in the three columns with the correct preterite endings for these regular verbs.

-er Verbs	*-ar* Verbs	*-ir* Verbs

Exercise 2

Imagine that you're at the mall with a group of friends. You split up to do your shopping, and now all of you are at the food court discussing what you bought. Use the elements below to make sentences in the preterite tense.

1. Max / un póster de Nirvana

_____

_____

2. Yo / una colonia (*cologne*) de Armani

_____

_____

3. Mis hermanos / unos discos compactos

_____

_____

4. Tú / un juego de computadora

_____

_____

5. Tú y Bianca / una blusas de última moda (*latest style*)

_____

_____

Exercise 3

Write the following sentences using the preterite form of the verb in parentheses.

1. Yo (pasar) un semestre en Guadalajara, México.

_____

_____

2. Yo (vivir) con una familia muy encantadora.

_____

3. La familia (enseñarme) mucho sobre la vida y la cultura mexicana.

_____

_____

4. Y ellos (aprender) mucho sobre mis costumbres americanas.

_____

_____

5. Mi novio, José, (extrañarme) mucho, y (escribirme) muchas cartas.

_____

_____

Exercise 4

Think about what you studied in your last history class. Write five history facts in Spanish using the correct preterite forms.

_____

_____

_____

_____

_____

_____

_____

_____

_____

_____

_____

_____

_____

50

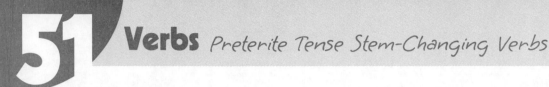

When stem-changing verbs are conjugated in the present tense, the stressed vowel of their stem changes. However, for *-ar* and *-er* verbs in the preterite tense, the stress remains the same as it is in the infinitive.

> *cerrar* (to close)
> Ana **cierra** la puerta.
> Ana **closes** the door.
>
> Ana **cerró** la puerta.
> Ana **closed** the door.

> *volver* (to come back)
> Simón **vuelve** a las cinco.
> Simón **returns** at 5 o'clock.
>
> Simón **volvió** a las cinco.
> Simón **returned** at 5 o'clock.

¡Atención!

Verbs that end in *-ir* and have a stem change in the present tense keep their stem change in the preterite tense.

El **repitió** la frase.
He **repeated** the phrase.

Verbs that have a present tense stem change from *e* to *ie* or *e* to *i* change from *e* to *i* in the preterite only with third-person singular (*él/ella/usted*) and third-person plural (*ellos/ellas/ustedes*) subjects.

	Singular	Plural
	yo preferí I preferred	*nosotros/as preferimos* we preferred
	tú preferiste you preferred	*vosotros/as preferisteis* you preferred
preferir (to prefer)	*él/ella prefirió* he/she/it preferred	*ellos/as prefirieron* they preferred
	usted prefirió you (formal) preferred	*ustedes prefirieron* you (formal) preferred

	Singular	Plural
	yo serví I served	*nosotros/as servimos* we served
	tú serviste you served	*vosotros/as servisteis* you served
servir (to serve)	*él/ella sirvió* he/she/it served	*ellos/as sirvieron* they served
	usted sirvió you (formal) served	*ustedes sirvieron* you (formal) served

Verbs that have a present tense stem change from *o* to *ue* change from *o* to *u* in the preterite only with third-person singular (*él/ella/usted*) and third-person plural (*ellos/ellas/ustedes*) subjects.

	Singular	Plural
	yo dormí I slept	*nosotros/as dormimos* we slept
	tú dormiste you slept	*vosotros/as dormisteis* you slept
dormir (to sleep)	*él/ella durmió* he/she/it slept	*ellos/ellas/ durmieron* they slept
	usted durmió you (formal) slept	*ustedes durmieron* you (formal) slept

Exercise 1

Fill in the blank with the correct preterite form of the verbs below.

1. cerrar: *yo*_____

2. encontrar: *nosotros*_____

3. mentir: *ellos*_____

4. seguir: *él*_____

5. pensar: *vosotros*_____

6. volver: *ustedes*_____

Exercise 2

The following word table has five hidden stem-changing verbs in preterite tense. Can you find them?

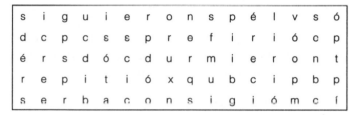

s	i	g	u	i	e	r	o	n	s	p	é	l	v	s	ó
d	c	p	c	s	s	p	r	e	f	i	r	i	ó	c	p
é	r	s	d	ó	c	d	u	r	m	i	e	r	o	n	t
r	e	p	i	t	i	ó	x	q	u	b	c	i	p	b	p
s	e	r	b	a	c	o	n	s	i	g	i	ó	m	c	í

Exercise 3

Rewrite the journal entry using the preterite tense.

Hoy me despierto tarde y pienso: «Tengo que conseguir un despertador nuevo. Este ya no sirve». Entonces, cansadísima, me visto y voy al almacén de electrónicos. El dependiente me dice: «Tenemos dos despertadores. ¿Cuál prefiere, señorita?». Me muestra los dos, pero sinceramente, no prefiero ninguno. El dependiente, impaciente, repite: «¿Señorita, cuál de los dos prefiere?». Su tono de voz me molesta, entonces decido posponer la compra. Pero cuando regreso a casa, me doy cuenta de que la pila en mi despertador está gastada. Solo tengo que cambiarla. Entonces así consigo un nuevo despertador.

_____

_____

_____

_____

_____

_____

_____

_____

_____

_____

_____

_____

_____

_____

59 Verbs *Preterite Tense Verbs with Spelling Changes*

Some verbs undergo spelling changes in the preterite tense to preserve the sound of their consonant.

For verbs that end in *-car, -c-* changes to *-qu-* in the first-person singular (*yo*).

Singular	
	*yo bus**qu**é*
	I look for
buscar (to look for)	*tú buscaste*
	you looked for
	él/ella/usted buscó
	he/she/it/you (formal) looked for

Other *-car* verbs that undergo a spelling change in the preterite include the following:

aplicar	to apply
comunicar	to communicate
dedicar	to dedicate
educar	to educate
indicar	to indicate
sacar	to take out
tocar	to touch/play music

For verbs that end in *-gar, -g-* changes to *-gu-* in the first-person singular (*yo*).

Singular	
	*yo lle**gu**é*
	I arrived
llegar (to arrive)	*tú llegaste*
	you arrived
	él/ella/usted llegó
	he/she/you (formal) arrived

Other *-gar* verbs that undergo a spelling change in the preterite include the following:

pagar	to pay
colgar	to hang
apagar	to put out/extinguish
encargar	to entrust
jugar	to play games or sports
negar	to deny
obligar	to obligate

For verbs that end in *-zar, -z-* changes to *-c-* in the first-person singular (*yo*).

Singular	
	*yo empe**c**é*
	I started
empezar (to start)	*tú empezaste*
	you started
	él/ella/usted empezó
	he/she/you (formal) started

Other *-zar* verbs that undergo a spelling change in the preterite include the following:

abrazar	to hug
almorzar	to eat lunch
comenzar	to begin
gozar	to enjoy
realizar	to fulfill
rezar	to pray

Verbs that end in *-aer, -eer,* and *-uir* take *-y-* in the third-person singular (*él/ella/usted*) and the third-person plural (*ellos/ellas/ustede*), instead of an *-i-*.

	Singular	Plural
	yo caí	*nosotros/as caímos*
	I fell	we fell
caer (to fall)	*tú caíste*	*vosotros/as caísteis*
	you fell	you fell
	*él/ella/usted ca**y**ó*	*ellos/ellas/ustedes ca**y**eron*
	he/she/it/you (formal) fell	they/you (formal) fell

The verb *oír* (to hear) also takes a *-y-* in the third-person singular (*él/ella/usted*) and the third-person plural (*ellos/ellas/ustede*), instead of an *-i*.

	Singular	Plural
oír (to hear)	*yo oí* I heard	*nosotros/as oímos* we heard
	tú oíste you heard	*vosotros/as oísteis* you heard
	él/ella/usted oyó he/she/it/you (formal) heard	*ellos/ellas/ustedes oyeron* they/you (formal) heard

Exercise 1

Complete the table with the correct preterite forms.

Verb	*yo*	*él*	*ellos*
pedir			
caer			
alcanzar			
pagar			
empezar			

Exercise 2

Fill in the blanks in the paragraph below with the correct preterite form of the verb in parentheses.

Yo (**1.**) _____ (*sacar*) la pelota del armario. Salí

afuera, y (**2.**) _____ (*empezar*) a rebotarla contra

la pared. «¡Julio, baja a jugar!», grité a su ventana. Pasó

media hora y no había bajado. Pasaron cuarenta y cinco

minutos. «Tal vez no me (**3.**) _____ (*oír*)», pensé.

Al final (**4.**) _____ (*concluir*) que no iba a bajar,

y (**5.**) _____ (*jugar*) solo con la pelota.

Exercise 3

Use the preterite tense to make five logical sentences from an element in each column.

mi padre	leer	un ruido en el sótano
yo	buscar	las luces
el profesor	explicar	la equación
la vecina	apagar	química
ellos	oir	el periódico
		el gato perdido

1. _____

_____

_____

2. _____

_____

_____

3. _____

_____

_____

4. _____

_____

_____

5. _____

_____

52

Some Spanish verbs have irregular stems in the preterite tense. These verbs are broken into three categories, based on their stem, but all share a common set of endings: *-e, -iste, -o, -imos, -isteis, -ieron.*

u-stem		i-stem		j-stem	
andar	(anduv-)	hacer	(hic-)	conducir	(conduj-)
estar	(estuv-)	querer	(quis-)	decir	(dij-)
tener	(tuv-)	venir	(vin-)	producir	(produj-)
poder	(pud-)			traer	(traj-)
poner	(pus-)				
saber	(sup-)				
haber	(hub-)				

La Excepción

The third-person singular (*él/ella/usted*) of *hacer* is *hizo,* not *hico.*

La Excepción

j-stem verbs take the *-eron* ending in the third-person plural (*ellos/ellas/ustedes*) form.

¡Atención!

Irregular preterites have no written accent marks. For example, the *ustedes* preterite tense form of the regular verb *comprar* is *compró* (accent present). The *ustedes* preterite tense form of the irregular verb *traer* is *trajo* (no accent present).

The verbs *dar, ver, ser,* and *ir* take regular *-er* endings in the preterite tense, but without the accents.

	Singular	Plural
dar (to give)	yo d**i** I gave	nosotros/as d**imos** we gave
	tú d**iste** you gave	vosotros/as d**isteis** you gave
	él/ella/usted d**io** he/she/it/you (formal) gave	ellos/ellas/ ustedes d**ieron** they/you (formal) gave

	Singular	Plural
ver (to see)	yo v**i** I saw	nosotros/as v**imos** we saw
	tú v**iste** you saw	vosotros/as v**isteis** you saw
	él/ella/usted v**io** he/she/it/you (formal) saw	ellos/ellas/ ustedes v**ieron** they/you (formal) saw

The verbs *ir* and *ser* are identical in the preterite. Context is used to determine which verb is being used.

	Singular	Plural
ir (to go)/ *ser* (to be)	yo fu**i** I went/was	nosotros/as fu**imos** we went/were
	tú fu**iste** you went/were	vosotros/as fuis**teis** you went/were
	él/ella/usted fu**e** he/she/it/ you (formal) went/ was/were	ellos/ellas/ ustedes fu**eron** they/you (formal) went/were

*La mujer **fue** a la peluquería. (ir)*
The woman **went** to the beauty salon.

***Fue** un error muy grave. (ser)*
It **was** a very serious error.

Exercise 1

Fill in the blanks with the correct preterite conjugations.

1. third-person plural of *ir*_____

2. first-person singular of *dar*_____

3. second-person singular of *ver*_____

4. first-person singular of *producir*_____

5. second-person plural of *poner*_____

6. first-person singular of *querer*_____

Exercise 2

Complete the crossword puzzle with the correct preterite form indicated by the clues.

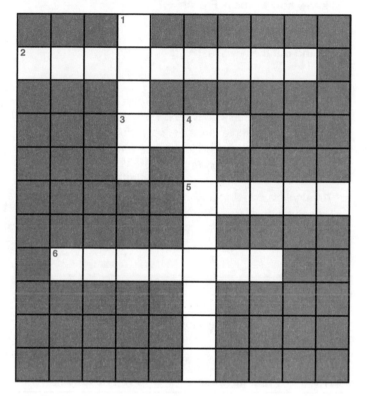

Across

2. nosotros _____ (andar)

3. ella _____ (saber)

5. tú _____ (dar)

6. tú _____ (ver)

Down

1. yo _____ (querer)

4. ellos _____ (poder)

Exercise 3

Conjugate the verbs below in the preterite tense to describe what happened on Christmas Eve at the Suárez residence.

1. todos / estar / en casa de los abuelos / antes de las nueve

_____

_____

_____

2. nosotros / poner / muchos regalos / debajo del árbol

_____

_____

_____

3. yo / tener / que ayudar con la comida

_____

_____

_____

4. mi tío / poner / música festiva

_____

_____

_____

5. los niños / ir / a dormir / a las once

_____

_____

_____

6. a medianoche / todos / decir / ¡Feliz Navidad!

_____

_____

_____

53

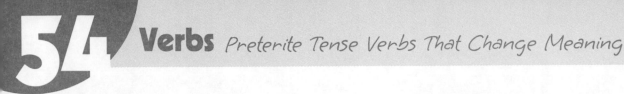

The verbs *poder*, *conocer*, *querer*, and *saber* change meaning from the present tense to the preterite.

Poder means *to be able* **in the present tense, but** *succeeded* **in the preterite tense.**

> ¿**Puedes** *ayudarme, por favor?*
> **Can** you help me, please?

> *Por fin* **pudiste** *alcanzar tu meta.*
> You finally **succeeded** in reaching your goal.
> = You **were** finally **able to** reach your goal.

> **Pude** *convencerle.*
> I **managed** to convince him.
> = I **was** finally **able** to convince him.

No poder means *to not be able* **in the present tense, but** *did not succeed* **or** *failed* **in the preterite tense.**

> **No puedo** *ir al cine.*
> I **cannot** go to the movies.

> **No pude** *terminar la tarea.*
> I **failed to** finish my homework.

Conocer means *to know* **in the present tense, but** *met* **(for the first time) in the preterite tense.**

> *Yo* **conozco** *a Marta.*
> I **know** Marta.

> *Yo* **conocí** *a Fernando en la fiesta.*
> I **met** Fernando (for the first time) at the party.

Querer means *to want* **in the present tense, but** *tried* **or** *attempted* **in the preterite tense.**

> *La niña* **quiere** *su muñeca.*
> The girl **wants** her doll.

> *Mi padre* **quiso** *abrir la ventana.*
> My dad **tried to** open the window.

No querer means *to not want* **in the present tense but** *refused* **in the preterite tense.**

> **No queremos** *estudiar.*
> We don't **want to** study.

> **No quisimos** *ir a la biblioteca.*
> We **refused to** go to the library.

Saber means *to know* **in the present tense but** *found out* **in the preterite tense.**

> **Sé** *hablar francés.*
> I **know how** to speak French.

> **Supe** *la noticia anoche.*
> I **found out** the news last night.

¡Atención!

Tener (to have) can signify possession in both the present and preterite tense. However, in the preterite tense, *tener* is often used to indicate when something first comes into someone's possession.

Tuve *noticias de Ana esta mañana.*
I **received** news from Ana this morning.

Exercise 1

Fill out the table with the English translation of each verb in the tenses provided.

Verb	Present Tense	Preterit Tense
poder		
conocer		
saber		
querer		

Exercise 2

Translate the following sentences into Spanish, using the correct verb in the preterite.

1. I met Mr. Paez at the fair last year.

_____

_____

_____

2. We weren't able to visit Iris yesterday.

_____

_____

_____

3. Eduardo tried to go to the party, but he had too much work.

_____

_____

_____

4. Last night, we found out the truth about Marta.

_____

_____

_____

5. The children refused to do their homework.

_____

_____

_____

Exercise 3

Complete the phrases with information about yourself.

1. Ayer mi mejor amigo supo...

_____

_____

_____

2. Mis padres no quisieron...

_____

_____

_____

3. Conocí a mi novio/novia en...

_____

_____

_____

4. Esta mañana no pude...

_____

_____

_____

5. El mes pasado quise

_____

_____

_____

54

As with the preterite tense, the imperfect tense is used to describe events that took place in the past. However, while the preterite expresses a single action or event, the imperfect expresses continuous or repeated actions.

Most verbs have a regular imperfect ending. Singular -ar verbs add -aba, -abas, and -aba. Plural -ar verbs add -ábamos, -abais, and -aban.

	Singular	Plural
cantar (to sing)	yo cant**aba** I used to sing	nosotros/as cant**ábamos** we used to sing
	tú cant**abas** you used to sing	vosotros/as c**antabais** you used to sing
	él/ella/usted cant**aba** he/she/it/you (formal) used to sing	ellos/ellas/ ustedes cant**aban** they/you (formal) used to sing

¡Atención!
Note that the first-person and third-person singular forms of -ar verbs are the same in the imperfect.

To form the imperfect, singular -er and -ir verbs add -ía, -ías, and -ía. Plural -er and -ir verbs add -íamos, -íais, and -ían.

	Singular	Plural
comer (to eat)	yo com**ía** I used to eat	nosotros/as com**íamos** we used to eat
	tú com**ías** you used to eat	vosotros/os com**íais** you used to eat
	él/ella/usted com**ía** he/she/it/you (formal) used to eat	ellos/ellas/ ustedes com**ían** they/you (formal) used to eat

	Singular	Plural
escribir (to write)	yo escrib**ía** I used to write	nosotros/as escrib**íamos** we used to write
	tú escrib**ías** you used to write	vosotros/as escrib**íais** you used to write
	él/ella/usted escrib**ía** he/she/it/you (formal) was/ used to write	ellos/ellas/ ustedes escrib**ían** they/you (formal) used to write

¡Atención!
Though many verbs have stem changes in the present and preterite tenses, these verbs do not have stem changes in the imperfect.

The imperfect is used to describe what was happening, used to happen, or happened repeatedly.

Andrés **llegaba** tarde a menudo.
Andrés **would arrive/arrived** late often.

Vivíamos en esta calle.
We used to live on this street.

The imperfect is also used to the describe circumstances surrounding an action or event in the past.

Cuando **era** joven, Francisco corría todas las mañanas.
When **he was** young, Francisco jogged every morning.

¡Atención!
The imperfect has several equivalents in English. For example, *corría* (the first-person singular imperfect form of *correr*) can translate as "I was running," "I would run," or "I used to run." Context is used to determine the exact meaning.

The imperfect is used to describe qualities of people or things in the past.

Gloria **era** rubia y **tenía** los ojos verdes.
Gloria **was** blonde and **had** green eyes.

The imperfect is used to express a state of mind in the past with the verbs *creer* (to believe), *pensar* (to think), *querer* (to want), and *saber* (to know).

> ***Creían*** *que era importante.*
> They **believed** it was important.

> ***Queríamos*** *comprar una casa nueva.*
> We **wanted** to buy a new house.

The imperfect expresses the time of day in the past.

> ***Eran*** *las siete.*
> **It was** seven o'clock.

The imperfect is used to describe a situation that was occurring in the past when another single action or event (expressed in the preterite) interrupted it.

> ***Almorzábamos*** *cuando nos llamó.*
> **We were eating** when he called us.

Exercise 1

Provide the imperfect form of the verb in parentheses. Include the subject pronoun in your answer.

1. first-person, plural (*hablar*)

_____

2. third-person, singular (*servir*)

_____

3. second-person, plural (informal, Spain) (*mentir*)

_____

4. second-person, singular (*querer*)

_____

5. third-person, plural (*decidir*)

_____

Exercise 2

Pepito is talking with his grandfather. Fill in the blanks below with the correct past tense form of the verb in parentheses.

—Abuelo, ¿cómo era la ciudad cuando tú eras pequeño?

—Pepito, la ciudad que veo hoy no es la ciudad de mi

juventud. Hace 50 años no (**1.**)_____ (haber)

contaminación. Los patos y los gansos (**2.**)_____

(nadar) libremente en los lagos. Tampoco (**3.**)_____

(haber) delitos. Yo (**4.**)_____ (poder) salir sólo y

mi padres no (**5.**)_____ (preocuparse) por mí.

Nosotros (**6.**)_____ (vivir) tranquilos. ¡Qué pena

que todo haya cambiado!

Exercise 3

Use complete sentences to answer the following questions about your younger days.

1. Cuando tenías 5 años, ¿qué te gustaba comer?

_____

_____

2. Cuando tenías 8 años, ¿con qué jugabas?

_____

_____

3. Cuando tenías 10 años, ¿cuándo te sentías enfermo/a?

_____

_____

4. Cuando tenías 12 años, ¿con quién discutías?

_____

_____

55

Only three verbs have irregular forms in the imperfect tense: *ir, ser,* and *ver*.

	Singular	Plural
ir (to go)	*yo* **ibá** I used to go	*nosotros/as* **íbamos** we used to go
	tú **ibas** you used to go	*vosotros/as* **ibais** you used to go
	él/ella/usted **iba** he/she/it/you (formal) used to go	*ellos/ellas/ustedes* **iban** they/you (formal) used to go
ser (to be)	*yo* **era** I used to be	*nosotros/as* **éramos** we used to be
	tú **eras** you used to be	*vosotros/as* **erais** you used to be
	él/ella/usted **era** he/she/it/you (formal) used to be	*ellos/ellas/ustedes* **eran** they/you (formal) used to be

	Singular	Plural
ver (to see)	*yo* **veía** I used to see	*nosotros/as* **veíamos** we used to see
	tú **veías** you used to see	*vosotros/as* **veíais** you used to see
	él/ella/usted **veía** he/she/it/you (formal) used to see	*ellos/ellas/ustedes* **veían** they/you (formal) used to see

Present Tense	Imperfect Tense
Yo **voy** *a la biblioteca.* I **go** to the library.	*Yo* **iba** *a la biblioteca.* I **was going** to the library.
El profesor Méndez **es** *un hombre muy agradable.* Professor Méndez **is** a very pleasant man.	*El profesor Méndez* **era** *un señor muy agradable.* Professor Méndez **was** a very pleasant man.
Te **vi** *en la cafetería.* I **saw** you in the cafeteria.	*Te* **veía** *en la cafetería.* I **used to see** you in the cafeteria.

Exercise 1

Complete the blanks with the correct imperfect form of *ir* and *ser*.

Singular	Plural
yo _____	nosotros _____
	nosotras _____
tú _____	vosotros _____
	vosotras _____
él _____	ellos _____
ella _____	ellas _____
usted _____	ustedes _____

Singular	Plural
yo _____	nosotros _____
	nosotras _____
tú _____	vosotros _____
	vosotras _____
él _____	ellos _____
ella _____	ellas _____
usted _____	ustedes _____

Exercise 2

Use context to determine the appropriate verb (*ir, ser,* or *ver*), and fill in the blank with the correct imperfect form.

1. Cuando mis padres _____ jóvenes, el mundo _____ menos peligroso.

2. Ellos _____ todos las noches a pasear en el parque. Nadie les molestaba.

3. Nunca _____ *graffiti* en las paredes porque la gente era más considerada.

4. Los vecinos _____ todos amigos, y cuando se _____ en la calle siempre se saludaban.

Exercise 3

Imagine what life was like for your parents or grandparents. Use the imperfect forms of *ser, ir,* and *ver* to compose five sentences describing their lives.

_____

_____

_____

_____

_____

_____

_____

_____

56

The action described by the verb is used to determine whether the imperfect or the preterite should be used. The following questions can help you decide whether the preterite is appropriate.

Does the verb express a specific action or event completed in the past? If so, the preterite is used.

> *La hermana de Paul **se casó** el año pasado.*
> Paul's sister **got married** last year.

Does the verb express an action or event that occurred at a specific point in time? If so, the preterite is used.

> *La clase **empezó** a las diez.*
> The class **started** at ten.

> *Ayer **terminé** mi tarea de física.*
> Yesterday I **finished** my physics homework.

Does the verb describe a series of actions or events completed in the past? If so, the preterite is used.

> *La profesora **entró** a la clase, **abrió** su libro y **escribió** en la pizarra.*
> The professor **entered** the room, **opened** her book, and **wrote** on the chalkboard.

Certain words and expressions are often associated with the preterite tense. These words express specific points in time in which an action occurred, or indicate how many times an action occurred.

ayer	yesterday
anteayer	the day before yesterday
una vez	once
dos veces	twice
el año pasado	last year
el martes pasado	last Tuesday (etc.)
de repente	suddenly

> ***Ayer** tomé el exámen de inglés.*
> **Yesterday** I took the English test.

> ***Tuve** que tomar el curso dos veces.*
> I **had to** take the course twice.

¡Atención!

Certain verbs are often in the preterite because they represent actions that do not take much time to complete. These verbs include *salir* (to leave), *entrar* (to enter), *recordar* (to remember), *empezar* (to start), *terminar* (to finish), *llegar* (to arrive), and *caerse* (to fall).

> *Mi mamá tropezó y **se cayó**.*
> My mom tripped and **fell**.

> ***Salimos** a las nueve de la noche.*
> We **left** at nine P.M.

Exercise 1

Indicate whether the statement is true or false for each scenario described below.

Use the preterite rather than the imperfect tense to say that...

1. _____ ...your brother graduated on May 30 of last year.

2. _____ ...you used to play basketball every day when you were in high school.

3. _____ ...the store you planned to visit was closing when you arrived.

4. _____ ...the exam that you're talking about ended promptly at 12:00.

5. _____ ...you went to the cafeteria, ordered a cheese sandwich, and then quickly ate it.

Exercise 2

Write one sentence in Spanish illustrating each rule described below.

You use the preterite...

1. To narrate a series of past actions or events.

   _____

   _____

   _____

2. To express the beginning or end of a past action.

   _____

   _____

   _____

3. To describe an action that has a specific ending in the past.

   _____

   _____

   _____

4. With punctual verbs such as *salir, entrar, recordar,* and *empezar.*

   _____

   _____

   _____

5. With expressions such as *el año pasado, ayer,* and *una vez.*

   _____

   _____

   _____

Exercise 3

Translate the following paragraph into Spanish using the proper past tense form.

Last Tuesday, a thief robbed me. That morning, I left at seven, and as usual, I bought some coffee and sat down to wait for the bus. It arrived only five minutes late. I got on the bus and greeted the driver. At the San Jacinto stop, a man dressed in black got on. He sat next to me. He smiled at me. I smiled back at him. The man got off at the next stop. And, without me noticing, the crook stole my backpack!

_____

_____

_____

_____

_____

_____

_____

_____

_____

_____

_____

_____

_____

_____

_____

_____

57

The action the verb describes is used to determine whether a situation calls for the imperfect or the preterite. The following questions can help you decide whether the imperfect is appropriate.

Does the verb express an action that was habitual or repeated in the past? If so, the imperfect is used.

*Carla **caminaba** todas las tardes por una hora.*
Carla **walked/used to walk** for an hour every afternoon.

Does the verb describe an ongoing or a continuous past event, with no definite start or end? If so, the imperfect is used.

*María Clara **corría** en la pista todos los días.*
María Clara **was running/used to run** on the track every day.

¡Atención!

Depending on the context, *corría* can mean *was running* or *used to run*.

Does the verb describe people, things, or states of mind in the past? If so, the imperfect is used.

*La mujer se **sentía** enferma.*
The woman **was feeling/felt** ill.

*La casa **tenía** tres pisos.*
The house **had** three floors.

¡Atención!

Nonaction verbs such as *amar* (to love), *ser* (to be), *estar* (to be), *desear* (to wish), *parecer* (to seem), *tener* (to have), and *hacer* (to do, in weather expressions) are generally used to give background information and almost always take the imperfect in the past tense.

***Parecía** que el amante de su esposa lo había asesinado.*
It **looked** like his wife's lover had killed him.

*Esa noche **hacía** mucho frío.*
It **was** very cold that night.

Certain words and expressions are often associated with the imperfect tense. These expressions suggest an action that took place habitually in the past.

todas las tardes	every afternoon
todos los (martes)	every (Tuesday)
siempre	always
mientras	while
frecuentemente	often
de niño	as a child
a menudo	often

The following table summarizes the differences between the preterite and imperfect tenses.

Preterite Tense	Imperfect Tense
Expresses specific actions or events completed in the past	Describes ongoing or continuous actions or events in the past
***Estudié** mucho.* I **studied** a lot.	*Kati **nadaba** en la piscina.* Kati **was swimming/used to swim** in the pool.
Expresses an action or event at a specific point in time	Describes habitual or repeated actions or events in the past
*Ayer **compramos** un carro nuevo.* Yesterday we **bought** a new car.	*Margarita **trabajaba** todos los días en una oficina.* Margarita **was working/used to work** every day in an office.
States a series of actions completed in the past	Describes qualities of people, things, or a states of mind in the past
*El señor **se sentó** y **empezó** a fumar su cigarro.* The man **sat down** and **began** to smoke his cigar.	*Al oír la noticia, su madre **estaba** muy contenta.* Upon hearing the news, her mother **was** very happy.

Exercise 1

The speaker below is describing his life as a child. Fill in the blanks with the correct past tense form of the verb in parentheses.

Cuando (**1.**) _____ (ser) niños, Amanda y

yo (**2.**) _____ (vivir) en Ecuador. Siempre

(**3.**) _____ (ir) a la playa, a *Montañita*, a pasar

el año nuevo. Allí casi siempre (**4.**) _____

(quedarse) con mi tío Pepe. Un año, cuando yo

(**5.**) _____ (tener) once años, mi familia

(**6.**) _____ (decidir) quedarse en un hotel.

Mi tío Pepe (**7.**) _____ (enfadarse) con

nosotros. (**8.**) _____ (decidir) entonces

regresar a su casa y aprovechar de su hospitalidad.

Exercise 2

Complete the sentences using either the imperfect or preterite tense based on the context provided.

1. A menudo mi hermano mayor... _____

_____

_____

2. Anoche mi novio/a... _____

_____

_____

3. De niño, mi primo... _____

_____

_____

4. La semana pasada el profesor... _____

_____

_____

Exercise 3

The speaker below is describing her second year in the university. Rewrite the paragraph in past tense using the preterite and imperfect where appropriate.

Durante mi segundo año en la universidad, conozco a Jaime en una clase de historia latinoamericana. Pronto nos hacemos muy buenos amigos. Jaime es una persona muy simpática. Le gusta mucho organizar fiestas salvajes en su apartamento. Un sábado, los vecinos se quejan de la música. Estamos haciendo mucha bulla. Deciden llamar a la policía. La policía llega, pero en vez de arrestarnos, ¡el agente empieza a bailar con una rubia!

_____

_____

_____

_____

_____

_____

_____

_____

_____

_____

_____

_____

58

117

Both the preterite and the imperfect tenses can be used in the same sentence.

The imperfect tense describes a situation that was going on in the past, while the preterite describes a past action or event that interrupted that ongoing situation.

*Catalina **hablaba** (imperfect) por teléfono cuando **sonó** (preterite) el timbre.*
Catalina **was speaking** on the phone when the doorbell **rang.**

¡Atención!

The imperfect is used to refer to general events, such as a daily walk. The preterite is used to refer to specific events, such as a walk taken on a particular day.

***Paseaba** por el parque todos los días.*
He **strolled** through the park every day.

***Paseó** por el parque el sábado.*
On Saturday, he **strolled** through the park.

In the presentation of an event, as in a news or fictional story, the imperfect tense is used to provide the background information (such as the time, mood, location, and weather) while the preterite tense describes what happened.

***Era** (imperfect) medianoche, y **caía** (imperfect) la lluvia. **Hacía** (imperfect) mucho frío, pero **salí** (preterit) de todas maneras. De repente, **me resbalé** (preterit) en un charco de agua, y **caí** (preterit) en la vereda.*

It **was** midnight, and it was **raining.** It **was** very cold, but I **went** out anyway. Suddenly, I **slipped** on a puddle of water and **fell** on the sidewalk.

Exercise 1

The speaker below is describing a scare he had one night. Fill in the blanks with the most appropriate verb, conjugated in either the imperfect or the preterite.

poner	tener
ser	apagarse
abrir	llover
abrir	leer
sonar	ver
ir	

(**1.**)_____ las nueve de la noche

cuando ¡de repente (**2.**)_____

todas las luces de la casa! (**3.**)_____

el libro que estaba (**4.**)_____ en

la mesa, y (**5.**)_____ a investigar.

Yo (**6.**)_____ mucho miedo. Afuera

(**7.**)_____ muy fuerte, y los truenos

(**8.**)_____ como un tambor.

(**9.**)_____ la ventana,

y (**10.**)_____ la causa del incidente:

un árbol se había caído en la línea eléctrica.

Exercise 2

Use the following phrases to write a short story about Francisco and María Fernanda. Use the preterite and imperfect tenses and add any missing words.

Francisco llevar a María Fernanda/a un restaurante muy elegante/ser su cumpleaños/pedir una comida de cuatro platos/disfrutar del postre/estar lleno de fresas, su fruta favorita/estar muy contenta/ besar a su esposo/Francisco abrir la billetera para pagar la cuenta/no tener dinero/el restaurante/no aceptar tarjetas de crédito/Francisco/tener que lavar los platos/¡Qué cumpleaños!

_____

_____

_____

_____

_____

_____

_____

_____

_____

_____

_____

_____

_____

_____

_____

_____

_____

Exercise 3

Write the first paragraph of a mystery story about a break-in at the school library. Set the scene using both the preterite and the imperfect tenses.

_____

_____

_____

_____

_____

_____

_____

_____

_____

_____

_____

_____

_____

_____

_____

_____

_____

_____

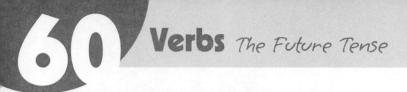

Verbs *The Future Tense*

In Spanish, there are several ways to express the future tense, or what will happen.

ir (to go) + *a* + infinitive	Mañana **vamos a ir** al supermercado. *Tomorrow **we're going to go** to the supermarket.*
present indicative tense	Mañana **vamos** al supermercado. *Tomorrow **we're going** to the supermarket.*
future tense	Mañana **iremos** al supermercado. *Tomorrow **we're going** to the supermarket.*

The future tense of all three types of regular verbs (*-ar, -er,* and *-ir*) is formed by adding to the infinitive form the endings *-é, -ás,* and *-á* for singular subjects and *-emos, -éis,* and *-án* for plural subjects.

cantar (to sing)	Singular	Plural
	yo cantar**é** I'm going to sing	nosotros/as cantar**emos** we are going to sing
	tú cantar**ás** you're going to sing	vosotros/as cantar**éis** you are going to sing
	él/ella/usted cantar**á** he/she/it/you (formal) are going to sing	ellos/ellas/ ustedes cantar**án** they/you (formal) are going to sing

comer (to eat)	Singular	Plural
	yo comer**é** I am going to eat	nosotros/as comer**emos** we are going to eat
	tú comer**ás** you are going to eat	vosotros/as comer**éis** you are going to eat
	él/ella/usted comer**á** he/she/it/you (formal) are going to eat	ellos/ellas/ ustedes comer**án** they/you (formal) are going to eat

escribir (to write)	Singular	Plural
	yo escribir**é** I am going to write	nosotros/as escribir**emos** he/she/it/you (formal) are going to write
	tú escribir**ás** you are going to write	vosotros/as escribir**éis** you are going to write
	él/ella/usted escribir**á** he/she/it/you (formal) are going to write	ellos/ellas/ ustedes escribir**án** they/you (formal) are going to write

¡Atención!

Because all future tense endings, except for *–emos,* have an accent mark, verbs that have an accent mark on the stem in the infinitive drop that accent in the future tense.

oír (to hear) → *oiré* (I'm going to hear)

The future tense of an irregular verb is formed by adding the future tense ending to the irregular stem.

Infinitive	Irregular Stem
decir	dir-
hacer	har-
poder	podr-
poner	pondr-
querer	querr-
saber	sabr-
salir	saldr-
tener	tendr-
venir	vendr-

La Excepción

The future tense of *hay* (there is/there are) is *habrá* (there will be).

Habrá *mucho que hacer la próxima semana.*
There will be a lot to do next week.

In addition to expressing events In the future, the future tense can also express curiosity or probability.

*¿Dónde **estarán** las Islas Canarias?*
I **wonder** where the Canary Islands are?

***Estarán** en África.*
They are **probably** in Africa.

Exercise 1

Use the phrases below to complete this sentence with the future tense.

En cinco o seis años…

1. hablar bien el español (nosotros)

_____

2. trabajar en una oficina en el centro (tú)

_____

3. ser una doctora famosa (Rosana)

_____

Exercise 2

Translate the following sentences into Spanish in two ways: first, by using the future tense, and second, by using the *ir a* + infinitive.

1. In ten years, I'll live in another city.

_____

_____

2. In five years, you will be married.

_____

_____

3. In two years, my sister will have a new house.

_____

_____

Exercise 3

What will the world be like in 2100? Make your predictions using the future tense. Write about transportation, food, housing, the political situation, the environment, or any other aspect of life.

Example: En 2100, muchas especies de animales desaparecerán.

_____

_____

_____

_____

_____

60

In English, an action that is in progress is expressed by combining the verb *to be* with the present participle (the *-ing* form). Spanish uses a similar construction to form the present progressive.

The present progressive is a compound tense formed by combining the present tense of the auxiliary verb *estar* (to be) with the present participle.

> *Estás esperando.* (present participle)
> You**'re waiting.**
>
> *Los niños* **están escribiendo.** (present participle)
> The children **are writing.**

¡Atención!

In the present progressive, the present participle remains the same no matter what the subject is. It is only *estar* that conjugates to agree with the subject.

The present participle is formed by dropping the *-ar*, *-er*, or *-ir* ending of the verb, and adding the following endings:

> *-ar* verbs → *-ando*
> esper**ando**   (waiting)
> jug**ando**   (playing)
>
> *-er* verbs → *-iendo*
> com**iendo**   (eating)
> corr**iendo**   (running)
>
> *-ir* verbs → *-iendo*
> escrib**iendo**   (writing)
> decid**iendo**   (deciding)

If the stem of an *-er* or *-ir* verb ends in a vowel, the present participle ending is *-yendo*.

> *leer* (to read) → le**yendo** (reading)
> *traer* (to bring) → tra**yendo** (bringing)

-ir verbs that have irregular stem changes in the present tense (e → i, e → ie, and o → ue verbs) retain those stem changes in the present participle form.

pedir (to ask)	→	**pidiendo** (asking)
seguir (to follow)	→	**siguiendo** (following)
sentir (to feel)	→	**sintiendo** (feeling)
preferir (to prefer)	→	**prefiriendo** (prefering)
dormir (to sleep)	→	**durmiendo** (sleeping)

¡Atención!

As in English, the present progressive can be used to talk about the weather.

> *Está* **lloviendo.**   It's **raining.**
> *Está* **nevando.**   It's **snowing.**

When used with the present progressive tense, object pronouns and reflexive pronouns must either precede the conjugated form of *estar* or be attached to the end of the present participle.

> *Josefina está vistiéndo***se.**
> Josefina is getting **herself** dressed.

¡Atención!

The present progressive in Spanish is *only* used to emphasize an action that is in progress at the time the speaker is talking. Unlike the present progressive in English, the present progressive in Spanish does *not* refer to an action that will occur in the future. For example, "Mateo is going to Europe tomorrow" would be translated as *Mateo va a Europa mañana.*

Exercise 1

What are you generally doing at the following times of day? Write complete sentences using the present progressive tense.

1. A las cinco de la mañana…

_____

_____

2. A mediodía…

_____

_____

3. A las ocho de la noche…

_____

_____

4. A las diez de la noche...

_____

_____

5. A la una de la mañana…

_____

_____

Exercise 2

Complete the crossword puzzle with the Spanish present participles of the verbs provided.

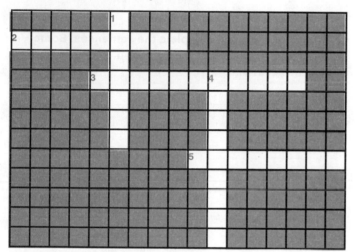

Across
2. sleeping
3. resting
5. living

Down
1. reading
4. feeling

Exercise 3

Look at each drawing below. State what is happening in complete sentences, using the present progressive tense.

1. _____

_____

2. _____

_____

3. _____

_____

4. _____

_____

61

69 Verbs *The Gerund*

When not accompanied by the auxiliary verb *estar* in the progressive tense, the present participle (*llorando, siendo, mintiendo*, and so on) can describe an action occurring at the same time as the main action of a sentence. In this case, the present participle functions as an adverb and is called a gerund.

A gerund can indicate the manner in which something is occurring.

> *La viuda entró al cuarto llorando.*
> The widow entered the room **crying.**

> *Fui al almacén cantando.*
> I went to the store **singing.**

A gerund can indicate why something is occurring.

> *Siendo una persona honrada, nunca pensó que alguien le mintiera.*
> **Being** an honest person herself, she never thought someone would lie to her.

> *Teniendo solo dos años, el niño no sabía la diferencia entre el bien y el mal.*
> **Being** only two years old, the boy didn't know the difference between right and wrong.

> *Estando las luces prendidas, el ladrón no entrará a la casa.*
> With the **lights on,** the robber won't enter the house.

> *Escuchando la voz del maestro en el corredor, los alumnos regresarán a sus puestos.*
> **Hearing** the teacher's voice in the hall, the students will return to their places.

A gerund can indicate the means by which something occurs.

> *Practicando, aprendí a tocar bien la guitarra.*
> **By practicing,** I learned how to play the guitar well.

> *Haciendo dieta, Marta logró perder diez quilos.*
> **By dieting,** Marta was able to lose ten kilos.

¡Atención!

In English, the present participle (-ing word) can also be used as an adjective. This is not the case in Spanish. In Spanish, only an adjective, a clause, or a preposition is used as the adjective.

existing problems =
   los problemas existentes (adjective)

a singing bird = *un pájaro que canta* (clause)

a book containing drawings =
   un libro con dibujos (preposition)

Exercise 1

Use the verbs below to complete the sentences. Some sentences will call for the infinitive form, and others will call for the gerund.

hablar
escuchar
hacer
reírse
poder

1. No voy al gimnasio con ustedes porque no me gusta

   _____ ejercicios.

2. No _____ cocinar, compró la cena.

3. Preparó el desayuno _____ la radio.

4. ¡Eso te pasa por _____ tanto!

5. Salió del cine _____ porque la película estuvo muy cómica.

124

Exercise 2

Complete the crossword puzzle with gerund forms of the verbs provided in the clues.

Across

2. beber

4. venir

5. oír

Down

1. pedir

3. entrar

Exercise 3

Translate the following sentences to Spanish using the proper form of the verb.

1. How interesting she is!

_____

_____

2. I need to buy some writing paper.

_____

_____

3. They have running water.

_____

_____

4. He was standing in the middle of the room.

_____

_____

5. I saw a vase containing many beautiful flowers.

_____

_____

The past progressive can be used to discuss ongoing actions in the past. There are two forms of the past progressive: the imperfect progressive and the preterite progressive. Both the imperfect progressive and the preterite progressive combine the present participle with different forms of the verb *estar* (to be).

The imperfect progressive is formed by combining the imperfect tense of the auxiliary verb *estar* with the present participle.

> ***Estábas esperando.***
> You **were waiting.**

> *Los niños **estaban escribiendo.***
> The children **were writing.**

¡Atención!

Note that a simple imperfect verb, without *estar*, can also be used to express ongoing actions in the past.

Esperabas.	You **were waiting.**
*Los niños **escribían.***	The children **were writing.**

The use of the imperfect progressive construction emphasizes that the action was in progress at a given time. *Los niños estaban escribiendo* (imperfect progressive) indicates that the children were actually writing, while *los niños escribían* (imperfect) suggests that the children could have been writing at any time.

The imperfect progressive refers to an ongoing action or event in the past that has no beginning or end. The imperfect progressive is often used to provide background information.

> *Los niños **estaban escribiendo** cuando entró el maestro.*
> The children **were writing** when the teacher walked in.

The preterite progressive is formed by using the preterite tense of *estar* with the present participle.

> *Tu **estuviste cantando.***
> You **were singing** (at that very moment).

> *La señora **estuvo cocinando.***
> The woman **was cooking** (at that very moment).

The preterite progressive indicates an action or event that is ongoing at a specific moment in the past. The exact time at which the event was happening is clear.

> *A las cinco y quarto de la tarde, **estuve pintando** la casa.*
> At five fifteen in the afternoon, I **was painting** the house.

¡Atención!

When used with the past progressive tenses, object pronouns and reflexive pronouns must either precede the conjugated form of *estar* or be attached to the end of the present participle.

> ***Estaba esperándote** en la esquina.*
> I **was waiting for you** on the corner.

Exercise 1

Change the following present progressive forms into the imperfect and preterite progressives.

1. estás durmiendo:

_____

_____

2. estáis leyendo:

_____

_____

3. estoy llorando:

_____

_____

4. está sintiendo:

_____

_____

5. estamos mintiendo:

_____

_____

Exercise 2

Rewrite the following sentences using the imperfect progressive form.

1. Los estudiantes se preparaban para el examen.

   _____

   _____

   _____

2. El vagabundo cantaba una canción de amor.

   _____

   _____

   _____

3. Maite hervía el agua.

   _____

   _____

   _____

4. Yo platicaba con mi mejor amiga.

   _____

   _____

   _____

5. El gato jugaba con el ratón.

   _____

   _____

   _____

Exercise 3

Use context to determine whether the imperfect progressive form or the preterite progressive form of the verb in parentheses should be used.

1. Cuando entró mi hermano a mi cuarto,

   _____(yo: desvestirse).

2. ¿Qué música _____

   (tú: escuchar) anoche cuando llamé?

3. ¿Dónde _____

   (ellos: vivir) tus padres durante la guerra civil española?

4. La señora _____

   (ella: cenar) hasta que sonó el teléfono.

5. Nosotros _____

   (nosotros: ver) la televisión toda la noche.

63

The present perfect is used to talk about what someone *has done* in the past.

The present perfect is a compound tense formed by combining the present tense of the auxiliary verb *haber* (to have) with the past participle.

Hemos comido en ese restuarante.
We**'ve eaten** at that restaurant.

¿*Has ido* a Perú?
Have you **been** to Peru?

¡Atención!

The present tense of *haber* is *yo he* (I have), *tú has* (you have), *él/ella ha* (he/she/it has), *nosotros/as hemos* (we have), *vosotros/as habéis* (you have), *ellos/as/ustedes han* (they/you have).

The past participle is formed by dropping the *-ar, -er,* or *-ir* ending of the infinitive verb and adding the following endings:

-*ar* verbs → -*ado*
esper**ado**   (waited)
jug**ado**   (played)

-*er* and -*ir* verbs → -*ido*
viv**ido**   (lived)
com**ido**   (eaten)

La Excepción

Some verbs have irregular stems in the past participle form. These verbs retain their irregular stems in the present perfect tense.

Infinitive	Past Participle
abrir	abierto
decir	dicho
descubrir	descubierto
escribir	escrito
hacer	hecho
morir	muerto
poner	puesto
resolver	resuelto
romper	roto
ver	visto
volver	vuelto

The present perfect indicates an action that began in the past and continues up to the present, or an action that took place in the past but is connected to the present.

Hemos esperado ya veinte minutos, y Marco todavía no *ha llegado.*
We**'ve waited** twenty minutes already, and Marco **hasn't arrived** yet.

As in English, the Spanish present perfect can indicate something that someone has just done (or something that has just occurred) in the recent past.

He trabajado cinco horas sin descansar.
I**'ve worked** five hours without resting.

Ha llovido mucho este mes.
It**'s rained** a lot this month.

¡Atención!

In the present perfect, *haber* is never separated from the past participle. If the word *no* or a pronoun is present in a sentence, it is placed before *haber*.

No lo he hecho.
I **haven't done** it.

Exercise 1

Match the subject pronouns in column A to the correct present perfect form in column B.

A	B
_____ **1.** yo	a. ha pensado
_____ **2.** ellos	b. habéis ido
_____ **3.** tú	c. he esperado
_____ **4.** ella	d. has comido
_____ **5.** vosotros	e. han bailado

Exercise 2

Provide the present perfect tense form of the following irregular verbs.

1. escribir _____

2. poner _____

3. ver _____

4. resolver _____

5. abrir _____

Exercise 3

You've been feeling sluggish and out of shape lately, so you've decided to do something about it. Write five sentences in Spanish using the present perfect tense to describe what steps you've taken to improve your physical health.

1. _____

_____

_____

2. _____

_____

_____

3. _____

_____

_____

4. _____

_____

_____

5. _____

_____

64

The past perfect, also called the pluperfect, is used to discuss what someone *had done* in the past. The past perfect describes an action that was completed in the past, before another action took place.

The past perfect is a compound tense formed by combining the imperfect tense of the auxiliary verb *haber* (to have) with the past participle.

> *Cuando llegué, la película **había empezado**.*
> When I arrived, the movie **had begun.**

> *Antes de ayer, nunca **habían comido** comida tailandesa.*
> Before yesterday, they **had** never **eaten** Thai food.

¡Atención!

The auxiliary verb *haber* agrees with the subject of the sentence, not the object.

> ***La señora había** abierto la ventanas.*
> **The woman had** opened the windows.

The past perfect is often used with *ya* (already) to express that an action or state occurred before another action. *Ya* is placed before *haber*.

*A medianoche **ya había cerrado** el restaurante.*
At midnight the restaurant **had already closed.**

¡Atención!

The verb *haber* is never separated from the past participle in the past perfect tense. With reflexive verbs, the reflexive pronoun is placed immediately before the verb *haber*.

> *Cuando se levantó Jaime, ya **me había levantado**.*
> When Jaime got up, I **had** already **gotten (myself) up.**

Exercise 1

Matilde is discussing her recent travels with Teodoro. Fill in their dialogue with the correct past perfect form of the verb in parentheses.

Teodoro: Antes de este año, ¿(**1.**)_____

(ir) al Ecuador?

Matilde: No. Solo (**2.**)_____ (visitar)

los países de América Central. (**3.**)_____

(ser) un gran gusto llegar a conocer a la ciudad de Quito.

Teodoro: ¿Y antes de este viaje (**4.**)_____

(probar) los *llapingachos*?

Matilde: ¡Pues no! Son una delicia que nunca

(**5.**)_____ (comer) en mi vida. Pero

que placer comerlos ahora!

Exercise 2

Describe what was going on at certain times in the past by completing the following phrases in the past perfect.

1. Hasta el año pasado, mi madre nunca...

_____

_____

2. Hasta este semestre, yo siempre...

_____

_____

3. Antes de 1999, mis hermanos nunca...

_____

_____

4. Cuando te llamé ayer, ya...

_____

_____

5. Antes de ir a la playa, nosotros...

_____

_____

Exercise 3

Which of the following had you done and not done by the time you graduated from high school? Write in complete sentences.

1. ir de _camping_

_____

_____

_____

2. bucear en el océano

_____

_____

_____

3. montar a caballo

_____

_____

_____

4. esquiar

_____

_____

5. escalar una montaña

_____

_____

_____

65

The future perfect tense is used to discuss what someone *will have done* or what *will have happened* by a specific time or before another action takes place in the future.

The future perfect is formed by combining the future tense of the auxiliary verb *haber* (to have) with the past participle.

> *Para el sábado,* **habremos comprado** *los libros.*
> By Saturday, we **will have bought** the books.

> *Para el año nuevo,* **habrá pagado** *la deuda.*
> By the new year, he **will have paid off** the debt.

The future perfect tense can also express probability in a past time. It can replace the preterite or present perfect tense, and can often translate as *I wonder* or *probably*.

> *¿Dónde* **se habrá escondido** *el gato?*
> I **wonder** where the cat **hid.**

> *El gato* **se habrá escondido** *en el sótano.*
> The cat **probably hid** in the basement.

¡Atención!

The expression *deber de*, followed by *haber* and the infinitive, can be substituted for the future perfect to express probability.

> **Deben de haber perdido** *las llaves.*
> They **must have lost** the keys.

¡Atención!

As with the other perfect tenses, the verb *haber* and the past participle must never be separated in the future perfect.

> *Para el año que viene,* **habré comprado** *un carro nuevo.*
> By next year, I **will have bought** a new car.

Exercise 1

Fill in the blanks with the future perfect tense of the appropriate verb below.

dejar
viajar
regresar
empezar
corregido
tomar

1. Para la semana que viene, nosotros _____

_____ el examen de historia. El

profesor los _____ antes

de las vacaciones.

2. Dentro de dos meses, mis padres _____

_____ a Buenos Aires. Y en dos meses y

medio, _____ a casa.

3. Para el año nuevo yo _____

de fumar, y tú _____

a ir al gimnasio todos los días.

Exercise 2

Add probability to the questions below by rewriting them using the future perfect.

1. ¿A dónde se mudaron José y Lucía?

   _____

   _____

   _____

2. ¿Cuánto le costo ese mueble a la señora Asunción?

   _____

   _____

   _____

3. ¿Se casaron los hijos de Carola?

   _____

   _____

   _____

4. ¿Quién se robó el dinero de la caja?

   _____

   _____

   _____

5. ¿El sobrino de Mario tuvo un accidente de carro?

   _____

   _____

   _____

Exercise 3

State your intentions for the new year by writing five resolutions using the future perfect tense.

Para el año que viene...

1. _____

   _____

   _____

2. _____

   _____

   _____

3. _____

   _____

   _____

4. _____

   _____

   _____

5. _____

   _____

   _____

66

67 Verbs *The Conditional Tense*

The conditional tense expresses what someone *would do* or what *would happen.*

The conditional tense is formed by adding to the infinitive forms of the three types of verbs (-ar, -er, and -ir) the endings -ía, -ías, and -ía for singular subjects and -íamos, -íais, and -ían for plural subjects.

	Singular	Plural
cantar (to sing)	yo cantaría I would sing	nosotros/as cantaríamos we would sing
	tú cantarías you would sing	vosotros/as cantaríais you would sing
	él/ella/usted cantaría he/she/it/you (formal) would sing	ellos/ellas/ustedes cantarían they/you (formal) would sing
comer (to eat)	yo comería I would eat	nosotros/as comeríamos we would eat
	tú comerías you would eat	vosotros/as comeríais you would eat
	él/ella/usted comería he/she/it/you (formal) would eat	ellos/ellas/ustedes comerían they/you (formal) would eat
escribir (to write)	yo escribiría I would write	nosotros/as escribiríamos we would write
	tú escribirías you would write	vosotros/as escribiríais you would write
	él/ella/usted escribiría he/she/it/you (formal) would write	ellos/ellas/ustedes escribirían they/you (formal) would write

¡Atención!

All conditional endings carry an accent. Verbs already carrying an accent mark in the infinitive drop that accent in the conditional.

oir (to hear) → **oiría** (I would hear)

The conditional form of an irregular verb is formed by adding the conditional ending to the irregular stem.

Infinitive	Irregular Stem
caber	cabr-
decir	dir-
haber	habr-
hacer	har-
poder	podr-
poner	pondr-
querer	querr-
saber	sabr-
salir	saldr-
tener	tendr-
valer	valdr-
venir	vendr-

The conditional is used to refer to the future in relation to a past action. The future expresses what *will happen*; the conditional expresses what *would happen*.

Me **promete** (present) *que no* **fumará** (future) *más.*
He **promises** me that he **won't smoke** again.

Me **prometió** (past) *que no* **fumaría** (conditional) *más.*
He **promised** me that he **wouldn't smoke** again.

The conditional tense is used to make a polite request.

¿Me **podrías** ayudar, por favor?
Would you **be able to** help me, please?

The conditional tense is used to soften a statement.

Me **gustaría** hablar con el Señor Guzmán.
I **would like** to speak with Mr. Guzmán.

The conditional tense is used to express curiosity or probability about something in the past. In these cases, the conditional tense translates as *I wonder, probably*, or *must have*.

¿Manolo y Claudia **llegarían** a tiempo al concierto?
I **wonder** whether Manolo and Claudia got to the concert on time.

*Él **pensaría** que estoy loca si llegara vestida así.*
He **would think** I was crazy if I arrived dressed like this.

¡Atención

The expression *deber de*, followed by the infinitive, can also express probability in the past.

***Deberían de estar** cansados.*
They **must have been** tired.

día. No quiero perder tanto tiempo.

—Tengo una sugerencia. Tú y Marta (**7.**) _____

(poder) ir al Palacio Real, y yo al Museo del Prado. Nos

(**8.**) _____ (ponerse) de acuerdo para

encontrarnos en el hotel a las siete de la noche. ¿Qué te

parece?

—Me parece genial.

Exercise 1

Provide the conditional tense for the following verbs and the given subjects.

1. saber (nosotros) _____

2. venir (tú) _____

3. pensar (vosotros) _____

4. decir (yo) _____

5. vivir (ustedes) _____

Exercise 3

You're giving advice to a friend who is looking for a job. Write five sentences in the conditional describing what you would do if you were in her place. Use *yo* + conditional (I would) to begin each sentence.

1. _____

_____

_____

2. _____

_____

_____

3. _____

_____

_____

Exercise 2

Jaime is discussing an upcoming trip to Madrid. Fill in the dialogue with the correct conditional form of the verb in parentheses.

—Jaime, ¿que te (**1.**) _____ (gustar) hacer en

Madrid?

—Pues, (**2.**) _____ (querer) ir primero al

Museo del Prado. Me (**3.**) _____ (encantar)

ver los cuadros de Goya y Velásquez.

—Yo (**4.**) _____ (preferir) ir primero al Palacio

Real. Yo (**5.**) _____ (decir) que una excursión

al Museo del Prado (**6.**) _____ (durar) todo el

4. _____

_____

_____

5. _____

_____

_____

67

All verbs are classified as expressing one of three moods: indicative, imperative, and subjunctive. Each mood describes the form the verb takes to show the attitude of the subject.

The indicative, the most common mood, is used to state facts and express certainty and reality. The imperative mood expresses commands. The subjunctive mood expresses feelings, opinions, suppositions, dreams, and speculations.

> *Es importante que **vayas** al doctor ahora mismo.*
> It's important that you **go** to the doctor right now.

> *Siento que tu **no puedas** venir mañana.*
> I'm sorry that you **can't** come tomorrow.

The present subjunctive of regular -ar verbs is formed by dropping the final -o from the first-person singular (yo) form of the present indicative, and adding -e, -es, and -e for singular subjects and -emos, -éis, and -en for plural subjects.

	Singular	Plural
cantar (to sing)	*yo cant**e*** I (want to) sing	*nosotros/as* cant**emos** we sing
	*tú cant**es*** you sing	*vosotros/as* cant**éis** you sing
	él/ella/usted cant**e** he/she/it/you (formal) sings	*ellos/ellas/* ustedes cant**en** they/you (formal) sing

The present subjunctive of regular -er and -ir verb add -a, -as, and -a for singular subjects and -amos, -áis, and -an for plural subjects.

	Singular	Plural
comer (to eat)	*yo com**a*** I eat	*nosotros/as* com**amos** we eat
	*tú com**as*** you eat	*vosotros/as* com**áis** you eat
	él/ella/usted com**a** he/she/it/you (formal) eats	*ellos/ellas/* ustedes com**an** they/you (formal) eat
escribir (to write)	*yo escrib**a*** I write	*nosotros/as* escrib**amos** we write
	*tú escrib**as*** you write	*vosotros/as* escrib**áis** you write
	él/ella/usted escrib**a** he/she/it/you (formal) writes	*ellos/ellas/* ustedes escrib**an** they/you (formal) write

Exercise 1

Provide the subjunctive form, given the subject in parentheses, for the verbs below.

1. estudiar (yo)

_____

2. aprender (ellos)

_____

3. escribir (nosotros)

_____

4. leer (tú)

_____

5. abrir (él)

_____

Exercise 2

Fill in the blank with the correct subjunctive form of the verb in parentheses.

1. Es bueno que los niños _____ (comer)

frutas, verduras, y cereales.

2. Es importante que tú _____ (estudiar)

todas las noches.

3. Es mejor que vosotros les _____ (escribir)

antes de llamarlos.

4. Es necesario que yo _____ (hablar) con el

profesor Morales, por favor.

5. Es importante que nosotros _____ (leer)

este capítulo con cuidado.

Exercise 3

Translate the following sentences into Spanish using the subjunctive form.

1. It's very important that you wash your dishes every night.

_____

_____

_____

2. It's necessary that she speak to her mother about the accident.

_____

_____

_____

3. It's good that we help Grandma.

_____

_____

_____

4. It's bad that they don't read a lot.

_____

_____

_____

5. It's important that Marta open the window while she cooks.

_____

_____

_____

68

Stem-changing and irregular verbs make slight changes in the subjunctive tense.

Verbs with irregular *yo* forms in the present indicative have the same irregularities in the present subjunctive.

Infinitive	Present Indicative	Present Subjunctive
conducir (to drive)	conduzco	conduzca
decir (to say)	digo	diga
traer (to bring)	traigo	traiga

-ar, -er, and -ir verbs with stem changes in the present indicative have the same stem changes in the subjunctive.

Infinitive	Present Indicative	Present Subjunctive
pensar (to think)	pienso	piense
mostrar (to show)	muestro	muestre
volver (to turn)	vuelvo	vuelva
pedir (to ask)	pido	pida

La Excepción

Stem-changing -ar and -er verbs do not change their stems in the *nosotros/nosotras* and *vosotros/vosotras* forms of the present indicative or present subjunctive.

Stem-changing -ir verbs, however, retain their stem changes in the *nosotros/nosotras* and *vosotros/vosotras* forms: *e* changes to *i*, and *o* changes to *u*.

Infinitive	Nosotros/as, Subjunctive	Vosotros/as, Subjunctive
pedir (to ask)	pidamos	pidáis
dormir (to sleep)	durmamos	durmáis
sentir (to hear)	sintamos	sintáis

Five verbs are irregular in the present subjunctive.

	Singular	Plural
dar (to give)	yo **dé**	nosotros/as **demos**
	tu **des**	vosotros/as **deis**
	él/ella/usted **dé**	ellos/ellas/ustedes **den**
estar (to be)	yo **esté**	nosotros/as **estemos**
	tu **estés**	vosotros/as **estéis**
	él/ella/usted **esté**	ellos/ellas/ustedes **estén**
ir (to go)	yo **vaya**	nosotros/as **vayamos**
	tu **vayas**	vosotros/as **vayáis**
	él/ella/usted **vaya**	ellos/ellas/ustedes **vayan**
saber (to know)	yo **sepa**	nosotros/as **sepamos**
	tu **sepas**	vosotros/as **sepáis**
	él/ella/usted **sepa**	ellos/ellas/ustedes **sepan**
ser (to be)	yo **sea**	nosotros/as **seamos**
	tu **seas**	vosotros/as **seáis**
	él/ella/usted **sea**	ellos/ellas/ustedes **sean**

Exercise 1

Complete the crossword puzzle with the correct subjunctive form of the verbs provided in the clues.

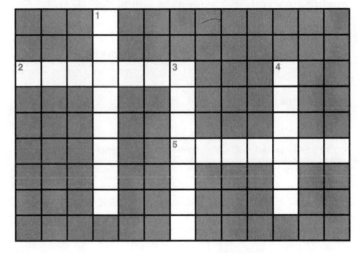

Down
2. saber (nostros)
5. traer (ellos)

Across
1. traducir (yo)
3. sentir (vostros)
4. jugar (yo)

Exercise 2

Complete the table with the subjunctive form of the following irregular verbs.

	estar	ir	ser
yo			
tú			
él			
nosotros			
vosotros			
ellos			

Exercise 3

Rewrite the sentences below using the subjunctive form of the verb in parentheses.

1. Mi madre dice que es importante que la gente (tener) compasión para los demás.

   _____

   _____

   _____

2. Es necesario que (haber) una reunión de los gerentes ésta tarde.

   _____

   _____

   _____

3. La enfermera de la escuela dice que es urgente que tú (ir) al médico.

   _____

   _____

   _____

4. Es mejor que mi hermano (conducir) más lento.

   _____

   _____

   _____

5. Es una desventaja que nosotros no (saber) más lenguas.

   _____

   _____

   _____

69

The subjunctive mood exists in English, but it is rarely used. In contrast, the subjunctive is used frequently in Spanish to express feelings, opinions, suppositions, dreams, and speculations.

The subjunctive is primarily used in dependent (subordinate) clauses introduced by a conjunction or relative pronoun, such as *que* (that).

*Temo **que** Susana no **pueda** ir con nosotros.*
I'm afraid **that** Susana won't **be able to** go with us tomorrow.

The subjunctive is used following a main clause containing a verb that gives advice, commands, demands, desires, suggests, or requests.

Catalina **sugiere**   *que* **vayamos** al cine.
(main clause/advice)   (subordinate clause/subjunctive)

Catalina **suggests** that we **go** to the cinema.

Other verbs and verb phrases that indicate advice and are commonly used with the subjunctive mood include the following:

aconsejar	to advise
desear	to wish
necesitar	to need
pedir	to ask for
querer	to want
sugerir	to suggest
es bueno que	it's good that
es importante que	it's important that

¡Atención!

When there is no change in the subject of the sentence from the main clause to the subordinate clause, the infinitive is used instead of the subjunctive.

*No quiero **ir** a la escuela.*
I don't want **to go** to school.

The subjunctive is used following a main clause containing a verb that expresses emotion.

Me **molesta**   *que*   **pienses** así.
(main clause/emotion)   (subordinate clause/subjunctive)

It **bothers** me that you **think** that way.

Other verbs and verb phrases that express emotion and are commonly used with the subjunctive mood include the following:

esperar	to hope, wish
gustar	to like
sorprender	to surprise
temer	to be afraid
es triste	it's sad

The subjunctive is used following a main clause containing a verb that expresses doubt, denial, or disbelief.

Dudan   *que* **seas** mi amigo.
(main clause/doubt)   (subordinate clause/subjunctive)

They **doubt** that you **are** my friend.

Other verbs and verb phrases that express doubt and are commonly used with the subjunctive mood include the following:

negar	to deny
no creer	to not believe
no es cierto	it's not true
no es seguro	it's not certain
es imposible	it's impossible
dudar	to doubt

The subjunctive is used with the verb *ojalá* or the expression *ojalá que*, which translates as *if only, I hope*, or *I wish*. The relative pronoun *que* can be omitted, though the subjunctive verb is necessary.

***Ojalá que pueda** ir contigo.*	**I hope that I can** go with you.
***Ojalá pueda** ir contigo.*	**I hope I can** go with you.

Exercise 1

Complete the sentences below with a subordinate clause using the subjunctive.

1. Te aconsejo que...

_____

_____

2. Les pido que...

_____

_____

3. Sugerimos que...

_____

_____

4. Deseo que...

_____

_____

5. Esperamos que...

_____

_____

Exercise 2

Determine if the sentences below call for the subjunctive. Circle the correct form of the verb.

1. Me molesta que tú no me escuches/escuchas.

2. Temo que mi hermana se pierde/pierda.

3. Queremos ir/vayamos a la playa este verano.

4. Dudo que ellos son/sean capaces de entender el problema.

5. Necesitamos comprar/compremos huevos para el desayuno.

Exercise 3

You're going to your first opera. What are your expectations? Use *ojalá* to form complete sentences in the subjunctive given the elements below.

1. nosotros / llegar / a tiempo

_____

_____

_____

2. haber / subtítulos / en inglés

_____

_____

_____

3. los cantantes / saber / sus papeles

_____

_____

_____

4. el escenario / ser / hermoso

_____

_____

_____

5. nuestros asientos / no estar / muy lejos del escenario

_____

_____

_____

The conditional perfect tense is used to discuss an action that *would have been completed* in the past. The present perfect subjunctive tense is used to discuss *what has happened* in the past. Both tenses combine the past participle with different forms of the auxiliary verb *haber* (to have).

The conditional perfect is formed by combining the future tense of the auxiliary verb *haber* with the past participle.

> Yo **habría preferido** ir al partido de fútbol que al partido de baloncesto.
> I **would have preferred** to go to the soccer match rather than the basketball game.

¡Atención!

The future tense of *haber* is *yo habría* (I will have), *tu habrías* (you will have), *él/ella habría* (he/she/it will have), *nosotros/as habríamos* (we will have), *vosotros/as habríais* (you will have), *ellos/as/ustedes habrían* (they/you will have).

The conditional perfect is used to express conjecture or possibility.

> Todos pensábamos que **habría consultado** primero con su doctor.
> We all thought that he **would have consulted** first with his doctor.

¡Atención!

The use of the conditional perfect implies that the action was not completed or did not take place.

The present perfect subjunctive is formed by combining the present subjunctive form of the auxiliary verb *haber* with the past participle.

> Espero que **hayas terminado** tus tareas.
> I hope you **have finished** your homework.

The present perfect subjunctive is always used in the subordinate clause, and indicates when an action occurred before the action expressed in the main clause.

> Me alegro que ustedes **se hayan divertido** tanto esta tarde.
> I'm pleased that you **had fun** this afternoon.

¡Atención!

The same conditions that call for the present subjunctive call for the present perfect subjunctive.

*Me preocupa que los niños todavía **no hayan regresado**.*
It worries me that the kids still **haven't returned**.

Exercise 1

Provide the correct form of the conditional perfect based on the subject in parentheses.

1. hacer (nosotros)

_____

2. vivir (ellos)

_____

3. presentar (yo)

_____

4. querer (vosotros)

_____

5. viajar (tú)

_____

Exercise 2

What would you have done in the following situations? Write your answers in complete sentences using the conditional perfect.

1. encontraste una bolsa de dinero en el bus

_____

_____

_____

2. te subiste al tren pero no tenías un billete

_____

_____

_____

3. quisiste ducharte pero no había agua caliente

_____

_____

_____

4. no estudiaste para tu examen de historia

_____

_____

_____

5. rompiste un plato antiguo de tu tía

_____

_____

_____

Exercise 3

Use the phrase in parentheses to rewrite each sentence using the present perfect subjunctive.

1. Saliste anoche con Alexandra. (No creo que)

_____

_____

_____

2. Jorge y Salvador aprendieron a bailar el tango. (Dudo que)

_____

_____

_____

3. Mi mejor amigo se casó. (Me alegro de que)

_____

_____

_____

4. Te fuiste de vacaciones a Chile. (Que bueno que)

_____

_____

_____

5. La sopa de pescado me dio un tremendo dolor de barriga. (Es imposible que)

_____

_____

_____

71

An adverbial clause is a group of words that modifies a verb and is introduced by a conjunction. Both the indicative and subjunctive mood can be used in adverbial clauses to show time, purpose or intention, or a condition or restriction imposed by an action. They answer the questions *where? when? how?* and *why?*

Common conjunctions that introduce adverbial time clauses include the following:

cuando	when
después de que	after
en cuanto	as soon as
hasta que	until
mientras	while
antes de que	before

The indicative mood is used after conjunctions showing time if the action has already taken place.

> *Cuando terminé de comer, lavé mi plato.*
> **When I finished** eating, I washed my plate.

The subjunctive mood is used after conjunctions showing time if the action has not been completed or is uncertain.

> *Cuando termine de comer, lavaré mi plato.*
> **When I finish eating,** I'll wash my plate.

¡Atención!

The subjunctive always follows the phrase *antes de que*.

Common conjunctions that introduce adverbial clauses expressing purpose or intention include the following:

a fin de que	in order that
para que	so that
de manera que	so as, so that
de modo que	so as
aunque	although, even if

The subjunctive mood is always used with *a fin de que* and *para que*.

> *Para que el niño mejore, tendrá que tomar penicilina.*
> **For** the child to **improve,** he'll need to take penicillin.

The subjunctive mood is used with *de modo que* and *de manera que* when expressing a purpose or intention.

> *Habla lento de modo que los niños entiendan.*
> Speak slowly **so that** the children **understand.**

The indicative is used with *de modo que* and *de manera que* when expressing the result of an action.

> *Hablaron lento de modo que todos los entendimos.*
> They spoke slowly **so that** we all **understood.**

Common conjunctions that introduce adverbial clauses establishing condition or restriction include the following:

a menos que	unless
sin que	without
con tal de que	provided that
en caso de que	in case

The subjunctive mood is always used with conjunctions introducing clauses that establish a condition or a restriction of an action.

> *Juana hablará con el jefe con tal de que tu vayas con ella.*
> Juana will talk to the boss **provided that** you **go** with her.

Exercise 1

Do the following conjunctions require a subjunctive verb or an indicative verb in the adverbial clauses they introduce? Note: Some may take either verb.

1. hasta que _____

2. a fin de que _____

3. de modo que _____

4. para que _____

5. con tal de que _____

Exercise 2

Translate the following sentence pairs into English using the correct mood in the adverbial clause.

1. When I finished studying, I closed my book.
   When I finish studying, I'll close my book.

   _____

   _____

   _____

   _____

2. As soon as the concert finished, the audience began to clap.
   As soon as the concert finishes, the audience will begin to clap.

   _____

   _____

   _____

   _____

3. I drive slowly so that mom doesn't get scared.
   I drove slowly, so mom didn't get scared.

   _____

   _____

   _____

   _____

Exercise 3

Is the subjunctive necessary? Circle the correct form of the verb in each sentence below.

1. Tan pronto como yo llego/llegue a casa, haré mis tareas.

2. En cuanto Julio llamó/llame, fui a buscarlo.

3. Cuando Juan saluda/salude a María, ella le sonríe.

4. La mamá de Marta le espera hasta que ella se baje/se bajó del bus.

5. Le daré el dinero después de que ella compre/compra la comida.

72

The past subjunctive (also called the imperfect subjunctive) is the past form of the present subjunctive.

The past subjunctive is used in the same situations as the present subjunctive, but to describe past events.

Present subjunctive: ***Quiero*** que **juegen** en el jardín.
I **want** them **to play** in the garden.

Past subjunctive: ***Quería*** que jugaran en el jardín.
I **wanted** them **to play** in the garden.

The past subjunctive is formed by dropping the *-ron* ending of the third-person plural (*ellos/ellas/ustedes*) form of the preterite, and adding *-ra, -ras, -ra, -ramos, -rais*, or *-ran*.

	Singular	Plural
hablar (to talk)	yo habla**ra**	nosotros/as hablá**ramos**
	tu habla**ras**	vosotros/as habla**rais**
	él/ella/usted habla**ra**	ellos/ellas/ustedes habla**ran**

Lenguaje en Práctica

Though it is rare, in some Spanish literature the past subjunctive takes another set of endings: *-se, -ses, -se, -semos, -seis*, and *-sen*.

Me dijo que me ***callase.***
He told me to **shut up.**

Verbs with irregular preterite forms use the same irregular stems and endings in the past subjunctive.

	Preterite	Past Subjunctive
estar (to be)	estuvieron	**estuviera**
hacer (to do)	hicieron	**hiciera**
tener (to have)	tuvieron	**tuviera**

Stem-changing verbs that end in *-ir* retain the vowel change from the third-person plural of the preterite.

	Preterite	Past Subjunctive
dormir (to sleep)	durmieron	**durmiera**
pedir (to ask)	pidieron	**pidiera**

Exercise 1

Fill in the blank with the correct past subjunctive form of the verb in parentheses.

1. Mi padre siempre quiso que yo _____ la medicina. (estudiar)

2. Fue una mala idea que tú _____ con Patricia. (hablar)

3. No creían que Marta _____ hacerlo. (poder)

4. No había nadie que _____ la historia. (creer)

5. Queríamos que ustedes _____ a la biblioteca. (ir)

Exercise 2

Rewrite the following present-tense sentences using the past subjunctive form.

1. Mis maestros me piden que yo estudie mucho.

   _____

   _____

   _____

2. Los padres de Orlando no quieren que mire mucho la televisión.

   _____

   _____

   _____

3. Busca amigos que sean aventureros.

   _____

   _____

   _____

4. Espero que tu vengas a la fiesta.

   _____

   _____

   _____

5. Queremos que tú pagues la cuenta.

   _____

   _____

   _____

Exercise 3

Use the past subjunctive to compose five sentences describing what your parents expected of you when you were younger.

1. _____

   _____

   _____

2. _____

   _____

   _____

3. _____

   _____

   _____

4. _____

   _____

   _____

5. _____

   _____

   _____

73

The past perfect (pluperfect) subjunctive is used to express feelings, opinions, suppositions, dreams, and speculations occurring prior to another action in the past.

The past perfect subjunctive is formed by combining the imperfect subjunctive of the auxiliary verb *haber* (to have) with the past participle.

> *No pensaron que **hubiéramos hablado** (past participle) con el director.*
> They didn't think that **we would have spoken to** the director.

> *Me molestó que no me **hubieras llamado** (past participle) antes.*
> It bothered me that you **hadn't called me** sooner.

¡Atención!

The imperfect subjunctive of *haber* is *yo hubiera* (I would have), *tu hubieras* (you would have), *él/ella/usted hubiera* (he/she/it would have), *nosotros/as hubiéramos* (we would have), *vosotros/as hubierais* (you would have), *ellos/as/ustedes hubieran* (they/you would have).

The past perfect subjunctive is used when the following two conditions are met: The verb in the main clause is in either the past or the conditional tense, and the action of the verb in the past perfect subjunctive tense took place before the action in the main clause.

> *El jefe quería que los albañiles **hubieran terminado** el trabajo antes de las cinco.*
> The boss wanted the bricklayers **to have finished** the job before 5:00.

¡Atención!

As with the other perfect tenses, the verb *haber* and the past participle must never be separated in the past perfect subjunctive. With reflexive verbs, the reflexive pronoun is placed immediately before the verb *haber*.

> *Era probable que **lo hubieran visto.***
> It was probable that **they had seen it.**

Exercise 1

Use the subject indicated in parentheses to provide the correct form of both the past subjunctive and the past perfect subjunctive for each verb.

1. deber (ella)

_____

_____

2. estudiar (ustedes)

_____

_____

3. oír (nosotros)

_____

_____

4. dormir (tú)

_____

_____

5. ver (yo)

_____

_____

Exercise 2

Complete the following sentences with the past perfect subjunctive of the verb in parentheses.

1. No habríamos comido el pollo si (nosotros, saber) que era tuyo.

   _____

   _____

   _____

2. No había nadie que (ver) el espectáculo.

   _____

   _____

   _____

3. Es posible que (ellos, ver) la policía y por eso se escaparon.

   _____

   _____

   _____

4. No era cierto que (yo, ir) con él al concierto.

   _____

   _____

   _____

5. Dudaba que (tú, decir) esa mentira.

   _____

   _____

   _____

Exercise 3

Imagine that the following events happened last week. How do you feel about them? Write down your reactions using the past perfect subjunctive.

1. Se murió la abuela de mi amiga.

   _____

   _____

   _____

2. Ganaste la lotería.

   _____

   _____

   _____

3. Tus amigos te hicieron una fiesta.

   _____

   _____

   _____

4. Tu novia/o rompió contigo.

   _____

   _____

   _____

5. Viajaste a El Salvador.

   _____

   _____

   _____

74

Like the English phrases *if only* or *I hope*, *ojalá que* is a phrase that expresses hope. *Ojalá que* always requires the subjunctive tense.

Lenguaje en Práctica

Ojalá is derived from the Arabic word meaning *Allah willing.*

The present subjunctive accompanies *ojalá que* to express hope that something happens in the present or will happen in the future.

> *¡Ojalá que no haga mucho calor esta tarde!*
> **I hope** it **isn't** too hot this afternoon.

The present perfect subjunctive accompanies *ojalá que* to express hope that something took place in the past.

> *¡Ojalá que tu hermano haya pasado sus exámenes!*
> **I hope** your brother **passed** his exams.

¡Atención!

Ojalá que is used with the present or present perfect subjunctive tenses to express a wish that may come true.

> *¡Ojalá que gane la lotería!*
> **I hope** I win the lottery.

> *Ojalá que mi mamá haya preparado la cena.*
> **I hope** my mom prepared dinner.

The past subjunctive accompanies *ojalá que* to express hope for something that is contrary to reality in the present.

> *¡Ojalá que hubiéramos comprado más pan!*
> **I wish we had bought** more bread. (though we didn't)

The past perfect subjunctive accompanies *ojalá que* to express hope for something that didn't happen.

> *¡Ojalá que hubieras estudiado más!*
> **I wish you had studied** more. (but you didn't)

Exercise 1

Rewrite the following sentences correctly.
Note: Some of the sentences do not have errors.

1. Ojalá que puedes ir con nosotros al Museo Central.

_____

_____

_____

2. Ojalá que María haya comprado las entradas.

_____

_____

_____

3. Ojalá que la entrada no cuesta demasiado.

_____

_____

_____

4. Ojalá que la cola no esté muy larga.

_____

_____

_____

5. Ojalá que todos nos divertimos.

_____

_____

Exercise 2

Translate the following sentences into Spanish using *ojalá que.*

1. I hope it doesn't rain this afternoon.

_____

_____

_____

2. I wish you hadn't fallen.

_____

_____

_____

3. I wish we had spent less money at the shopping center.

_____

_____

_____

4. I hope you remembered to get eggs.

_____

_____

_____

5. I hope the restaurant is good.

_____

_____

_____

Exercise 3

You're at the airport on your way to Puerto Rico. Things aren't going so well. Write complete sentences using *ojalá que* **and the past subjunctive to express how you hoped things would have been.**

1. el avión / salir a tiempo

_____

_____

_____

2. yo / conseguir un asiento en la ventanilla

_____

_____

_____

3. no haber tanta gente

_____

_____

_____

4. yo / poder llevar la navaja que me regaló mi abuelo

_____

_____

5. mis padres / quedarse conmigo por un rato

_____

_____

_____

75

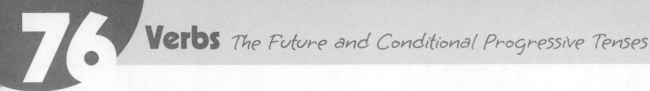
Progressive tenses express ongoing actions. They can also express possibility. Both the future and conditional progressive combine the present participle with different forms of the auxiliary verb *estar* (to be).

The future progressive refers to an ongoing action in the future. It is formed by combining the future tense of the auxiliary verb *estar* with the present participle.

> *Mañana, a las ocho de la noche, **estarás cenando.***
> Tomorrow, at 8 P.M., **you'll be having dinner.**

The future progressive also expresses probability in the present.

> *—¿Qué hace Javier?*
> *—No estoy seguro. **Estará leyendo** su libro.*

> "What's Javier up to?"
> "I'm not sure. **He must be reading** his book."

The conditional progressive refers to an ongoing action that is in the future, when the referent is in the past. It is formed by combining the present conditional tense of the auxiliary verb *estar* with the present participle.

> *Carmen me dijo que tú **estarías cenando** a las ocho de la noche.*
> Carmen told me that **you would be having dinner** at 8 P.M.

The conditional progressive can also express probability in the past.

> *—¿Por qué estaba llorando Paco?*
> *—No sé. **Estaría disgustado** porque perdió la apuesta con Ramón.*

> "Why was Paco crying?"
> "I don't know. **Maybe he was upset** because he lost his bet with Ramón."

In the progressive tenses, object pronouns and reflexive pronouns must either precede the conjugated form of *estar* or be attached to the end of the participle. *Estar* and the participles must not be separated.

> *Maite **estará cepillándose** los dientes.*
> Maite **must be brushing** her teeth.

> *Les dije que yo **me estaría preparando** para la presentación a las dos.*
> I told them I **would be preparing myself** for the presentation at 2 P.M.

Exercise 1

Complete the following sentences using the future progressive.

1. ¿Piensas que ya acabó el examen de Fátima?

   Creo que sí, ya _____

   _____ (llegar a casa)

2. ¿Sabes si ya empezó la película?

   Sí, ya _____

   _____ (terminar)

3. ¿Crees que ya llegaron tus hermanas?

   Sí, ya _____

   _____ (registrándose en la recepción del hotel)

4. ¿Sabes si aterrizó el avión?

   Seguro. Los señores _____

   _____ (recoger sus maletas)

5. ¿Sabes si terminó la operación?

   Sí, Manuel _____

   _____ (despertarse)

Exercise 2

What do you think the following people are doing right now? Use the future progressive in sentences that express the probability of their actions in the present.

1. El presidente venezolano Hugo Chávez

_____

_____

_____

2. Tu profesor/a de español

_____

_____

_____

3. Gloria Estefan

_____

_____

_____

4. Salma Hayek

_____

_____

_____

5. Tu mejor amigo

_____

_____

_____

Exercise 3

Form logical responses to the questions below. Use the conditional progressive tense to express probability in the past.

1. ¿Por qué está enfadada tu madre?

_____

_____

_____

2. ¿Por qué no atendió a la clase Marta?

_____

_____

_____

3. ¿Por qué perdieron el partido de fútbol?

_____

_____

_____

4. ¿Por qué cancelaron el vuelo a Santo Domingo?

_____

_____

_____

5. ¿Por qué le castigaron a Pedro?

_____

_____

_____

16

Si (if) clauses express actions that may occur if particular conditions are met. A sentence with a *si* clause consists of a condition (the *si* clause) and a result (the result clause). The condition in a *si* clause can either be real or contrary to reality.

Real conditions describe situations that are likely, certain, or factual. Real conditions are expressed using the indicative form of the verb in both the *si* clause and the result clause.

> *Si **estudias** más, **sacarás** mejores notas.*
> If you **study** more, you **will receive** better grades.

> *Si **comes** esa comida picante, te **va a doler** el estómago mañana.*
> If you **eat** that spicy food, your stomach **will hurt** tomorrow.

Conditions that run contrary to fact are expressed using either the imperfect or past perfect (pluperfect) subjunctive in the *si* clause, depending on when the action takes place.

Action in *Si* Clause	*Si* Clause	Result Clause
present time	imperfect subjunctive	conditional (preferred for simple tenses) or imperfect subjunctive
in the past	past perfect subjunctive	conditional perfect or past perfect subjunctive

> *Si **tuviera** (conditional) más tiempo libre, **iría** (imperfect) a la playa.*
> If **I had** more free time, **I'd go** to the beach.

> *Si **hablara** (conditional) italiano, **leería** (imperfect) La Divina Comedia.*
> If **I spoke** Italian, **I'd read** The Divine Comedy.

> *Si mi hermano **se hubiera casado** (past perfect subjunctive) con Rosa, los dos **habrían sido** (conditional perfect) más felices.*
> If my brother **had married** Rosa, they both **would have been** happier.

A *si* clause is used to express a habitual event in the past. In these cases, the verbs in both clauses are in the imperfect tense.

> *Mi familia siempre **iba** a la cabaña si no **hacía** mucho frío.*
> My family always **went** to the cabin if it **wasn't** too cold.

¡Atención!

The placement of the *si* clause does not change the meaning of the sentence.

Si puedes venir, *llámame.*
If you can come, call me.

Llámame **si puedes venir.**
Call me **if you can come.**

Exercise 1

Fill in the blanks with the correct form of the verbs in parentheses. Begin each *si* clause with the past subjunctive.

1. Laura _____ (ver) esa obra de arte si _____ (entradas).

2. Si Matías _____ (ganar) la lotería, _____ (comprar) una casa en Buenos Aires.

3. Si Jaime _____ (poder), _____ (resolver) el problema matemático.

4. Danilo _____ (dormir) hasta las once si _____ (tener) tiempo libre.

5. Si ustedes _____ (invitarnos), nosotros _____ (venir) a visitarles.

Exercise 2

Santiago grew up in the country. How would his life be if he had grown up in the city instead? Use the prompts to write complete sentences. Begin each *si* clause with the past perfect subjunctive.

1. Result clause: tomar el metro
Si clause: trabajar en la ciudad

_____

_____

_____

2. Result clause: llevar un traje elegante
Si clause: ganarse la vida en una empresa

_____

_____

_____

3. Result clause: asistir al teatro
Si clause: vivir en la ciudad

_____

_____

_____

4. Result clause: comer en un restaurante
Si clause: no tener ganas de cocinar

_____

_____

_____

5. Result clause: salido a una discoteca
Si clause: conocer a una muchacha bonita

_____

_____

_____

Exercise 3

What would you do if...? What would you have done if...? Complete the sentences below with a result clause in the proper form.

1. Si yo ganara la lotería…

_____

_____

2. Si yo me hubiera casado joven…

_____

_____

_____

3. Si yo me mudara a España…

_____

_____

4. Si yo fuera presidente…

_____

_____

5. Si yo tuviera más tiempo…

_____

_____

_____

17

The imperative mood expresses a command. Formal commands with *usted* or *ustedes*, both affirmative and negative, are always expressed with the present subjunctive.

In the formal imperative mood, the verb takes the same form as it does in the present subjunctive.

	bailar (to dance)	*comer* (to eat)	*escribir* (to write)
usted	baile	coma	escriba
ustedes	bailen	coman	escriban

Stem-changing verbs retain their stem change in the formal imperative mood.

Cierren la ventana, por favor. — **Close** the window, please.
Vuelva pronto. — **Come back** soon.
Sirvan la limonada. — **Serve** the lemonade.

Verbs with an irregular *yo* form retain their irregularity in the formal imperative mood.

Infinitive	*usted/ustedes*
conocer	conozca/conozcan
decir	diga/digan
hacer	haga/hagan
oír	oiga/oigan
poner	ponga/pongan
salir	salga/salgan
tener	tenga/tengan
traer	traiga/traigan
ver	vea/vean

Verbs that end in -*gar*, -*car*, and -*zar* have a spelling change in the imperative form.

jugar (to play) → *jue**gu**e/jue**gu**en*
marcar (to mark) → *mar**qu**e/mar**qu**en*
cazar (to hunt) → *ca**c**e/ca**c**en*

There are five verbs that have irregular formal imperative forms.

dar (to give) → ***dé/den***
estar (to be) → ***esté/estén***
ir (to go) → ***vaya/vayan***
saber (to know) → ***sepa/sepan***
ser (to be) → ***sea/sean***

¡Atención!

Pronouns are attached to the end of the verb in affirmative commands.

*Sírva**se**, por favor.* — Serve **yourself,** please.

Pronouns are placed before the verb in negative commands.

*No **se** preocupe, señora.* — Don't worry, ma'am.

Exercise 1

Provide both the affirmative and negative formal imperative forms for each of the following verbs.

1. salir (usted)

_____

_____

2. dar (ustedes)

_____

_____

3. sacar (usted)

_____

_____

4. ir (ustedes)

_____

_____

5. volver (usted)

_____

_____

Exercise 2

You are the Spanish professor for today. Turn the following phrases into classroom commands.

1. llegar a tiempo

_____

_____

2. leer la lección

_____

_____

3. traer los libros a clase

_____

_____

4. estudiar los verbos

_____

_____

5. no hablar inglés

_____

_____

Exercise 3

You are giving your neighbor, Paco, advice on how to be a more productive member of society. Use the phrases below to create sentences in the formal imperative mood.

1. despertarse más temprano

_____

_____

2. afeitarse cada mañana

_____

_____

3. vestirse mejor

_____

_____

4. bañarse con más frecuencia

_____

_____

5. buscar un trabajo

_____

_____

78

Familiar imperative forms (commands) are used with people who would normally be addressed as *tú*.

Affirmative familiar commands have the same form as the third-person singular (*él/ella*) of the present indicative.

> *cambiar* (to change) → **cambie**
> *correr* (to run) → **corre**
> *pedir* (to ask) → **pide**

Negative familiar commands have the same form as the present subjunctive.

> *cambiar* → no **cambies**
> *correr* → no **corras**
> *pedir* → no **pidas**

Several verbs have irregular forms in the familiar imperative mood.

Infinitive	*tú*
decir	*di*
hacer	*haz*
ir	*ve*
poner	*pon*
salir	*sal*
ser	*sé*
tener	*ten*
venir	*ven*

The first-person plural form of the subjunctive is used for affirmative and negative *nosotros/as* commands.

> *ir* (to go) → *(no)* **vayamos**
> *limpiar* (to clean) → *(no)* **limpiemos**
> *tener* (to have) → *(no)* **tengamos**

¡Atención!

Pronouns are attached to the end of the verb in affirmative commands.

*¡Siénta**te**!*	Sit down!
*¡Sentámos**nos**!*	Let's sit down!

Pronouns are placed before the verb in negative commands.

*No **te** vayas.*	Don't leave.
*No **nos** vayamos.*	Let's not leave.

Exercise 1

Use the prompts below to form affirmative and negative informal commands for each verb.

1. correr (tú)

_____

_____

2. hacer (nosotros)

_____

_____

3. venir (tú)

_____

_____

4. temer (nosotros)

_____

_____

5. pedir (tú)

_____

_____

Exercise 2

Rewrite each negative command as an affirmative command, and each affirmative command as a negative command.

1. No barras el piso.

_____

_____

2. Plancha la ropa.

_____

_____

3. No prepares el desayuno.

_____

_____

4. No pongas la radio.

_____

_____

5. Vete al supermercado.

_____

_____

Exercise 3

You're teaching someone how to make scrambled eggs. Use the familiar imperative form to write out the steps he should take.

_____

_____

_____

_____

_____

_____

_____

_____

_____

_____

_____

_____

_____

_____

_____

79

The infinitive (*trabajar, comer, vivir,* and so on) form of a verb can function as a noun in Spanish. In English, the present participle (-ing form) would generally be used in this role.

The infinitive can function as the subject of another verb in a sentence. That verb is always conjugated in the third-person singular.

> ***Hacer ejercicios*** *es bueno para la salud.*
> **Doing exercises (exercising)** is good for your health.

Lenguaje en Práctica

Sometimes the definite article *el* precedes the infinitive. This is a stylistic variation and does not alter the meaning of the sentence.

> ***Mentir*** *es un vicio./**El mentir** es un vicio.*
> **Lying** is a vice.

The infinitive can function as the direct object of a verb.

> *Tenemos que **ir** a la biblioteca esta tarde.*
> We have **to go** to the library this afternoon.

> *Mi abuela quiere **aprender** el francés.*
> My grandmother wants **to learn** French.

The infinitive can function as an object of a preposition.

> *La señora Moncayo se fue **sin despedirse.***
> Mrs. Moncayo left **without saying goodbye.**

> *¡Eso te pasa **por tomar** tanto alcohol!*
> That's what you get **for drinking** so much alcohol!

The following words and phrases are generally followed by the infinitive. Some of the prepositions, however, can also be followed by nouns or pronouns, depending on the intended meaning.

hay que, tener que	it is necessary to	posible de	possible that
algo que	something that	imposible de	impossible that
nada que	nothing	antes de	before
poco que	a little	después de	after
fácil de	easy to	para, por	for

difícil de	difficult/hard to	sin	without
algo que	something that	en vez de	instead of

> ***Hay que comprar*** *una nueva refrigeradora.*
> **It is necessary to buy** a new refrigerator.

> *Ese problema matemático es **difícil de entender**.*
> That math problem is **hard to understand.**

The construction *al* (upon) + the infinitive is used to express an action that occurs at the same time as the verb in the main clause.

> ***Al entrar,*** *vi a todos mis hermanos.*
> **Upon entering,** I saw all my brothers and sisters.

Exercise 1

Indicate whether the infinitive below is functioning as the subject of the verb, the direct object of the verb, or the object of a preposition.

1. Es peligroso **hacer** demasiado ejercicio.

_____

2. Margarita se casó sin **avisarnos.**

_____

3. Queremos **ir** a la playa este verano.

_____

4. Es bueno **estudiar.**

_____

5. Antes de **comer,** hago la tarea.

_____

Exercise 2

Rewrite the following sentences correctly.
Note: Some of the sentences do not have errors.

1. No les gusta cantando.

_____

_____

2. Estoy cansada de correr.

_____

_____

3. El anuncio dice: «No fumando».

_____

_____

4. Pensaban viajar al Caribe este invierno.

_____

_____

5. Al saliendo, no se les olvide llevarse el paraguas.

_____

_____

Exercise 3

Create logical endings to the sentences below using an infinitive.

1. En vez de…

_____

_____

2. Tenemos que…

_____

_____

3. Para…

_____

_____

4. Antes de…

_____

_____

5. Hay que…

_____

_____

80

In Spanish, as in English, there are two different ways to indicate that someone else has spoken: direct speech and indirect speech.

Direct speech uses direct quotes to report the exact words of the original speaker.

>—Te llamo mañana —dijo Jaime.
> "I'll call you tomorrow," said Jaime.

>Alejandro me preguntó: «¿Cuándo vamos al concierto?».
>Alejandro asked me, "When are we going to the concert?"

Indirect speech reports the words of the original speaker without using a direct quote. Indirect speech is indicated with a subordinate *que* clause.

>**Direct:**
>—Pati, **estoy cenando** —dijo Aurora.
>"Pati, **I'm having dinner**," said Aurora.

>**Indirect:**
>Aurora le dijo a Pati **que estaba cenando.**
>Aurora told Pati **that** she **was having dinner.**

Indirect speech generally requires a complex verb change to report speech.

Tense in Direct Speech		Tense in Indirect Speech
Present Indicative	→	**Imperfect Indicative**
—Canta. "She sings."		Dijo que cantaba. He said that she was singing.
Present Subjunctive	→	**Imperfect Subjunctive**
—Dudo que vayas. "I doubt that you'll go."		Dijo que dudaba que fueras. He said that he doubted you would go.
Present Perfect Indicative	→	**Past Perfect Indicative**
—Nos han visto. "They've seen us."		Dijo que nos habían visto. He said they had seen us.
Present perfect Subjunctive	→	**Past Perfect Subjunctive**
—Pienso que se hayan ya ido. "I think they already left."		Dijo que pensaba que se hubieran ya ido. He said that he thought that they had already left.

Tense in Direct Speech		Tense in Indirect Speech
Preterite	→	**Past Perfect Indicative**
—Te vi. "I saw you."		Dijo que te había visto. He said that he had seen you.
Future	→	**Present Conditional**
—Iré mañana. "I'll go tomorrow."		Dijo que iría al día siguiente. He said that he would go the next day.
Future Perfect	→	**Perfect Conditional**
—Habré terminado para el martes. "I will have finished by Tuesday."		Dijo que habría terminado para el martes. He said he would have finished by Tuesday.
Imperative	→	**Imperfect Subjunctive**
—Limpia tu cuarto. "Clean your room."		Dijo que limpiara mi cuarto. He told me to clean my room.

Some verb tenses do not change from direct speech to indirect speech.

Tense in Direct Speech		Tense in Indirect Speech
Imperfect	→	**Imperfect**
—Iban al parque. "They were going to the park."		Dijo que se iban al parque. He said they were going to the park.
Past Perfect	→	**Past Perfect**
—Ya habíamos cenado. "We had already had dinner."		Dijo que habíamos ya cenado. He said that we had already had dinner.
Conditional	→	**Conditional**
—Si fuera rico, compraría una casa. "If I were rich, I'd buy a house."		Dijo que si fuera rico, compraría una casa. He said that if he were rich, he'd buy a house.

Exercise 1

Rewrite the following sentences using indirect speech.
Begin each sentence with *Dijo que* (he or she said that).

1. Los muchachos van al cine.

_____

_____

2. Juan siempre llega tarde.

_____

_____

3. La señora quería un café con leche.

_____

_____

4. El policía capturó al criminal.

_____

_____

5. La cena está servida.

_____

_____

Exercise 2

Rewrite the following indirect sentences correctly.
Note: Some of the sentences do not have errors.

1. —Daniel irá el jueves. → Dijo que Daniel iba el jueves.

_____

_____

2. —Si Carolina ganara el premio, estaría muy contenta. →
Dijo que si Carolina ganara el premio, estaría muy contenta.

_____

_____

3. —Duda que tu vayas. → Dijo que duda que tu vayas.

_____

_____

4. —La familia había ya regresado a casa. → Dijo que la
familia hubiera ya regresado a casa.

_____

_____

5. —Habrá terminado el trabajo para el lunes → Dijo que
habría terminado el trabajo para el lunes.

_____

_____

Exercise 3

What has been told to you in the past few weeks? Use
indirect speech to complete the sentences below.

1. Mi hermana me dijo que…

_____

_____

2. Mi amigo me dijo que…

_____

_____

3. Mi profesor me dijo que…

_____

_____

4. Mi doctor me dijo que…

_____

_____

81

Point of view and time can change when moving from direct speech to indirect speech.

References to people and things (both for the subject and the object) change from direct to indirect speech, as the point of view changes. Other elements, such as verbs, articles, and pronouns, must also change.

Direct Speech		Indirect Speech
—Me voy. "I'm leaving."	→	Él dijo que se iba. He said that he was leaving.
—Te di tu libro. "I gave you your book."	→	Ella dijo que te había dado su libro. She said that she had given you his book.
—No voy contigo. "I'm not going with you."	→	Ella me dijo que no iba conmigo. She told me she wasn't coming with me.
—Vamos a visitar a la abuela. "We're going to visit our grandmother."	→	Dijeron que iban a visitar a la abuela. They said they were going to visit their grandmother.

Expressions used to reference time often change from direct speech to indirect speech.

ahora (now)	→	entonces (then)
—**Ahora** te llamo. "I'll call you **now**."		Dijo que **entonces** le llamaba. He said he would call me **then**.
ayer (yesterday)	→	el día anterior (the day before)
—**Ayer** terminé. "I finished **yesterday**."		Dijo que había terminado **el día anterior**. He said that he had finished **the day before**.

anoche (last night)	→	la noche anterior (the night before)
—**Anoche** fuimos al cine. "We went to the movies **last night**."		Dijo que habían ido al cine **la noche anterior**. He said that they had gone to the movies **the night before**.
mañana (tomorrow)	→	el próximo día (the next day)
—Iré **mañana**. "I'll go **tomorrow**."		Dijo que iría **el próximo día**. He said he would go **the next day**.
la semana pasada (last week)	→	la semana anterior (the week before)
—**La semana pasada** fuimos a Río de Janeiro. "**Last week** we went to Río de Janeiro."		Dijo que **la semana anterior** habían ido a Río de Janeiro. He said that they had gone to Río de Janeiro **the week before**.

Exercise 1

Change the following sentences from indirect to direct speech. Pay close attention to changes in reference to people.

1. La señora le dijo que iría al doctor.

_____

_____

2. Mi mamá me dijo que lavara los platos.

_____

_____

3. Dijo que dudaba que tú estuvieras bravo.

_____

_____

4. Dijo que iban al museo.

_____

_____

5. El delincuente dijo que el guardia les había visto.

_____

_____

Exercise 2

Match the time expressions in column A to their likely counterparts in column B.

A	B
Direct Speech	**Indirect Speech**
_____ **1.** anoche	a. entonces
_____ **2.** mañana	b. el día anterior
_____ **3.** la semana pasada	c. la semana anterior
_____ **4.** ahora	d. el próximo día
_____ **5.** ayer	e. la noche anterior

Exercise 3

Complete the sentences in indirect speech below.

1. —María, vendré a buscarte mañana a las ocho —dijo José. José le prometió a María que...

_____

_____

_____

2. —No creo que la carta llegue hasta mañana. Pedro dijo que...

_____

_____

_____

3. —Mi esposa dio a luz la semana pasada —dijo el padre. El padre dijo que...

_____

_____

_____

4. —Ahora voy al banco. Mi padre dijo que...

_____

_____

_____

5. —Anoche entró un ladrón al almacén, y se robó todo el dinero. El policía explico que...

_____

_____

_____

82

83 Verbs *Active vs. Passive Constructions*

The *voice* of a sentence can be either active or passive, depending on whether the subject or the object of the verb is emphasized. Spanish uses the active and passive voices much as English does.

In the active voice, the subject generally performs the action described by the verb. In the passive voice, the subject is acted upon.

Active:
Juan abrió la puerta.
Juan opened the door.

Passive:
La puerta fue abierta por Juan.
The door was opened by Juan.

Lenguaje en Práctica

As in English, the active voice is preferred in Spanish, particularly if the subject is a person. A sentence written in passive voice in English would most likely be translated into Spanish using the active voice:

The man was punished.
= *Castigaron al hombre.* (active)
≠ *El hombre fue castigado.* (passive)

The passive construction in Spanish is similar to the passive construction in English: subject + *ser* (to be) + past participle + *por* (by) + agent (doer).

Todos mis amigos han sido invitados por Javier.
All of my friends **have been invited by Javier.**

La cena fue servida por Claudia.
Dinner **was served by Claudia.**

In the passive voice, the past participle agrees in gender and number with the subject and acts as an adjective.

La casa fue construida por mis bisabuelos.
The house was **built** by my great-grandparents.

La huérfana fue educada por monjas.
The orphan was **educated** by nuns.

La Excepción

In passive voice in English, the agent (doer) may be omitted or implied, particularly in the case of signage or official instructions. In Spanish, however, the reflexive construction is preferred over the passive voice, with the pronoun *se* replacing the agent. For example, the passive English sentence *Spanish is spoken here* is translated as:

Aquí se habla español.
People speak Spanish here. (literally)

¡Atención!

The passive voice can also be formed with the verb *estar* (to be). When constructed with *ser*, the passive voice shows a process (how something came to be). When constructed with *estar*, the passive voice simply shows the result of an action.

La torta fue hecha por el cocinero.
The cake **was** made by the cook.

La torta estaba hecha.
The cake **was** (already) made.

Exercise 1

Form logical sentences by matching column A with column B.

A	B
_____ 1. Los poemas de Pablo Neruda	a. fueron ocupadas por estudiantes
_____ 2. Los libros	b. fueron interrogados por la policía.
_____ 3. Durante la manifestación, las casas	c. han sido traducidos a muchos idiomas.
_____ 4. Los vecinos de la víctima	d. fueron construidas por el gobierno.
_____ 5. Nuevas viviendas	e. fueron publicados por Editorial Cátedra.

Exercise 2

The following sentences are written in the active voice. Rewrite each using the passive voice.

1. Mi madre preparó el almuerzo para todos los niños.

_____

_____

_____

2. El cartero entregó todos los paquetes.

_____

_____

_____

3. Los trabajadores construirán el edificio.

_____

_____

_____

4. El bibliotecario ha preparado el folleto.

_____

_____

_____

5. Un arquitecto americano diseñó el Museo Guggenheim en Bilbao.

_____

_____

_____

Exercise 3

Rewrite the following sentences correctly. Note: Some of the sentences do not have errors.

1. Mis padres son queridos por mis amigos.

_____

_____

_____

2. Las casas fueron destruida por el viento.

_____

_____

_____

3. Las comidas fue preparada por el cocinero.

_____

_____

_____

4. El oleoducto será construido por Repsol.

_____

_____

_____

5. El hombre fueron atacados por dos perros.

_____

_____

_____

83

In Spanish, there are two verbs that can express the meaning of the English phrase *to know*: *saber* and *conocer*. Though their literal meaning is the same, these words are not interchangeable. Context dictates which verb should be used.

Saber means *to know* when referring to a piece of information.

> *¿**Sabes** mi dirección?*
> **Do you know** my address?

> *Paco **sabe** muchas palabras en árabe porque salió con una muchacha libanesa.*
> Paco **knows** a lot of Arabic words because he dated a Lebanese girl.

When followed by the infinitive, *saber* means *to know* how to do something.

> *Sé **hablar** español.*
> **I know how to speak** Spanish.

> *¿**Sabes manejar** PowerPoint?*
> **Do you know how to use** PowerPoint?

¡Atención!

In the preterite tense, the meaning of *saber* changes from *to know* to *found out*.

> *Ayer **supe** que mi hermano se había quebrado la pierna.*
> Yesterday **I found out** that my brother had broken his leg.

Conocer means *to know someone* or *to be familiar with something.*

> *Conozco a Luis.*
> **I know** Luis.

> *No **conozco** la ciudad.*
> **I'm not familiar with** the city.

¡Atención!

In the preterite tense, the meaning of *conocer* changes from *to know* to *met* (*for the first time*) or *began to know.*

> *La semana pasada **conocí** a tu primo, Javier.*
> Last week **I met** your cousin, Javier.

Exercise 1

Use context to determine whether *saber* or *conocer* should be used in the sentences below.

1. Mi hermano mayor _____ conducir.

2. Nosotros no _____ a Costa Rica.

3. _____ ustedes el número de Carlos?

4. Yo _____ bien los cuadros de Picasso.

5. Ellas todavía no _____ a tu novio.

Exercise 2

Combine elements from each column below to form five logical sentences. Determine whether *saber* or *conocer* is appropriate in each case.

Shakira	(no) saber	cantar
Penélope Cruz y Antonio Banderas	(no) conocer	actuar
Jennifer López		mi abuela
tú		hablar dos
yo		lenguas
		extranjeras

1. _____

_____

_____

2. _____

_____

_____

3. _____

_____

_____

4. _____

_____

_____

5. _____

_____

_____

Exercise 3

How do you know? Determine which of the choices below would _not_ correctly complete each sentence.

1. Anita no sabe…
a. dónde vivo
b. usar un mapa
c. mi ciudad

2. Nosotros conocemos…
a. el museo de arte moderno
b. dibujar
c. el artista Velásquez

3. Ustedes queréis conocer…
a. hablar español
b. el Ecuador
c. los animales de las Islas Galápagos

4. La cocinera sabe…
a. preparar la carne
b. los ingredientes
c. el dueño del restaurante

5. Yo conozco…
a. el Río Amazonas
b. un guía muy bueno
c. como identificar plantas e animales

Exercise 4

Write down six things you know using _saber_ and _conocer_ three times each.

1. _____

_____

_____

2. _____

_____

_____

3. _____

_____

_____

4. _____

_____

_____

5. _____

_____

_____

6. _____

_____

_____

84

In Spanish there are two verbs that express the meaning of the English phrase *to ask*: *pedir* and *preguntar*. These words are not interchangeable, and their usage depends on context.

Pedir means *to ask for* or *to request* an item. It does not take a preposition.

> *La señora **pidió** un café con leche.*
> The lady **asked for** a coffee with milk.

> *El mendigo me **pidió** una limosna.*
> The beggar **asked me for** alms.

Pedir que is used to ask someone to do something, or to request that someone perform a task.

> *Le **pedí que** me despertara a las diez.*
> I **asked her** to wake me up at ten.

¡Atención!

The use of *pedir que* in the main clause requires that the subjunctive tense be used in the subordinate clause.

> *Te **pido que** no me **molestes,** por favor.*
> I'm **asking that** you not **bother** me, please.

Preguntar is used to ask for information about something. Preguntar must be accompanied by a preposition (*qué, cuándo, si,* etc.), depending on what is being asked for.

> *La señora le **preguntó si** tenía un mapa.*
> The lady **asked if** he had a map.

> *Les **preguntaré qué** quieren.*
> I'll **ask** them **what** they want.

Preguntar is used in direct speech when quoting a question. In these cases, preguntar does not need a preposition.

> *Agustín le **preguntó:** «¿De dónde eres?».*
> Agustín **asked** her, "Where are you from?"

¡Atención!

Be careful with false cognates related to questions. *Una pregunta* means *a question*. *Una cuestión* means *a matter*.

> *Tengo **una pregunta.***
> I have **a question.**

> *Es **una cuestión** de gusto.*
> It's **a matter** of taste.

Exercise 1

Match the clues in column A with the correct uses of *pedir* and *preguntar* in column B.

A	B
_____ 1. This means *a question*.	a. una questión
_____ 2. This makes a request.	b. preguntar
_____ 3. This asks someone to do something.	c. una pregunta
_____ 4. This means *a matter*.	d. pedir que
_____ 5. This asks information about something.	e. pedir

Exercise 2

Fill in the blank with the correct form or *pedir* or *preguntar*. Use the preterite tense in your answer.

1. Yo le _____ a Juan que me ayudara.

2. Roberto _____: —¿Cuándo nos

   vamos?

3. Anoche los niños _____ mil preguntas

   antes de acostarse.

4. Irina me _____ un favor.

5. El guardia me _____ mi identificación.

Exercise 3

Translate the following sentences into Spanish using the correct verb for *ask*.

1. Don't ask me for money, because I don't have any.

   _____

   _____

   _____

2. If you want to pay the bill, you need to ask the waiter to bring it to you.

   _____

   _____

   _____

3. The secretary asked me what I was there for.

   _____

   _____

   _____

4. He asked her, "Are you really seventeen?"

   _____

   _____

   _____

5. The clerk asked her to fill out a form.

   _____

   _____

   _____

85

In Spanish there are several verbs that express the meaning of the English phrase *to take. Llevar, tomar,* and *sacar* are the most commonly used of these verbs. They are not interchangeable, and their usage depends on context.

Llevar means *to take someone or something to a specified location or in a specified direction. Llevar* is similar to the English verb *to bring.*

> *Voy a **llevar** a mis padres a la estación.*
> I'm going **to bring** my parents to the station.

¡Atención!

Spanish distinguishes between movement away from the speaker (*llevar*) and movement toward the speaker (*traer*).

> *Te **llevo** el lápiz si me **traes** el sacapuntas.*
> I'll **bring** you the pencil if you **bring** me the sharpener.

Tomar has several uses related to *take. Tomar* can mean *to drink, to take* (as in, a mode of transportation), or *to take* (as in, an object).

> ***Tengo*** *que tomar el tren hasta mi casa.*
> I have to **take** the train to my house.

> *No dejes que el niño **tome** cerveza.*
> Don't let the little boy **drink** (literally, **take**) beer.

> ***Tomó*** *el control remoto y cambió el canal.*
> He **took** the remote control and changed the channel.

¡Atención!

The *tú* and *usted* form of *tomar* (*toma/tome*) is used when handing an object to someone.

> —*Tienes un destornillador?*
> —*Sí. **Toma.***

"Do you have a screwdriver?"
"Yes. **Here.**"

Sacar means *to remove something,* or *to take something out.*

> *El dentista me **sacó** un diente.*
> The dentist **removed** my tooth.

> *¿Me ayudas a **sacar** la basura?*
> Will you help me **take out** the trash?

Exercise 1

Choose the form of *to take* for each given context.

1. To take in a specific direction:
   a. tomar
   b. llevar
   c. sacar

2. Movement toward the speaker:
   a. llevar
   b. sacar
   c. traer

3. To remove something:
   a. sacar
   b. llevar
   c. tomar

4. To take for someone's use:
   a. sacar
   b. traer
   c. tomar

5. Movement away from the speaker:
   a. llevar
   b. traer
   c. tomar

Exercise 2

Translate the following sentences into Spanish using the correct verb for *to take.*

1. What would you like to drink?

_____

_____

_____

2. He took his dish to the table and sat down.

_____

_____

_____

3. "Can we take you home?" "No, thank you, I'll take the bus."

_____

_____

_____

4. My father took out the trash.

_____

_____

_____

5. Here's the book you were asking about. Take it.

_____

_____

_____

Exercise 3

Juanita's papá wants to take her to the station. Complete their dialogue with the correct form of *to take.*

—Juanita, te vamos a (**1.**) _____ a la estación.

—No, papá, puedo (**2.**) _____ el metro. No es

lejos, y no quiero que se molesten.

—Bueno, hija, pero te voy a ayudar con las maletas. Ya te las

(**3.**) _____. ¿Te las dejo afuera?

—Papá, yo las (**4.**) _____. Sé que te duele la

espalda.

—Juanita, ¡me tratas como un anciano! (**5.**) _____

la llave de la casa. Cuando regreses de tu viaje, ¡tal vez

encontrarás a un hombre menor!

Exercise 4

Create one sentence that uses all three forms of *to take:*
llevar, tomar, **and** *sacar.*

_____

_____

_____

_____

_____

Ir, salir, and *dejar* all mean *to go,* or *to leave.* They are not interchangeable and their usage depends on context.

Ir indicates movement toward a specific destination.

*Anoche **fui** a un restaurante nuevo.*
Last night I **went to** a new restaurant.

***Vamos** al campo.*
We're **going to** the countryside.

The reflexive form of *ir* (*irse*) indicates movement away from an understood (unspecified) location, as in *to leave.*

*La señora Capello **se fue.***
Mrs. Capello **left.**

*Arturo **se va** a las cinco y media.*
Arturo is **leaving** at five thirty.

¡Atención!

Ir (to go) has an irregular conjugation in the present tense.

Singular	Plural
*yo **voy*** I **go**	*nosotros/as **vamos*** we **go**
*tu **vas*** you **go**	*vosotros/as **vais*** you **go**
*él/ella/usted **va*** he/she/it/you (formal) **go**	*ellos/ellas/ustedes **van*** they/you (formal) **go**

Salir indicates movement out of an enclosed area.

*Las muchachas **salieron** a la playa.*
The girls **went out** to the beach.

*Esta noche **saldremos** a las seis.*
Tonight we'll **go out** at six.

¡Atención!

Salir and *irse* are very similar in meaning. They can both be used to express movement out of an enclosed area, such as a building. *Salir* indicates that the person is expected to return shortly. With *irse,* there is no indication of a time frame. Additionally, when using *irse,* the location from which the subject is leaving is not specified.

*Ignacio **salió** de casa hace media hora.*
Ignacio **left** home an hour ago. (He'll return soon.)

*Cuando Luis terminó su postre, **se fue.***
When Luis finished his dessert, he **left.** (There is no indication of when he'll return.)

Salir expresses movement associated with travel and means of transportation.

*El tren **sale** a la una en punto.*
The train **leaves** at one P.M. sharp.

Dejar means *to leave something somewhere* or *to leave someone with someone else.* Dejar must be followed by a noun or pronoun.

*¡**Dejaste tu mochila** en el taxi!*
You **left your backpack** in the taxi!

*Todas las mañanas, **dejo mi perro** con mis padres.*
Every morning, I **leave my dog** with my parents.

Exercise 1

Match the definition in column A with the verbs in column B.

	A		B
_____	**1.** To leave someone or something		a. irse
_____	**2.** To go away		b. ir
_____	**3.** To go out of an enclosed area		c. salir
_____	**4.** To go toward a specific location		e. dejar

Exercise 2

Translate the following sentences into English using the correct verb for _to go_ or _to leave_.

1. Raquel and Claudia are going out tonight.

_____

_____

_____

2. What time does your flight leave?

_____

_____

_____

3. Could you please leave me at the corner?

_____

_____

_____

4. She left her suitcase with the hotel receptionist.

_____

_____

_____

5. Luis got mad and left.

_____

_____

_____

Exercise 3

The paragraph below describes a trip recently taken to Barcelona. Fill in the blanks with the correct forms of _ir, salir,_ and _dejar._

Los turistas (**1.**) _____ de su hotel

temprano para (**2.**) _____ al aeropuerto.

Su vuelo (**3.**) _____ esa mañana. Habían

estado en Barcelona dos semanas, y era tiempo de

(**4.**) _____. El viaje les había encantado:

(**5.**) _____ a muchos lugares turísticos,

y todas las noches (**6.**) _____ a

restaurantes y bares. El taxista los (**7.**) _____

en el aeropuerto, y todos estaban tristes de que se terminara

el viaje.

87

Poner, meter, and *guardar* can all be used to express the English phrase *to put*. They are not interchangeable, and their usage depends on context.

In most contexts, *poner* means *to put*. *Poner* itself does not specify where the item is being placed. The rest of the sentence offers specific information about location.

> **Pon** el conejo en la jaula.
> **Put** the rabbit in the cage.

> **Puso** la maleta debajo de la cama.
> He **put** the suitcase under the bed.

¡Atención!

Poner can also mean *to set*, as in a table, or *to turn on*, as in a TV, radio, or other appliance.

> Antonia, puedes **poner** la mesa por favor?
> Antonia, could you please **set** the table?

> Fede **puso** la tele y empezó a mirar el partido de fútbol.
> Fede **turned on** the TV and started to watch the soccer game.

The reflexive form of *poner* (*ponerse*) means *to put something on* (clothes, for example).

> **Me** voy a **poner** los aretes de oro.
> I'm going **to put** on my gold earrings.

When used with an adjective, *ponerse* means *to become* as in a change of mood, form, or state.

> Mi mamá **se puso** histérica cuando perdió su bolsa.
> My mom **became** hysterical when she lost her purse.

¡Atención!

Ponerse is used to form several common expressions:

ponerse + adjective	to become, to turn
ponerse a + infinitive	to begin to, to set about
ponerse de acuerdo	to come to an agreement

> Al oír la noticia, el niño **se puso pálido.**
> On hearing the news, the child **turned pale.**

> El día **se puso gris.**
> The day **turned gray.**

> La niña **se puso a cantar.**
> The girl **began to sing.**

> Por fin **se pusieron de acuerdo.**
> Finally, they **came to an agreement.**

Meter means *to put something inside of something else*.

> El niño **metió** el pulgar en la boca.
> The boy **put** his thumb in his mouth.

> **Metí** el carro en el garaje.
> I **put** the car in the garage.

Guardar means *to put away*, or *to save*.

> **Guardemos** todos los juguetes.
> Let's **put away** all the toys.

> Voy a **guardar** los dulces para comer luego.
> I'm going **to save** the sweets to eat later.

Exercise 1

Choose the correct verb for *put* for each of the following situations.

1. to put the clean laundry on the dresser:
   a. meter
   b. poner
   c. guardar

2. to put away your clothing:
   a. poner
   b. meter
   c. guardar

3. to put your socks in the drawer:
   a. meter
   b. poner
   c. ponerte

4. to put on your clean jeans:
   a. meter
   b. guardar
   c. ponerte

5. to put the wet laundry in the dryer:
   a. guardar
   b. meter
   c. poner

Exercise 2

Rewrite the following sentences correctly.
Note: Some of the sentences do not have mistakes.

1. Guardó la mano en el bolsillo.

_____

_____

2. Ayúdame a poner la mesa, por favor.

_____

_____

3. Se puso histérica cuando supo que había pasado.

_____

_____

4. Daniela, ¿puedes meter la televisión?

_____

_____

5. Métete las botas antes de salir.

_____

_____

Exercise 3

Complete the crossword puzzle with the correct form of the verb in parentheses that completes each sentence below

Across

4. ¿Vas a _____ los dulces? Quiero uno más. *(guardar)*

5. Aida, ¿Podrías _____ la mesa, por favor? *(poner)*

Down

1. Hijo, ¡no salgas sin _____ tu chaqueta! *(ponerse)*

2. No te _____ nerviosa: el avión no se va a estrellar. *(poner)*

3. Panchito, ¡no _____ el dedo en la mermelada! *(meter)*

88

89 Special Verbs *Romper/se) vs. Descomponerse*

The verbs *romper(se)* and *descomponerse* both mean *to break*, though each verb has specific uses depending on what is being conveyed.

Romper means both *to break* and *to tear,* as in an object.

> *El espejo está **roto**.*
> The mirror is **broken.**

> *La cortina está **rota**.*
> The curtain is **torn.**

The reflexive verb *romperse* is used with an article of clothing to mean *to tear something*. *Romperse* can also be used with parts of the body.

> *La niña **se rompió** el vestido mientras bajaba por la resbaladera.*
> The girl **tore her** dress while she was going down the slide.

> *Cuando mi abuela se cayó, **se rompió** la pierna.*
> When my grandmother fell, she **broke her** leg.

The reflexive verb *descomponerse* is used to say that something is out of order or not functioning. *Decomponerse* is most often used with machines.

> *Se descompuso el teléfono celular.*
> The cellphone **broke.**

> *No me prestes tu reloj. Temo que **se descomponga**.*
> Don't lend me your watch. I'm afraid **it** will **break.**

The expression *estar descompuesto* means *to be broken,* often in reference to a machine.

> *Voy en tren porque mi carro **está descompuesto**.*
> I'm taking the train because my car **broke down.**

> *Necesito una lámpara nueva porque la que tengo **está descompuesta**.*
> I need a new lamp because the one I have **is broken.**

Exercise 1

Decide which of the situations below call for *romper* and which call for *descomponer*?

	A. romper	**B. descomponer**

_____ **1.** You break a dish

_____ **2.** Your printer is damaged

_____ **3.** Your elevator is out of order

_____ **4.** You tear your shirt

_____ **5.** Your air conditioner isn't working

Exercise 2

Rewrite the following sentences correctly.
Note: Some of the sentences do not have mistakes.

1. No podemos escuchar la radio porque está rota.

_____

_____

_____

2. Mi chaqueta está rota: ¿Quién la puede reparar?

_____

_____

_____

3. La bandeja de vidrio está descompuesta.

_____

_____

_____

4. Se rompió el despertador de Consuelo.

_____

_____

_____

5. ¿Te rompiste de nuevo la falda?

_____

_____

_____

Exercise 3

A family friend and her toddler are visiting your apartment. The toddler destroys everything within his reach. Write five sentences in Spanish explaining what was damaged.

1._____

_____

_____

2._____

_____

_____

3._____

_____

_____

4._____

_____

_____

5._____

_____

_____

89

90 Special Verbs *Pensar vs. Creer*

Pensar and *creer* often confuse Spanish students because of their similar meanings. *Pensar* primarily means *to think*. *Creer* means *to believe*, but can translate as *to think* in certain contexts.

Pensar en is used to express the basic act of *thinking* about someone or something.

> Siempre **pienso en** mi madre cuando huelo ese perfume.
> I always **think about** my mother when I smell that perfume.

> ¿**En** qué **piensas**?
> What are you **thinking about**?

Pensar de translates to *to think* when eliciting an opinion about something or someone. This expression is only used in direct or indirect interrogatives.

> ¿Qué **piensas de** este restaurante?
> What do you **think about** this restaurant?

> No le dije que **pensaba de** su comentario.
> I didn't tell him what I **thought about** his comment.

Pensar + infinitive translates to *to think* when expressing a plan to doing something.

> ¿Qué **piensan hacer** este verano?
> What do you **plan on doing** this summer?

> **Pienso ir** a Barcelona.
> I'm **thinking about going to** Barcelona.

Pensar que and creer que can both be used to express *to think that,* when stating a personal opinion.

> **Pienso que** es una persona muy humilde.
> I **think that** he is a very humble person.

> **Creo que** es una persona muy humilde.
> I **think that** he is a very humble person.

¡Atención!

When *creer* is used in the negative form (*no creer*), it must be followed by a verb in the subjunctive.

> **No creo** que **sea** él.
> I **don't think** (that) **it's** him.

> Mi padre **no creía** que **fuera** importante ir a la cita.
> My father **didn't think** (that) **it was** important to go to the appointment.

Creer en is used to express belief or faith in something or someone.

> Mi amigo cristiano **cree en** Dios.
> My Christian friend **believes in** God.

> **Creo en** tus habilidades.
> I **believe in** your abilities.

Exercise 1

Match the *to think* phrases in column A to their appropriate English equivalents in column B.

A	B
_____ **1.** creer en	a. to think about doing something
_____ **2.** pensar que	b. to think about someone
_____ **3.** pensar + infinitive	c. to have faith in
_____ **4.** pensar en	d. to think about something (opinion)
_____ **5.** pensar de	e. to think that

Exercise 2

Translate the following sentences from English to Spanish.

1. What do you think about the novel we read in class?

_____

_____

2. Do you believe in God?

_____

_____

3. I think he's mad at me.

_____

_____

4. I'm always thinking about you.

_____

_____

5. Magdalena doesn't think she looks good.

_____

_____

Exercise 3

Answer the following questions in Spanish using the correct expression to explain what you think or believe.

1. ¿Qué piensas hacer este verano?

_____

_____

2. ¿Qué piensas de tu mejor amigo?

_____

_____

3. ¿En qué piensas todos los días?

_____

_____

4. ¿Qué piensas del presidente?

_____

_____

5. ¿En qué crees?

_____

_____

90

The verb *gustar* is used to express a liking for something. *Gustar* literally means *to be pleasing*, though it often is translated as *to like*.

> *Me **gusta** la clase de inglés.*
> I **like** English class. (literally, The class **pleases** me.)

> *¿No te **gustó** la película?*
> You didn't **like** the movie? (literally, The movie didn't **please** you?)

Gustar is always preceded by an indirect object pronoun, and it always agrees with the subject, which generally follows it.

> *Te **gusta** el libro.*
> You **like** the book.

> *Te **gustan** los libros.*
> You **like** the books.

Gustar can be followed by an infinitive if the subject (the thing that is pleasing) is an action (expressed by a verb or clause) instead of a noun. In these cases, the infinitive is treated as a third person singular subject.

> *Me gusta **comer** a las ocho de la mañana.*
> I like **to eat** at eight in the morning.

> *Me gusta **correr, saltar** y **brincar.***
> I like to **run, jump,** and **hop.**

¡Atención!

Because the literal translation of *gustar* is *to be pleasing,* the subject that is performing the action of the verb is the thing that pleases, *not* the individual who is pleased.

In the sentence *Me gusta el café* (I like coffee), *el café* is the subject, not *me*. Inserting the first person pronoun *yo* (I) at the beginning of this sentence (*yo me gusta el café*) would be incorrect.

The phrase *a* + noun/pronoun is often used with *gustar* to clarify or emphasize. This construction normally precedes the indirect object pronoun.

> **Clarity:**
> ***A mí** me gusta leer, pero **a ti** te gusta cantar.*
> I like to read, but **you** like to sing.

> **Emphasis:**
> ***A Teodoro** le gusta la música rock.*
> **Teodoro** likes rock music.

¡Atención!

A noun or pronoun cannot precede the indirect object pronoun + *gustar* unless *a* is present.

A Teo le gusta la música rock.
≠ *Teo le gusta la música rock.* (grammatically incorrect)
Teo likes rock music.

The conditional form of *gustar* (*gustaría*) + the infinitive means *would like to do* or *would not like to do*.

> *Me **gustaría ir** a Egipto.*
> I **would like to go** to Egypt.

> *No nos **gustaría comer** pollo.*
> We **would not like to eat** chicken.

¡Atención!

Several other verbs are also preceded by the indirect object pronoun and function in a way that is grammatically similar to *gustar*.

encantar (to be charmed by)
molestar (to be bothered by)
preocupar (to worry)
faltar/hacer falta (to be lacking, to need)
doler (to be painful, to cause sorrow)
parecer (to seem)
placer (to be pleasing, to be pleased)

> *Me **molesta** tu tono de voz.*
> Your tone of voice **bothers me.**

> *¿**Te duele** mucho la herida?*
> Is the wound very **painful**?

Exercise 1

Fill in the blanks below with the correct form of *gustar*.

1. ¿Te _____ las galletas que hice ayer?

2. Mamá, creo que te _____ mucho el concierto que vamos a ver esta noche.

3. Me _____ mucho ir contigo, pero hoy estoy muy ocupado.

4. A Diana le _____ viajar por Suramérica, comer comida buena, y conocer a gente nueva.

5. No creo que les _____ esta sopa.

Exercise 2

Who likes what? Construct sentences using the correct forms of *gustar* or *no gustar* based on the prompts.

1. el vino (tú)

   _____

   _____

2. la música clásica (yo, no)

   _____

   _____

3. el invierno (los estudiantes)

   _____

   _____

4. los parques de atracciones (los chicos, no)

   _____

   _____

5. bailar en discoteca (María Fernanda)

   _____

   _____

Exercise 3

Create sentences using *gustar* and the *a* + noun/pronoun construction along with the following elements.

1. tú / películas románticas

   _____

   _____

2. tú hermano / películas cómicas

   _____

   _____

3. todos nosotros / películas de ciencia ficción

   _____

   _____

4. vosotros / películas de aventura

   _____

   _____

Exercise 4

You have just subscribed to an online dating website. Write an online profile about yourself expressing your likes and dislikes.

   _____

   _____

   _____

   _____

   _____

   _____

   _____

   _____

An *idiom* is an expression that cannot be understood by analyzing its literal meaning. The verb *tener* (to have) is used in many Spanish idioms. Most of these expressions would take the verb *to be* in English.

Tener...años expresses age in years and translates as *to be...years old.*

> *Juan Martín* **tiene** *siete* **años.**
> Juan Martín **is** seven **years old.**

Tener ganas de translates in English as *to feel like*, and expresses preference.

> *¿Tienes ganas de ir al cine?*
> **Do you feel like** going to the movies?

Tener miedo de translates in English as *to be afraid of*.

> *Tengo miedo de los ratones.*
> **I'm afraid of** mice.

Tener prisa translates in English as *to be in a hurry*.

> *¡Vamos! Tengo prisa.*
> Let's go! I'm **in a hurry.**

Tener que translates in English as *to have to*, and expresses an obligation or duty.

> *Tenemos que hacer las tareas.*
> We **have to** do our homework.

(No) tener razón translates in English as *to be right/ wrong*.

> *Tenías razón: Marta es cubana.*
> **You were right:** Marta is Cuban.

Tener sueño translates in English as *to be sleepy*.

> *El bebé tiene sueño.*
> The baby **is sleepy.**

Tener hambre translates in English as *to be hungry*.

> *Margarita tiene hambre.*
> Margarita **is hungry.**

Tener sed translates in English as *to be thirsty*.

> *Tengo sed. Quiero agua.*
> **I'm thirsty.** I want water.

Exercise 1

Translate the following sentences from Spanish to English using the appropriate *tener* expression.

1. Tengo mucho sueño: pienso tomar una siesta.

_____

_____

2. ¿Cuántos años tiene Tomás?

_____

_____

3. Siempre tienes prisa, Daniel.

_____

_____

4. Catalina tiene que limpiar el piso.

_____

_____

5. ¿De qué tienes miedo, Abuelo?

_____

_____

Exercise 2

Match the idiomatic expressions below to their English equivalents.

_____ **1.** tener sueño

a. to be afraid of

_____ **2.** tener ganas de

b. to be sleepy

_____ **3.** tener prisa

c. to be right

_____ **4.** tener razón

d. to feel like

_____ **5.** tener miedo

e. to be in a hurry

Exercise 3

Fill in the blanks with the correct idiomatic expression.

1. Es el cumpleaños de mi bisabuela: _____

   99 _____.

2. Es mejor que te acuestes. Veo que _____

   mucho _____.

3. Si _____, es más rápido ir en bicicleta.

4. ¿_____, María? Toma un vaso de agua.

5. Hoy _____ terminar mi ensayo.

Exercise 4

Complete the cross word below by inserting the correctly conjugated form of *tener* to fit the following situations.

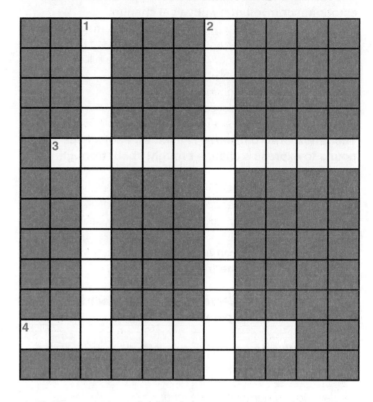

Across

3. describing what I am afraid of (tengo miedo)
4. telling her age (tiene años)

Down

1. expressing his hunger (tiene hambre)
2. saying we are sleepy (tenemos sueños)

92

There are several ways to express *to become* in Spanish, most of which use the reflexive verbs.

The reflexive verb *ponerse* is used to describe an emotional or involuntary physical change.

> *La señora **se puso** muy enojada cuando vio la cuenta.*
> The lady **got** very angry when she saw the bill.

> ***Me puse** roja cuando me besó.*
> I **got** red when he kissed me.

The reflexive verb *hacerse* is used with adjectives and nouns to express a change brought about through personal effort.

> ***Se hizo rico** trabajando de día y de noche.*
> He **became rich** by working day and night.

> *Los niños **se hicieron amigos.***
> The children **became friends.**

The reflexive verb *volerse* is used with adjectives to express a sudden or permanent change.

> *No te **volverás** activo si nunca sales de casa.*
> You won't **become** active if you never leave your home.

> *La ciudad puede **volverse** inhóspita si las lluvias no cesan.*
> The city may **become** inhospitable if the rains don't cease.

The reflexive verb *convertirse en* is used to express a transition from one state or thing to another (either natural or fantastic).

> *El dios romano **se convirtió** en árbol.*
> The Roman god **became** a tree.

> *La oruga **se convirtió** en mariposa.*
> The caterpillar **became** a butterfly.

Exercise 1

Translate the following sentences from English to Spanish using the correct *to become* verb.

1. My mother-in-law drives me crazy (makes me become crazy).

_____

_____

_____

2. I became sad when I heard the bad news.

_____

_____

_____

3. The seed became a beautiful tree.

_____

_____

_____

4. Juan Romero became a doctor.

_____

_____

_____

5. Don't get angry, dad.

_____

_____

_____

Exercise 2

Describe the kind of a change expressed in each sentence below.

1. La señora se puso muy enferma.

_____

_____

_____

2. En el cuento, el niño se convirtió en robot.

_____

_____

_____

3. Te volviste loco cuando viste a los dos juntos.

_____

_____

_____

4. Se hizo famoso cantando.

_____

_____

_____

5. Sin oxígeno, se puso azul.

_____

_____

_____

Exercise 3

Complete the following sentences with your own information.

1. Me pongo triste cuando...

_____

_____

_____

2. Quisiera convertirme en...

_____

_____

_____

3. Me vuelvo callado cuando...

_____

_____

_____

4. Me pongo rojo cuando...

_____

_____

_____

5. Pienso hacerme...

_____

_____

_____

93

The verb *to miss* can have several meanings in English. In Spanish, each of these meanings is expressed with a different verb.

Echar de menos, hacer falta, or **extrañar** can all be used to express a longing for someone or something.

> **Echo de menos** *a mi hermana.*
> **I miss** my sister.

> **Extraño** *mucho a Colombia.*
> **I miss** Colombia very much.

> *María,* **me haces falta** *cuando tú no estás.*
> María, **I miss you** when you're not here.

Perder means *to miss* when referring to mode of transportation (bus, plane, and so on).

> *Llegamos tarde y* **perdimos** *el bus.*
> We arrived late and **we missed** the bus.

> **Perdimos** *el vuelo a Guadalajara.*
> **We missed** the flight to Guadalajara.

The reflexive form of *perder* (*perderse*) **is used to indicate that a show or event has been missed.**

> **Me perdí** *la nueva película de Antonio Banderas.*
> **I missed** Antonio Banderas's new film.

> *Qué pena que* **te hayas perdido** *el concierto de Maná.*
> What a shame that **you missed** the Maná concert.

Faltar is used to express a lack of something or to indicate that something is missing.

> *Me* **faltan** *palabras para describir mi alegría.*
> I'm **lacking** words to describe my happiness.

> *Conté mi dinero: me* **falta** *un billete de cien euros.*
> I counted my money: I'm **missing** one 100-euro bill.

Faltar a means *to miss an appointment*, **or expresses a failure to attend a meeting.**

> *Los estudiantes buenos nunca* **faltan a** *clase.*
> Good students never **miss** class.

> *Estaba enfermo, entonces* **faltó a tres** *clases.*
> He was sick, so he **missed three** classes.

Exercise 1

Match the correct verb to each of the given situations.

_____ **1.** you miss your grandparents	a. perderse
_____ **2.** you missed your train	b. faltar
_____ **3.** you missed a show	c. perder
_____ **4.** you missed class	d. extrañar

Exercise 2

Correct the mistakes in the following sentences.
Note: Some of the sentences do not have mistakes.

1. Arturo perdió clase porque perdió el bus.

   _____

   _____

2. Echo de menos a mi mejor amigo.

   _____

   _____

3. Perdí el show de comedia de Carlos Mencía.

   _____

   _____

4. Estás listo, ¿o te falta algo?

   _____

   _____

5. No pierdas el tren – es el último del día.

   _____

   _____

Exercise 3

Complete the sentences below with the correct *to miss* verb.

1. Anoche mi prima se enfermó. Por eso _____ la obra teatral.

2. Andas muy tarde. Temo que _____ el bus.

3. Complete las oraciones con las palabras que

   _____.

4. No te pongas muy triste. Es normal _____ a la familia cuando uno viaja.

5. No pudimos salir hasta que encontramos los papeles que

   nos _____.

Exercise 4

Who is the person you miss the most? Write a short paragraph about what you miss about this person. Be sure to use the correct Spanish form of *to miss*.

_____

_____

_____

_____

_____

_____

_____

_____

_____

_____

_____

_____

94

There are several words and expressions used in Spanish to express the many ways that someone or something can be wrong.

The masculine singular adjective *malo* is used to express a moral or ethical wrong.

> *El criminal hizo algo muy **malo**.*
> The criminal did something very **wrong**.

> *Es **malo** mentir a tus padres.*
> It's **wrong** to lie to your parents.

No tener razón and estar equivocado can both be used when stating that a person is wrong or incorrect. These expressions are interchangeable.

> *Marta **no tiene razón**. Hoy no es jueves sino miércoles.*
> Marta is **wrong.** It's not Thursday but Wednesday.

> *Usted **está equivocado**. La respuesta es cinco.*
> You're **wrong.** The answer is five.

The reflexive verb *equivocarse* can also be used to state that someone is wrong.

> *A mi padre no le gusta **equivocarse**.*
> My father doesn't like **being wrong.**

> *Me **equivoqué** cuando te dije que Marta había terminado la tarea.*
> I **was wrong** when I told you Marta had finished the assignment.

The adjectives *incorrecto* and *equivocado* can both be used to indicate that a piece of information or an answer is wrong.

> *La respuesta está **incorrecta**.*
> The answer is **wrong.**

> *Tus calculaciones están **equivocadas**.*
> Your calculations are **wrong.**

The adverb *mal* is also used to indicate that information is wrong.

> *Marcaste **mal** el número.*
> You dialed the number **incorrectly.**

The negative expressions *no... adecuado* or *no... apropiado* can signify something that is inappropriate.

> ***No** es el momento **adecuado** para hablar de ese asunto.*
> It's the **wrong** moment to talk about this matter.

> ***No** es el tiempo **apropiado** para pensar en ti mismo.*
> It's the **wrong** time to think about yourself.

The verb *pasar* is used when the state or condition of something is wrong or amiss.

> *¿Qué te **pasa**, Lucho?*
> What's **wrong,** Lucho?

> *Algo le **pasa** al teléfono.*
> Something's **wrong** with the telephone.

Exercise 1

Which verb would be used to translate *wrong* in the following sentences?

_____ **1.** This is the **wrong** place to talk about your boss.	a. *pasar*	
_____ **2.** Katia, you have to admit that you were **wrong.**	b. *malo*	
_____ **3.** It is **wrong** to murder.	c. *incorrecto*	
_____ **4.** What's **wrong** with the computer?	d. *no adecuado*	
_____ **5.** I just dialed the **wrong** number.	e. *equivocarse*	

Exercise 2

Fill in the blanks with the correct expression of *wrong*.

1. Marcaste un número _____.

2. No es el sitio _____ para discutir los amores.

3. Leí _____ su nombre.

4. Es muy _____ robarle a tu amigo.

5. ¿_____ a la grabadora? Ya no funciona.

Exercise 3

Correct the mistakes in the following sentences.
Note: Some of the sentences do not have mistakes.

1. Julio, no le pegues a tu hermana. Eso es muy equivocado

   _____

   _____

   _____

2. ¡Esta sopa tiene demasiada sal! La receta no tiene razón.

   _____

   _____

   _____

3. Aquí no vive la familia Cuevas. Usted se ha equivocado de casa.

   _____

   _____

   _____

4. Jaime, yo tengo razón, y tú estás malo.

   _____

   _____

   _____

5. La dependiente escribió mal mi dirección.

   _____

   _____

   _____

Exercise 4

What are three things you've done wrong? Write in complete sentences using the correct word for *wrong*.

1. _____

   _____

   _____

2. _____

   _____

   _____

3. _____

   _____

   _____

95

The verb *quedar* and its reflexive form, *quedarse,* have many possible meanings depending on how they are used in a sentence.

Quedar can translate as *to be* in questions asking for the location of a place.

> —¿Dónde **queda** el supermercado?
> —**Queda** a dos cuadras.

> "Where **is** the supermarket?"
> "It **is** two blocks away."

Quedar can translate as *to have left* to express how much of something is remaining. Often in these cases, *quedar* is accompanied by an indirect object pronoun.

> Me **quedan** cinco pesos.
> I **have** five pesos **left.**

> **Quedan** ocho libros nuevos.
> There **are** eight new books **left.**

The reflexive verb *quedarse* is used to express that someone is in a particular emotional or physical state.

> El accidente causó que la señora **se quedara ciega.**
> The accident caused the woman **to go blind.**

> **Te queda muy bien** tu nuevo peinado.
> Your new hairdo **looks very good on you.**

> Cuando vi su maquillaje, **me quedé sorprendido.**
> When I saw her makeup, **I was surprised.**

Quedarse can also translate as *to stay.*

> Cuando voy a San Antonio, **me quedo** con mis suegros.
> When I go to San Antonio, **I stay** with my in-laws.

> El gato **se quedó** debajo del armario.
> The cat **stayed** under the dresser.

The expression *quedarse con* is used to indicate that something has been kept or retained. The expression *quedarse sin* is used to express that something has been depleted, or used up.

> **Se** puede **quedar con** el cambio.
> You **can keep** the change.

> **Nos quedamos sin** gasolina.
> We **ran out of** gasoline.

Exercise 1

Match the uses of *quedar* in the sentences below to their approximate English translation.

_____ **1.** La niña **se quedó** aterrorizada.	a. to stay
_____ **2.** La escuela **queda** muy cerca.	b. to have left
_____ **3.** Me **quedé** con mi tía Alfonsa.	c. to run out of
_____ **4.** ¿Cuántas manzanas te **quedan**?	d. to be in a particular emotional state
_____ **5.** El soldado **se quedó** sin munición.	e. location with to be

Exercise 2

Translate the following sentences into Spanish using the correct form of *quedar*.

1. Keep my jacket.

   _____

   _____

   _____

2. Where's the nearest bus stop?

   _____

   _____

   _____

3. We have only five days left in Santo Domingo.

   _____

   _____

   _____

4. The man was left lame because of the accident.

   _____

   _____

   _____

5. When we visited Quito, we stayed with Doña Elisa and Don Fernando.

   _____

   _____

   _____

Exercise 3

What are three things you've kept, and three things you've run out of? Use *quedarme con* and *quedarme sin* to compose six complete sentences.

1. _____

   _____

   _____

2. _____

   _____

   _____

3. _____

   _____

   _____

4. _____

   _____

   _____

5. _____

   _____

   _____

6. _____

   _____

96

The verbs *estar* and *haber* both indicate the existence of people or things. However, their uses differ depending on the context.

***Estar* means *to be in a specific location. Estar* always takes a subject.**

> *Los cuadernos están en el escritorio.*
> **The notebooks are** on the desk.

> *Los niños están en el parque.*
> **The children are** in the park.

***Haber* (to have) refers to the existence of a person or thing, and translates as *there is/are. Haber* has no subject and is always conjugated in the third person singular.**

> *Hay cuadernos en el escritorio.*
> **There are** notebooks on the desk.

> *Había niños en el parque.*
> **There were** children in the park.

***Hay* is a special third person singular conjugation of *haber*, when *haber* is used to mean *there is* or *there are. Hay* is always conjugated in the third person singular.**

> *Hay una mosca en la sopa.*
> **There is** a fly in the soup.

> *Hay dos moscas en la sopa.*
> **There are** two flies in the soup.

> *Había dos mujeres en la oficina.*
> **There were** two women in the office.

> *Hubo dos accidentes en la calle González Suárez.*
> **There were** two accidents on González Suárez Street.

> *Ojalá no **haya** otro accidente.*
> I hope **there are** no more accidents.

Exercise 1

The following paragraph describes Señor Bustamante's class. Fill in the blanks with the correct form of *estar* or *haber*.

(**1.**)_____ diez estudiantes en la clase del

Señor Bustamante. Algunos (**2.**)_____ sentados

cerca de la ventana, charlando, y otros (**3.**)_____

esperando pacientemente al maestro. Hoy día

(**4.**)_____ mucho que cubrir en clase. Va a

(**5.**)_____ un examen el viernes. Pero con tal

de que no (**6.**)_____ el Señor Bustamante, los

estudiantes no estudiarán.

Exercise 2

Rewrite the following sentences correctly.
Note: Some of the sentences do not have mistakes.

1. No creo que haya suficientes horas en el día para hacer este trabajo.

   _____

   _____

   _____

2. No están suficientes fondos para cubrir su cheque, señora.

   _____

   _____

   _____

3. Sofía, ¿dónde está la mantequilla?

   _____

   _____

   _____

4. El libro que usted busca hay en la Biblioteca Nacional.

   _____

   _____

   _____

5. Está un problema grave con el programa.

   _____

   _____

   _____

Exercise 3

Two people are discussing a problem with their computer. Translate their dialogue into Spanish using the correct forms of *estar* and *haber*.

"Is there a problem with your laptop?"
"Yeah, I'm afraid that it's broken."
"What a shame. Look, there's a computer repair store close to my house. I'll give you the address.... Here it is."
"Thanks. Is the technician there now?"
"I think so. And if he's not in today, there are two others who can help."
"What a disaster! My essay is due tomorrow at 8:30 A.M.!"

_____

_____

_____

_____

_____

_____

_____

_____

_____

_____

_____

_____

_____

_____

98 Special Verbs *Verbs Used for People and Machines*

In English, certain verbs have special idiomatic uses when they are used to describe the actions of people or machines. In Spanish, however, there are separate verbs to describe certain actions, depending on whether the subject is a person or a machine.

Correr (to run) and *trabajar* (to work) both describe the **actions of a person or living thing.** ***Andar*** **or** *funcionar* **(to run/to function/to work) are used when the subject is a machine.**

> Yo **corro** todas las mañanas.
> I **run** every morning.

> Mi madre ha **trabajado** toda la vida.
> My mother has **worked** her whole life.

> Mi motocicleta **anda** bien.
> My motorcycle **runs** well.

> La televisión no **funciona**.
> The television isn't **working**.

Comenzar **and** *empezar* **(to begin/to start) are used when the subject is a person or event.** ***Arrancar*** **(to start) is used when the subject is a machine, such as a vehicle or engine.**

> El concierto **empieza** a las nueve.
> The concert **starts** at nine.

> **Arranqué** el carro y me fui.
> I **started** the car and I left.

The compound verb *salir corriendo* **means** *to run out,* **and describes the actions of a person or people. The reflexive verb** *acabarse* **is used when a thing has run out or been depleted.**

> La gente, desesperada, **salió corriendo** del edificio.
> The people, desperate, **ran out of** the building.

> **Se** nos **acabó** el azúcar.
> We **ran out of** sugar.

Salir **(to leave) can mean** *to go out* **when referring to the actions of a person. The reflexive verb** *apagarse* **is used when a thing goes out, such as a light.**

> Anoche **salimos** con Magda y Fabián.
> Last night we **went out** with Magda and Fabián.

> Cuando **se apagaron** las luces, todas las niñas gritaron.
> When the lights **went out,** all the girls screamed.

Exercise 1

Which of the verbs below refer to machines, and which refer to people? Match the verbs to the references.

	A. people	B. machines
_____ **1.** salir		
_____ **2.** arrancar		
_____ **3.** funcionar		
_____ **4.** correr		
_____ **5.** trabajar		

Exercise 2

Circle the appropriate verb to be used in each sentence below.

1. El reloj de la cocina ya no trabaja/funciona.

2. Cuando compré este carro hace tres años, corría/ andaba muy bien.

3. Ernesto salió/apagó la luz y cerró la puerta.

4. Entregamos el examen incompleto porque corrimos fuera de/se nos acabó el tiempo.

5. La obra teatral arranca/comienza en cinco minutos.

Exercise 3

Translate the following sentences into Spanish using the correct verb to describe the action taking place.

1. The children were running in the park.

_____

_____

_____

2. The motor stopped running.

_____

_____

_____

3. I'm going to start the car so it gets warm.

_____

_____

_____

4. When did the movie start?

_____

_____

_____

5. Turn out the lights.

_____

_____

_____

6. We went out at eight.

_____

_____

_____

Exercise 4

Use the following word pairs to construct three sets of sentences. In each set, write one sentence from the perspective of a person, and one sentence from the perspective of a machine.

correr and _andar_
salir and _apagarse_
trabajar and _funcionar_

1. _____

_____

_____

_____

2. _____

_____

_____

_____

3. _____

_____

_____

_____

98

Spanish, like English, has many prefixes that can modify the meaning of a word. Many prefixes come from Latin, an ancestor of the Spanish language. Other prefixes come from Greek.

Prefixes can be attached to the beginning of nouns, verbs, adverbs, and adjectives. Some common prefixes and their meanings include:

Prefix	Meaning	Example
a-	without	**a**moral (amoral)
ante-	before	**ante**ayer (day before yesterday)
anti-	against	**anti**ácido (antacid)
auto-	self	**auto**biografía (autobiography)
bi-, bis-, biz-	two	**bi**sección (bisection)
contra-	against, counter	**contra**ataque (counter attack)
con-	with	**con**vivir (coexist)
de-, des-	undo	**des**armar (disarm)
ex-	former, out	**ex**traer (take out, remove)
homo-	same	**homó**nimo (homonym)
inter-	between, among	**inter**acción (interaction)

Prefix	Meaning	Example
mal-	bad	**mal**estar (discomfort)
mono-	one	**mono**grafía (monograph)
poli-	many	**poli**técnico (polytechnic)
pre-	before	**pre**natal (prenatal)
pro-	instead of	**pro**nombre (pronoun)
re-	again	**re**leer (reread)
semi-	medium	**semi**círculo (semicircle)
seudo-	false	**seudó**nimo (pseudonym)
super-	superior	**super**intendente (superintendent)
sub-	under	**sub**marino (submarine)
tele-	at a distance	**tele**fono (telephone)
uni-	one	**uni**cornio (unicorn)

Exercise 1

Match the following prefixes to their English definitions.

_____ **1.** sub-   a. self

_____ **2.** con-   b. before

_____ **3.** auto-   c. at a distance

_____ **4.** ante-   d. under

_____ **5.** tele-   e. with

Exercise 2

Use the prefixes to determine the meaning of each word below.

1. maltratar: _____

2. repaso: _____

3. subsuelo: _____

4. anticuerpo: _____

5. intercambio: _____

Exercise 3

Translate the following sentences from Spanish into English.

1. El automóvil se chocó contra la motocicleta.

_____

_____

_____

2. Espero que lleguemos a la semifinal del campeonato.

_____

_____

_____

3. La mona despioja a su bebé.

_____

_____

_____

4. La psíquica predijo un terremoto.

_____

_____

_____

5. Tienes que deshuesar al pescado antes de comerlo.

_____

_____

_____

99

Suffixes are endings that can be added to a word to modify its meaning. Though suffixes are used in both English and Spanish, they are much more common in Spanish.

Some Spanish suffixes are very similar to their English equivalents. Most of these suffixes derive from Latin or Greek.

Suffix	English Equivalent	Example
-arquía	-archy	an**arquía** (anarchy)
-ático	-atic	fan**ático** (fanatic)
-ble	-ble	proba**ble** (probable)
-cidio	-cide	homi**cidio** (homicide)
-ción	-tion	ac**ción** (action)
-cracia	-cracy	buro**cracia** (bureaucracy)
-dad	-ity	varie**dad** (variety)
-esa, -iz, -isa	-ess	cont**esa** (countess)
-fobia	-phobia	xeno**fobia** (xenophobia)
-ismo	-ism	aut**ismo** (autism)
-ista	-ist	rac**ista** (racist)
-itis	-itis	tendin**itis** (tendinitis)
-tude	-tude	vicisi**tud** (vicissitude)
-or, -ora	-er	lect**or** (reader)
-osa, -oso	-ous	luj**oso** (luxurious)

A diminutive word is formed by replacing the last letter of the noun with the diminutive suffix. The diminutive suffixes (-*ito*/-*ita* and -*illo*/-*illa*) make a noun smaller (literally or figuratively). These suffixes are very common in Spanish. -*Ito*/-*ita* and -*illo*/-*illa* can often be used interchangeably and agree with the noun in gender.

perro (dog) → perr**ito** (little dog)

canasta (basket) → canast**illa** (little basket)

¡Atención!

If the noun ends in a consonant,–**c**ito/–**c**ita and –**ec**illo/–**ec**illa are used. The final consonant on the noun is not removed.

almacén (store) → almacen**cito** (little store)

pan (bread) → pan**ecillo** (little bread)

Augmentative suffixes (-*ote*, -*ota*, -*ón*, -*ona*, -*azo*, –*aza*) make a noun larger (literally or figuratively). Though the augmentative suffixes are interchangeable, their use with specific words follows certain stylistic patterns that are learned through experience. To form an augmentative noun, add the augmentative suffix to the end of the word. If the word ends in vowel, that vowel is dropped before the suffix is added.

mujer (woman) → mujer**ona** (big woman)

conejo (rabbit) → conej**azo** (big rabbit)

¡Atención!

The augmentative suffixes can be used to overemphasize size or importance. They are often used to mock or ridicule and are meant as insults in this context. Care should be taken when using words with these suffixes.

grande (large) → grand**ote** (huge; monstrously large)

Ricardo es un **grandote.**
Ricardo is a **huge** man.

Exercise 1

Match the following suffixes to their English equivalents.

_____ **1.** -dad   a. -er

_____ **2.** -isa   b. -tion

_____ **3.** -ora   c. -ess

_____ **4.** -ción   d. -ist

_____ **5.** -ista   e. -ity

Exercise 3

Use diminutive and augmentative suffixes to create two new words for each noun below.

1. gato: _____, _____

2. mesa: _____, _____

3. libro: _____, _____

4. cocina: _____, _____

5. árbol: _____, _____

Exercise 2

Complete the crossword puzzle with the Spanish translation of the word provided.

Across

4. claustrophobia

Down

1. marvelous
2. dentist
3. actress

100

Irregular & Special Usage Spanish Words

Note: phonetic pronunciation in parentheses

Adverbs

a la una/a las dos, etc: (a la OO-na/a las dos, etc.): *at one o'clock/at two o'clock, etc.*

a veces (a VE-ses): *sometimes*

abajo (a-BA-ho): *below*

acá (a-KAH): *over here*

adelante (a-de-LAN-te): *in front*

adentro (a-DEN-tro): *inside*

ahora (a-OR-a): *now*

allá (a-YA): *over there*

algo (AL-go): *a bit, rather*

anoche (a-NO-che): *last night*

antes (AN-tes): *before*

apenas (a-PE-nas): *barely*

aquí (a-KEE): *here*

arriba (a-REE-ba): *above*

así (a-SEE): *like that*

ayer (a-YER): *yesterday*

bastante (bas-TAN-te): *a lot*

bien (be-YEN): *well*

casi (CA-see): *almost*

cerca (SER-ka): *close*

claramente (cla-ra-MEN-te): *clearly*

cuanto (COOAN-to): *as much, how much*

de día (de DEE-a): *during the day*

de noche (de NO-che): *at night*

de pronto (de PRON-to): *suddenly*

debajo (de-BA-ho): *underneath*

delante (de-LAN-te): *in front*

después (des-POOES): *after*

detrás (de-TRAS): *behind*

encima (en-SEE-ma): *on top*

entonces (en-TON-ses): *then*

hoy (oy): *today*

lejos (LE-hos): *far*

luego (LOOE-go): *later*

mal (mal): *badly*

mañana (ma-NYA-na): *tomorrow*

más (mas): *more*

medio (ME-deeo): *half*

mejor (me-HOR): *better*

menos (ME-nos): *less*

mientras (mee-EN-tras): *during*

mucho (MOO-cho): *a lot*

muy (mooy): *very*

nada (NA-da): *not at all*

nunca (NOON-ca): *never*

ojalá que (o-ha-LA ke): *hopefully*

peor (pe-OR): *worse*

poco (PO-co): *a little*

siempre (see-EM-pre): *late*

sólo (SO-lo): *only*

tanto (TAN-to): *so much*

tarde (TAR-de): *always*

temprano (tem-PRA-no): *early*

todavía (to-da-VEE-a): *still*

ya (ya): *already*

Adjectives

aquel / aquella (a-KEL / a-KE-ya): *that*

aquellos / aquellas (a-KE-yos / a-KE-yas): *those*

eso / esa (E-so / E-sa): *that*

esos / esas (E-sos / E-sas): *those*

este / esta (ES-te / ES-ta): *this*

estos / estas (ES-tos / ES-tas): *these*

Nouns

artista, M/F sing. (ar-TEES-ta): *artist*

dentista, M/F sing. (den-TEES-ta): *dentist*

estudiante, M/F sing. (es-too-DIAN-te): *student*

la capital, F sing. (ka-pee-TAL): *capital city*

cliente, M/F sing. (klee-EN-te): *client*

cólera, M sing. (KO-le-ra): *cholera*

cólera, F sing. (KO-le-ra): *anger*

cura, M sing. (KOO-ra): *priest*

cura, F sing. (KOO-ra): *cure*

miel, F sing. (MEE-yel): *honey*

papa, M sing. (PA-pa): *pope*

papa, F sing. (PA-pa): *potato*

pianista, M/F sing. (pee-a-NEES-ta): *pianist*

piel, F sing. (PEE-yel): *skin*

sal, F sing. (sal): *salt*

turista, M/F sing. (too-REES-ta): *tourist*

Definite & Negative Words

algo (AL-go): *something*

alguna vez (al-GOO-na ves): *sometime, ever*

algunas veces (al-GOO-nas VE-ses): *sometimes*

alguien (AL-gyen): *someone, anyone*

alguno / alguna (al-GOO-no / al-GOO-na): *some, someone, any*

algunos / algunas (al-GOO-nos / al-GOO-nas): *some, several, any*

cualquier / cualquiera (KOOAL-keeyer): *anybody, any*

de alguna manera (de al-GOO-na ma-NE-ra): *somehow*

de ninguna manera (de neen-GOO-na ma-NE-ra): *in no way*

en alguna parte (en al-GOO-na PAR-te): *somewhere*

en ninguna parte (en neen-GOO-na PAR-te): *nowhere*

jamás (ja-MAS): *never*

nada (NA-da): *nothing, not anything*

nadie (NA-dee-ye): *no one, not anyone, nobody*

ni...ni (nee...nee): *neither...nor*

ni siquiera (nee see-KYE-ra): *not even*

ninguno / ninguna (neen-GOO-no / neen-GOO-na): *no one, none*

no (no): *no, not*

nunca (NOON-ka): *never*

o...o (o...o): *either...or*

siempre (SEEYEM-pre): *ever / always*

sí (see): *yes*

también (tam-BEEYEN): *also, too*

tampoco (tam-PO-ko): *not either, neither*

todavía no (to-da-VEE-a no): *not yet*

ya no (ya no): *no longer*

Irregular & Special Usage Spanish Words

Prepositions

cerca de (SER-ka de): *near, close to*

a (a): *at, to*

a causa de (a CAOO-sa de): *because of*

a pesar de (a pe-SAR-de): *in spite of*

acerca de (a-SER-ca de): *about, concerning*

además de (a-de-MAS de): *in addition to, besides*

al lado de (a LA-do de): *next to, beside*

ante (AN-te): *before*

antes de (AN-tes de): *before*

aunque (AOON-ke): *although*

bajo (BA-ho): *under*

con (kon): *with*

contra (KON-tra): *against*

de (de): *of, from*

debajo de (de-BA-ho de): *under, beneath*

delante de (de-LAN-te de): *in front of, before*

dentro de (DEN-tro de): *inside, within*

desde (DES-de): *from, since*

después de (des-POOES de): *after*

detrás de (de-TRAS de): *after, behind*

durante (doo-RAN-te): *during*

en (en): *in, into, on, at*

en vez de (en ves de): *instead of*

encima de (en-SEE-ma de): *on, on top of, over*

enfrente de (en-FREN-te de): *in front of, opposite*

entonces (en-TON-ses): *so, then*

entre (EN-tre): *between, among*

excepto (ex-SEP-to): *except*

frente a (FREN-te a): *in front of, opposite*

fuera de (FOOE-ra de): *outside of, beyond*

hacia (A-seeya): *toward*

hasta (AS-ta): *to, up to, as far as, until*

lejos de (LE-hos de): *far from*

no...ni (nee...nee): *neither...nor*

no obstante (no ob-STAN-te): *nevertheless*

o (o): *or*

o...o (o...o): *either...or*

para (PA-ra): *for*

pero (PE-ro): *but*

por (por): *for*

por delante de (por de-LAN-te de): *in front of*

porque (POR-ke): *because*

según (se-GOON): *according to*

sin (seen): *without*

sin embargo (seen em-BAR-go): *nevertheless*

sino (SEE-no): *but rather*

sobre (SO-bre): *on, over, about, on top of*

tras (tras): *after*

y (ee): *and*

Time Expressions

a las (a las): *at*

de la mañana (de la ma-NYA-na): *in the morning, A.M.*

de la noche (de la NO-che): *in the evening, P.M.*

de la tarde (de la TAR-de): *in the afternoon, P.M.*

en punto (en POON-to): *sharp*

y cuarto (ee KWAR-to): *quarter past*

y media (ee ME-dya): *half past*

Interrogative Words

¿Adónde? (a-DON-de): *To where?*

¿Cómo? (KO-mo): *How?*

¿Cuál? (kwal): *Which one?*

¿Cuáles? (KWA-les): *Which ones?*

¿Cuándo? (KWAN-do): *When?*

¿Cuánto/a? (KWAN-to / KWAN-ta): *How much?*

¿Cuántos/as? (KWAN-tos / KWAN-tas): *How many?*

¿De dónde? (de DON-de): *From where?*

¿Dónde? (DON-de): *Where?*

¿Qué? (ke): *What? Which?*

¿Quién? (kee-YEN): *Who?*

¿Quiénes? (kee-YEN-es): *Who?* (plural)

¿Por qué? (por ke): *Why?*

Irregular Verbs

abrir (a-BREER): *to open*

caber (ca-BER): *to fit in*

conocer (co-no-SER): *to know*

dar (dar): *to give*

decir (de-SEER): *to say*

descubrir (des-koo-BREER): *to discover*

escribir (es-cree-BEER): *to write*

estar (es-TAR): *to be*

haber (a-BER): *to have*

hacer (a-SER): *to do, make*

ir (eer): *to go*

morir (mo-REER): *to die*

oír (o-EER): *to hear*

parecer (pa-re-SER): *to appear/to seem*

poder (po-DER): *to be able to*

poner (po-NER): *to put*

querer (ke-RER): *to want/love*

resolver (re-SOL-ver): *to resolve*

romper (rom-PER): *to break*

saber (sa-BER): *to know*

salir (sa-LEER): *to go out*

ser (ser): *to be*

tener (te-NER): *to have*

traer (TRA-er): *to bring*

venir (ve-NEER): *to come*

ver (ver): *to see*

valer (va-LER): *to be worth*

volver (vol-VER): *to come back / return*

Irregular & Special Usage Spanish Words

Expressions That Require the Infinitive

algo que (AL-go ke): *something that*

antes de (AN-tes de): *before*

después de (des-POOES de): *after*

difícil de (dee-FEE-seel de): *difficult / hard to*

en vez de (en ves de): *instead of*

fácil de (FA-seel de): *easy to*

hay que (ay ke): *it is necessary to*

imposible de (eem-po-SEE-ble de): *impossible that*

nada que (NA-da ke): *nothing*

para (PA-ra): *for*

poco que (PO-ko qe): *a little*

por (por): *for*

posible de (po-SEE-ble de): *possible that*

sin (seen): *without*

tener que (te-NER ke): *it is necessary to*

Other

palabra aguda (pa-LA-bra a-GOO-da): *a word that is stressed on its final syllable*

palabra llana (grave) (pa-LA-bra YA-na (gra-ve)): *a word that is stressed on its second-to-last syllable*

palabra esdrújula (pa-LA-bra es-DROO-hoo-la): *a word that is stressed on any syllable that comes before the second-to-last syllable*

Glossary of Grammar Terms

adjectival: A word or phrase that is related to or functions like an adjective and is used to describe a noun. For example: *The woman **who wrote the book** is my sister.* In this sentence, *who wrote the book* is an adjectival phrase that describes the noun *woman*.

adjective: A word that describes the quality or state of a noun. In the example *the **beautiful** dog, beautiful* is an adjective that describes the quality of *dog*.

adverb: A word that describes or enhances the meaning of a verb, adjective, another adverb, or sentence. An adverb answers *How? Where?* or *When?* In English, most adverbs end in *–ly*. For example: *slowly, hourly, softly*. Other common adverbs include: *there, now, yesterday*.

article: A word used in combination with a noun to indicate if that noun is definite (specific) or indefinite (generic). English has two articles: *the* (definite article) and *a/an* (indefinite article).

auxiliary: A verb that is used in combination with another verb when forming a specific tense or mood. In English, common auxiliary verbs include *to have* and *to be*. For example: *She **is** running, and he **has been** waiting.*

cardinal numbers: Numbers that are used when counting to describe how many of an item are present: *one, two, three...*

comparative: The form of a word, or the word construction, that is used to compare specific qualities between two things. In English, the comparative is generally formed by adding *–er* or *more/less* to an adjective or adverb. For example: *fast**er**, **more/less** intelligent*.

compound sentence: A sentence that has one main (independent) clause and one or more subordinate (dependent) clauses. *My father is generous* is an independent clause, and it can be part of a compound sentence when combined with a dependent clause: *My father is generous **when he gives me an allowance.***

conditional clause: A sentence or clause that describes a situation that is dependent on a condition explained by another clause or sentence. In English, conditional clauses generally begin with *if, unless,* or another conjunction with a similar meaning. For example: *I'll buy the cake **unless you don't want it.***

conditional mood: The form of a verb used when describing an imaginary situation that would happen in the future if a specific condition is met. In English, the conditional mood is formed with the auxiliaries *would* or *could* and a verb. For example: *I **would go** to the movies if you pay for my ticket. If you have enough time and money, we **could see** two movies.*

conjugation: The possible form a verb can take in a given tense to express person, number, and mood. In English, for example, the present tense conjugation of the verb *to be* is *am, are,* and *is*. The past tense conjugation for *to be* is *was* and *were*.

conjunction: A word that joins two or more words, phrases, or sentences. Conjunctions are either coordinating or subordinating, depending on how the two elements relate to each other. *And, but, because, unless,* and *if* are examples of common conjunctions in English.

coordinating conjunction: A conjunction that joins two elements that are on the same grammatical level, such as noun + noun, adjective + adjective, independent clause + independent clause. The coordinating conjunctions in English are *and, but, or, for, nor, yet,* and *so. The boy **and** the girl are swimming. The house is on fire, **and** the firemen are on the way.*

declarative sentence: A statement of fact or state of being, as opposed to a question, exclamation, or command. For example: *I would like to have pizza. The weather is nice. She has been working hard.*

declension: A group of nouns, pronouns, or adjectives that undergo the same kind of changes according to number, gender, and, in some languages, case.

demonstrative: A word that refers to a noun in terms of its proximity to the speaker. In English, demonstratives include *this, that, these,* and *those*.

dependent clause: See **subordinate clause**

direct object: The direct object in a sentence is usually a noun or pronoun that is directly affected by the action of the verb. The direct object will generally answer the question *what do you do (with the verb)?* In the sentence *I wrote **a letter,*** the noun *letter* is the direct object because it is directly affected by the verb (*wrote*).

disjunctive: A word used to establish a relationship of contrast or opposition between two or more things or events. For example, the preposition *but* is disjunctive: *I am stronger, **but** you are faster.*

future tense: A tense used to refer to events that have not yet occurred but will or are likely to happen. In English, the future tense can be formed in two ways: with the auxiliary *will* + a verb (*I **will read** that book tomorrow*) or with the present of *to be* + *going to* + a verb (*I **am going to read** that book tomorrow*).

future perfect tense: The future perfect refers to an event that is either currently in progress and will be finished in the future or that will begin and be finished in the future. In English, the

Glossary of Grammar Terms

future perfect is formed with the auxiliary *to have* in future tense (*will have*) + the past participle of a verb. For example: *I will have finished my project by the time you come back.*

gerund: A verb in a form ending in *-ing*. For example: *eating, writing, reading.* Gerunds can function as nouns in a sentence (***Smoking** is bad for you*). They are also the verb form used after a preposition (*Thanks **for** calling me back*).

imperative: The form of a verb used to give commands or orders. In the imperative form, the subject is often implied and is therefore omitted. The imperative can be either affirmative or negative. For example: *Go! Come! Don't speak! Don't eat!*

imperfect tense: A past tense form used to discuss repeated, habitual, or continued actions in the past. Though considered a separate tense in some languages, the imperfect tense is not considered a separate tense in English, and it is equivalent to the simple past and past progressive tenses. The imperfect is commonly formed using *used to* or *would*: *I **used to** visit my grandparents every Sunday. I **would** visit them every week.*

indefinite adjective: An adjective that refers to an undefined or inexact number or quantity. Common indefinite adjectives in English are *some, all, many, few, more, most,* and *several.*

independent clause: See **main clause**

indicative mood: The verb form used in declarative sentences or questions. The indicative is the most commonly used mood in most languages. For example: *She bought a cake. Are you OK?*

indirect object: The indirect object of a verb expresses who or what has been affected indirectly by the action of the verb. The indirect object is the receiver or beneficiary of the action and answers the question *To/for whom?* In the sentence *I wrote you a letter,* the pronoun *you* is the indirect object because it benefits from the action (the written letter).

infinitive: The base form of a verb. In English, the infinitive is expressed with the particle *to* + the verb. The infinitive is the form of the verb defined in a dictionary. For example: *to go, to eat, to come, to dance.*

interjections: A single word or phrase that conveys a strong emotion or an attitude, such as shock, surprise, delight, or disgust. Common interjections include *Ouch! Wow! Oh! Yuck!*

interrogative adjective: An adjective used in forming a question, asking for definition or clarification, and distinguishing among various choices. In English, interrogative adjectives include *what, which, who, whom,* and *whose.*

invariable: A word that never changes form, regardless of tense, number, or person. In English, prepositions are invariable. Verbs, however, are not because they change form depending on the tense and, occasionally, subject.

main (independent) clause: A sentence that expresses a complete thought on its own and does not depend on another clause to create meaning. For example: *I like cake. They have been traveling. Math is difficult.*

modal verb: In English, modal verbs are auxiliary verbs that express an attitude (doubt, desire, need) about the event expressed by another verb. Modal verbs are also used to make requests and ask permission. Modal verbs include *can, could, may, might, must, have to, should, shall, will,* and *would.* For example: *I **would** like to go to the movies. I **can** speak French.*

modify/qualify: To use a word or group of words to give further information about another noun or phrase, sometimes resulting in a change of meaning and/or form. Words are considered **modifiers** when they come before the word they alter. Words are considered **qualifiers** when they come after the word they alter. In the sentence *The **yellow** taxi **from New York**,* the adjective *yellow* modifies *taxi* and *from New York* qualifies it.

mood: All sentences are said to be in a specific mood, depending on the attitude and intentions of the speaker. The specific form of a past, present, or future tense verb in a given sentence indicates the mood.

nominal: A word or phrase that is related to or functions like a noun. For example: *I liked **what she gave me.*** In this sentence, *what she gave me* is a nominal phrase or clause because it functions like a noun describing *what I liked.* This nominal phrase is a direct object and can be replaced by a pronoun: *I liked **it.***

noun: A word referring to a person, an animal, a thing, a place, or an abstract idea. For example: *Steve, dog, teacher, book, California, love, freedom.*

object pronoun: Words used in place of the direct object in a sentence. The object pronouns in English are *me, you, him, her, it, us,* and *them.* In the sentence *I like cake,* the noun *cake* is the direct object and can be replaced by the direct object pronoun *it*: *I like **it.***

ordinal numbers: Numbers used when designating the place of items listed in a sequence: *first, second, third, fourth,* and so on.

participle (past and present): A verb form used as an adjective. The present participle is used in progressive tenses with the verb *to be* (*I am **reading***). The past participle is used in perfect tenses and in the passive voice with the verb *to be* (*the homework was **made***). In English, the present participle is formed by adding *-ing* to the verb (*I am **dancing,** they are **walking***), and the past participle is formed by adding either *-ed* to the verb (*danc**ed**, walk**ed***), or *-en* instead (*writt**en**, brok**en***). Some past participles are irregular (*sing/**sung**, eat/**ate***).

partitive adjective: A phrase used to express quantity when distinguishing a piece from the whole or when referring to an uncountable noun. For example: *a piece of cake, a slice of bread, a bunch of grapes, a pinch of salt.*

past tense: The verb tense used to describe events that occurred in the past. For example: *She **walked** to the store. He **ran** to the house.*

past perfect (pluperfect) tense: A past tense form that refers to an event completed in the past, prior to the beginning of another event that also occurred in the past. In English, the pluperfect tense is formed with the auxiliary *to have* in past tense (*had*) + the past participle. For example: *I **had read** the book before you told me the ending.*

possessive adjective: An adjective that indicates ownership or possession. In English, the possessive adjectives are *my, your, his, her, its, our, their.*

possessive pronoun: A pronoun that replaces a possessive adjective and its noun. In English, the possessive pronouns are *mine, yours, his, hers, its, ours, yours, theirs.* For example: *I bought my house. It is **mine.***

preposition: A word used to join nouns, adjectives, and pronouns with other words to indicate ownership, physical location, direction, or time. Prepositions are invariable, meaning they never change form. Some common English prepositions include *about, before, but, for, from, in, at, of,* and *on.* For example: *She sat **on** the bench. I left **before** you got there.*

present tense: The tense that describes an action taking place in present time or an action that is habitual. Present tense can also be used to describe facts or states of being in the present. For example: *She **reads** a book. I **go** to the movies every day. Madrid **is** the capital of Spain.*

present perfect tense: A past tense form that refers to an action that has been completed, occurred within a specific time period, or has results that continue up to a specific point in time. In English, the present perfect is formed with the auxiliary *to have* in present tense (*have, has*) + the past participle. For example: *I **have been** to New York twice. She **has finished** her homework.*

preterite tense: A past tense form used to discuss an action completed in the past, an action that happened only once, or an action that interrupted another in the past. For example: *I **saw** the movie yesterday. I **ran** into you while you were walking.* The preterite is also known as the simple past in English, though in some languages there is a distinction between the preterite and other past tenses.

progressive tenses: A progressive tense expresses an action that is in progress or is developing at a given time. Progressive tenses in English are formed with the auxiliary *to be* + the present participle (*-ing* form of a verb). A progressive action can be expressed in present tense (*I **am reading** a book now*), past (*She **was taking** notes during class*), and future (*We **will be eating** pizza next Saturday*).

pronoun: A word that replaces a noun or a noun phrase. English pronouns come in three forms: subject pronouns (for example, *I* and *we*), object pronouns (*me* and *us*), and possessive pronouns (*my/mine* and *our/ours*).

qualify: See *modify.*

reflexive verb: A verb used to imply that the subject is performing an action on itself. In English, reflexive verbs are expressed with the pronoun *self* (*myself, herself, themselves,* etc.) or are implied by the verb alone. For example: *I **hurt myself.** I was **shaving.***

relative pronoun: Relative pronouns introduce a sentence or clause that gives additional information about a noun. The relative pronouns in English are *who, whom, whose, which,* and *that.* In the sentence *The man **who** called was my father*, the clause *who called* provides additional information about the noun *man.*

subject pronoun: Pronouns that replace the subject of a sentence. Subject pronouns have the same gender and number as the noun they replace. The subject pronouns in English are *I, you, he, she, it, we, you, they,* and *one.* In the sentence *My mother is nice,* the noun phrase *my mother* can be replaced by the subject pronoun s*he: **She** is nice.*

subjunctive mood: The verb form used to express wishes, desires, emotions, uncertainty, and hypothetical or nonfactual situations. For example: *If I were you, I wouldn't go.*

subordinate (dependent) clause: A clause that does not express a complete idea on its own. A subordinate clause must be used with another clause or sentence (called a **main clause** or **independent clause**). In the sentence *They told me that she was not coming, that she was not coming* is the subordinate clause, since it does not form a complete idea on its own.

Glossary of Grammar Terms

subordinating conjunction: A conjunction that joins an independent clause with a dependent clause. Common subordinating conjunctions in English include *after, before, because, since, although, if, unless, until, while,* and *even if. I am going outside* **even if** *it is cold.*

superlative: The form of a word or the word construction used to show the most or the least in quantity, quality, or intensity. In English, the superlative is formed by adding *–est* or *most/least* to an adjective or adverb. For example: *tall***est,** **most** *difficult.*

tense: Tense conveys when in time an event happened, how long it lasted, and whether the event has been completed. All tenses can be divided into one of three groups: present, past, and future. The specific form of a verb in a given sentence indicates the tense.

verb: A word that refers to an action or a state of being. For example: *to eat, to write, to read.*

voice: Voice indicates whether emphasis is placed on the person or thing causing the action or on the person or thing receiving the action. The voice of a sentence is either **active** or **passive.** In the **active voice,** the subject is the person or thing performing the action: ***She visited*** *the school.* In the **passive voice,** the subject is receiving the action of the verb: ***The school is visited*** *by her.* Two sentences can be written in different voices but still carry the same meaning. For example: *I ate the cake* (active voice). *The cake was eaten by me* (passive voice).

Answer Key

Workout 1 .... p. 2

Exercise 1
1. 4,5%
2. $3.041,10
3. 1,02%
4. 2.501.034,03
5. 99,98

Exercise 2
1. 2.040
2. 100,10
3. 1.3712,11
4. 4.787,04
5. 78.414,55

Exercise 3
1. Julieta: ¿Me amas, Romeo? / Me amas, Romeo.
   Romeo: ¡No puedo vivir sin ti! / No, puedo vivir sin ti.
2. Señor Suárez: ¿Tienes un dólar? / Tienes un dólar.
   Señor Espinosa: ¡No tengo 25 centavos! / No, tengo 25 centavos.
3. Aurelio: ¿Quieres ir a la discoteca? / Quieres ir a la discoteca.
   Elisa: No me parece mala idea. / No, me parece mala idea.
4. Mamá: No estás feliz, Jaimito. / ¿No estás feliz, Jaimito?
   Jaimito: No estoy feliz. / ¡No, estoy feliz!
5. Maristela: Me vas a dejar. / ¿Me vas a dejar?
   Juan: Sí, no me quieres. / Si no me quieres.

Exercise 4
—Hernán, ¿me prestas dinero? —preguntó Guillermo.
—¿Para qué lo quieres? —contestó Hernán.
—Pues tengo una deuda. —dijo Guillermo.
—¿Y cuánto necesitas, hermano?
—Necesito 1.100 pesos.
—¡Tanto! —exclamó Hernán—. Estás loco. ¿Qué tipo de deuda es?
—Una deuda a mi novia. Ayer salimos a comer, fuimos al teatro y después a bailar. Soy tan bobo que me olvidé la billetera. ¡Y ahora Rosa espera el reembolso!

Workout 2 .... p. 4

Exercise 1
palabras agudas: canción, profesor
palabras llanas: biblioteca, computadora
palabras esdrújulas: película, periódico

Exercise 2
1. no accent
2. fútbol
3. electrónico
4. no accent
5. algodón
6. música
7. silla
8. colchón
9. no accent
10. portátil

Exercise 3
1. c
2. a
3. e
4. b
5. d

Exercise 4
Fátima López tiene 28 años y vive en Queens, New York. **Nació** en **México** pero ha vivido en los Estados Unidos por quince años. **Fátima** enseña **inglés** a inmigrantes hispanos. A **Fátima** le gusta ayudar a la gente hispana. —Yo **también** tuve que aprender el **inglés** —dice—.Todos necesitamos un poco de apoyo.

Fátima tiene dos hermanos. **José** vive en **Asunción,** Paraguay y **Ramón** vive en Puebla, **México. Fátima** extraña a sus hermanos. —Quisiera vivir juntos como cuando **éramos** pequeños —dice—. Es **difícil. Algún día,** si **Diós** quiere, viviremos, por lo menos, en el mismo **país.**

Workout 3 .... p. 6

Exercise 1
Masculine: sabor, rey, barril, camino
Feminine: vaca, actriz, libertad, carrera

Exercise 2
1. Mi tía vive en Nicaragua.
2. La reina vive en un gran castillo.
3. Mi padre está en casa.
4. El señor Méndez es profesor de matemática.
5. El hombre es actor.

Exercise 3
Possible answers:
1. libro
2. papel
3. garaje
4. hombre
5. maleta

6. universidad
7. declaración
8. mujer

Exercise 4
1. consejo
2. situación
3. mañana
4. baño
5. ducha
6. toalla
7. papel
8. novia
9. broma
10. hombre

Workout 4 .... p. 8

Exercise 1
Masculine: poema, mapa, papá, idioma
Feminine: miel, foto, capital, mano

Exercise 2
1. día: masculine, "Nouns that end in -a are feminine."
2. radio: feminine, "Nouns that end in -o are masculine."
3. sal: feminine, "Nouns that end in -l are masculine."
4. planeta: masculine, "Nouns that end in -a are feminine."
5. moto: feminine, "Nouns that end in -o are masculine."
6. piel: feminine, "Nouns that end in -l are masculine."

Exercise 3
1. b
2. e
3. a
4. f
5. d
6. c

Exercise 4
1. el artista
2. la cliente
3. la cura
4. el consonante
5. la capital
6. el tío
7. el hijo
8. el conductor
9. la chica
10. el turista

Workout 5 .... p. 10

Exercise 1

					P					
			J	U	E	V	E	S		
					C		X			
					E		Á			
					S		M			
						L	E	Y	E	S
							N			
C							E			
A	C	T	R	I	C	E	S			
S										
A										
S										

Exercise 2
1. monedas
2. lápiz
3. monos
4. hermana
5. países
6. conductor
7. computadora
8. actrices
9. leopardos
10. nacionalidad

Exercise 3
1. Tengo tres libros en mi mochila.
2. Hay tres relojes en la vitrina.
3. Hay dos lápices, un borrador y un cuaderno en el escritorio.
4. Hay cuartro personas en el tren.

Workout 6 .... p. 12

Exercise 1
1. el, los
2. la, las
3. el, los
4. el, las
5. el, los
6. la, las

Exercise 2

1. e
2. d
3. a
4. c
5. b

Exercise 3

1. La casa de Laura es blanca.
2. Mañana vamos al restaurante nuevo.
3. Correct
4. Correct
5. El agua está sucia.
6. Es el carro del vecino.

Exercise 4
Possible answers:

las sillas
el pastel
el regalo
la música
los helados

Workout 7 .... p. 14

Exercise 1

1. unos
2. una
3. un
4. unas
5. una

Exercise 2

1. un
2. unos
3. un
4. unas
5. una

Exercise 3
Possible answers:

Hay una señora el almacén.
Hay unos niños en el corredor.
Hay unos aretes bonitos en la joyería.
Hay un libro interesante en la librería.
Hay unas muchachas en la entrada.

Exercise 4

1. Hay una chica en mi clase.
2. Veo unos niños afuera.
3. Es un curso de literatura.
4. Son unas amigas de Pancho.
5. ¿Quieres una pera o unas bananas?

Workout 8 .... p. 16

Exercise 1

				F			
				E		V	
				R		I	
		B	J	O	V	E	N
		U		C		J	
		E		E		A	
L	I	N	D	A	S		
		O					
		S					

Exercise 2

1. h
2. a
3. b
4. c
5. c

Exercise 3
Possible answers:

1. Shakira es hermosa.
2. Mis amigas son simpáticas.
2. Antonio Banderas es arrogante
4. Mis padres son malos.
5. Enrique Iglesias es talentoso.

Exercise 4
Possible answers:

1. Soy alta y delgada
2. Mis ojos son oscuros
3. Tengo una sonrisa muy alegre
4. Mi cara es bonita
5. Tengo pelo largo.

Workout 9 .... p. 18

Exercise 1

1. este borrador
2. aquel diccionario
3. ese lápiz
4. estas plumas

Answer Key

5. aquellos mapas
6. esa calculadora

Exercise 2
1. e
2. b
3. a
4. c
5. d

Exercise 3
1. Estos
2. Ese
3. esos
4. esos
5. aquellos
6. aquellos

Workout 10 .... p. 20

Exercise 1
1. f
2. d
3. a
4. e
5. b
6. c

Exercise 2
1. circle: problema, dinero
2. circle: hijos, profesores
3. circle: tía, ventana
4. circle: disco compacto
5. circle: televisión

Exercise 3
1. la computadora suya
2. mis llaves
3. la cámara tuya
4. nuestro carro
5. la televisión mía
6. nuestra casa

Workout 11 .... p. 22

Exercise 1
1. Este perro es travieso. / Es travieso este perro.
2. Vi una chica simpática.
3. Mis libros son pesados. / Son pesados mis libros.
4. Los estudiantes inteligentes pasan el examen difícil.
5. Salma Hayek es una actriz talentosa.

Exercise 2
1. Correct
2. Me gustan las manzanas rojas.
3. Mi mamá lee novelas románticas.
4. Correct
5. Mis amigos estudiosos sacan buenas notas.

Exercise 3
1. h
2. f
3. e
4. a
5. b
6. d
7. c
8. g

Workout 12 .... p. 24

Exercise 1

Singular	Plural
yo	nosotras(F)
	nosotros (M)
tu (formal)	vosotras (F)
usted (informal)	vosotros (M)
	ustedes (N)
ella (F)	ellas (F)
él (M)	ellos (M)

Exercise 2
1. él
2. yo
3. ella
4. tú
5. nosotras
6. usted
7. ellos
8. ustedes or vosotros

Exercise 3
1. e
2. c
3. d
4. a
5. b

Exercise 4
Tú: your younger cousin, your father, a classmate
Usted: your professor, the bus driver, your elderly neighbor

Workout 13 .... p. 26

Exercise 1
1. c
2. a
3. b
4. b
5. a

Exercise 2
1. e
2. f
3. b
4. a
5. c
6. d

Exercise 3
1. tuyo
2. suyo
3. nuestras
4. mío
5. vuestro

Workout 14 .... p. 28

Exercise 1
1. c
2. d
3. b
4. e
5. a

Exercise 2
1. Correct
2. Alexandra escucha el CD de Jennifer López. Alexandra lo escucha.
3. Lupe y Daniel miran el partido de la Copa Mundial. Lupe y Daniel lo miran.
4. Correct
5. Vosotras estudiáis las lecciones. Vosotras las estudiáis.

Exercise 3
Possible answers:
1. No, no los tengo.
2. Los compré en la librería.
3. Sí, la necesito.
4. No, no te oigo.
5. La vamos a ver mañana.

Workout 15 .... p. 30

Exercise 1
1. True
2. False. When *a* precedes the indirect object, include the indirect object *le* or *les*.
3. True
4. False. The third person singular indirect object pronoun is *le*, while the third person singular direct object pronouns are *lo* or *la*.
5. True

Exercise 2
1. les
2. nos
3. me
4. le
5. te

Exercise 3
1. Les compró diez discos compactos.
2. Me compró unos aretes de plata.
3. Le compró una muñeca de porcelana.

Exercise 4
1. A
2. B
3. A
4. B
5. A

Exercise 5
Possible answers:
1. Le escribo mensajes electrónicos a mis padres.
2. Les mando cartas postales a mi profesor de español.
3. No le presto a nadie mi computadora.
4. Le compraría un disco de Luis Miguel a mi hermana menor.
5. Le regalaría un obsequio muy caro mi novia.

Workout 16 .... p. 32

Exercise 1
1. Jaime me lo regaló.
2. Tu padre te la dio.
3. Ustedes se la prestaron.
4. Ellas te la piden.
5. El camarero nos los sirve.

Exercise 2
1. Se los vendí.
2. Te las traemos.
3. Quiero leertela.
4. ¿Nos las guardáis?
5. Os la canto.

Answer Key

Exercise 3
1. Tomó una manzana y me la dio.
2. Marisela se la mandó.
3. Se lo quiero prestar.
4. ¿Nos la (lo) vas a dar? / ¿Nos la (lo) vas a dar?
5. La (lo) compré y se la (lo) enseñé.

Workout 17 .... p. 34

Exercise 1

	V				C					
N	O	S	O	T	R	O	S			
	S				N					
	O				M					E
	T			M	I					L
	R				G					L
	O			C	O	N	T	I	G	O
	S									S

Exercise 2
1. b
2. e
3. a
4. c
5. d

Exercise 3
1. Raúl está al lado de ella.
2. Andrea está al lado de él.
3. Andrea está delante de él.
4. Andrea está cenando con ellos.
5. Raúl y Juan Carlos están cenando con ellas.

Workout 18 .... p. 36

Exercise 1
1. lo que
2. quienes
3. que
4. lo que
5. quien

Exercise 2
1. d
2. c

3. a
4. b
5. e

Exercise 3
1. Fuimos a la nueva librería que está cerca de la escuela.
2. Delia tiene un hermano mayor que estudia en la Universidad Central. / Delia tiene un hermano mayor quien estudia en la Universidad Central.
3. El vendedor de relojes que nos ayudó estaba muy informado.
4. Fui a una doctora chilena que se llamaba Zorayda Preto. / Fui a una doctora chilena quien se llamaba Zorayda Preto.
5. Cristina, quien estudia matemáticas, es muy inteligente.

Workout 19 .... p. 38

Exercise 1
1. sencillamente
2. difícilmente
3. rápidamente
4. energéticamente
5. sensiblemente

Exercise 2
1. Llego facilmente a la universidad en autobús.
2. Correct
3. Cuando veo la television, mi hermano cambia el canal constantemente.
4. María está totalmente confundida.
5. Correct

Exercise 3
Possible answers:
inteligente/inteligentemente, fabuloso/fabulosamente, paciente/pacientemente
1. Mi amiga siempre responde inteligentemente a mis preguntas.
2. Ella siempre se viste fabulosamente.
3. Mi amiga siempre espera pacientemente cuando llego tarde.

Workout 20 .... p. 40

Exercise 1

a	d	e	l	a	n	t	e	u	p	l	h	l	k	a	a
p	d	é	o	a	r	r	i	b	a	e	d	m	i	o	q
a	v	a	d	r	f	s	i	l	w	j	p	é	h	d	u
s	w	b	n	x	p	z	q	b	g	o	i	p	a	j	í
d	e	t	r	á	s	r	l	n	e	s	r	m	b	p	i

Exercise 2

1. Yo hago la tarea lentamente.
2. Ahora el profesor nos examina menos.
3. Tú estudias más que Julio.
4. Esta clase es peor que la otra.
5. El profesor enseña mal.

Exercise 3

1. debajo
2. mal
3. lejos
4. así
5. aquí

Workout 21 .... p. 42

Exercise 1

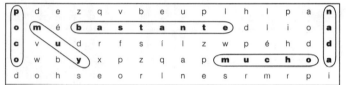

Exercise 2
Possible answers:

1. Yo miro la televisión de vez en cuando.
2. Yo nunca duermo en el tren.
3. Yo leo un libro todos los días.
4. Yo siempre saco la basura.
5. Yo lavo los platos a menudo.

Exercise 3

El fin de semana me gusta relajarme. El sábado nunca me despierto antes de las once o doce. Me ducho, y después almuerzo. A veces veo la televisión. Si no hay nada en la televisión, leo un libro o una revista. De noche no hay nada que hacer en my apartamento. Prefiero salir con mis amigos. Casi siempre vamos al la misma discoteca. Se llama "Blues." Me gusta much bailar. Regreso a casa muy temprano la próxima mañana, y mi rutina empieza de nuevo el domingo!

Workout 22 .... p. 44

Exercise 1

1. Tengo pocos amigos.
2. Me gusta mucho la música *reggaetón*.
3. El verano pasado fuimos a bastantes fiestas.
4. Mi primo viaja de vez en cuando a Perú.
5. Juegan mal al tenis.

Exercise 2

1. Mi tía es una mujer alta.
2. Tú hablas muy alto, Marta.

3. Hoy lavé mucha / bastante ropa.
4. Juan, mi vecino, es un hombre bajo.
5. Estos días como muy poco.

Exercise 3
Possible answers:

1. Soy un gato **muy** perezoso.
2. Duermo **mucho.**
3. Tengo **pocos** amigos porque nunca salgo a la calle.
4. Como **bastante** pero siempre tengo hambre.
5. Soy un gato **malo** porque rasguño a la gente.

Workout 23 .... p. 46

Exercise 1

1. Ernesto es tan inteligente como un profesor universitario.
2. La casa de Ernesto es tan grande como la mía.
3. Ernesto tiene tantos hijos como Jorge.
4. El hijo de Ernesto duerme tanto como su hija.
5. Ernesto lee tantos libros como su esposa.

Exercise 2

1. Mi sopa es tan caliente como la tuya.
2. Mi padre canta en la ducha tanto como mi hermano.
3. Manuel juega fútbol tan mal como Nancy.
4. Tu novia es tan bonita como Paulina Rubio.
5. Mi casa tiene tantas habitaciones como la suya.

Exercise 3
Possible answers:

1. Soy tan perfeccionista como mi madre.
2. Me visto tan bien como mi madre.
3. Tengo tantos amigas como mi madre.

Workout 24 .... p. 48

Exercise 1

1. más
2. menos
3. tanto como
4. menos
5. más

Exercise 2

1. La música de *los* Aterciopelados es mejor que la música de Fobia.
2. Esta emisora de radio es peor que esa.
3. Los Héroes del Silencio tocan mejor en conceierto que Los Enanitos Verdes.
4. Los miembros de la banda son menores que nosotros.
5. Las canciones de Beto Cuevas son menos interesantes que las de Andrea Echeverri.

Answer Key

Exercise 3

1. The chicken at Pío Pío and the chicken in other restaurants.
2. El pollo del Restaurante Pío Pío es más rico que el pollo de otros restaurantes / Servimos el pollo al horno que también tiene menos grasa que el pollo en otros restaurantes.
3. más, menos

Workout 25 .... p. 50

Exercise 1

1. mejor, el mejor
2. peor, el peor
3. menor, el menor
4. mayor, el major

Exercise 2

Exercise 3
Possible answers:

1. *Flor Cuencana* es el restaurante más elegante de la ciudad.
2. *El Hotelcito* es el hotel menos caro de la ciudad.
3. *El Museo Central* es la atracción turística más bonita de la ciudad.
4. *La Floresta* es en barrio menos peligroso de la ciudad.

Workout 26 .... p. 52

Exercise 1

1. d
2. e
3. a
4. b
5. c

Exercise 2

1. pero
2. sino
3. pero
4. sino

Exercise 3

Juan nunca se viste de negro. Siempre viene a clase, porque nunca se levanta tarde. Nunca se enoja con sus amigos. Por eso siempre mantiene sus amistades.

Workout 27 .... p. 54

Exercise 1

							T			
					N	A	D	I	E	
			N			M				
			I			B				
			N			I				
T			G			E				
A	L	G	U	I	E	N				
M			N							
P			O							
O										
C										
O										

Exercise 2

1. Conozco a alguien en Barcelona.
2. Alguien en la Ciudad de México me mandó un paquete.
3. Aunque sea invierno, veo algunos patos en el lago.
4. No he hablado con nadie esta mañana.
5. A Roberto no le gustó este libro. No le gustó ese libro tampoco.

Exercise 3

1. Los fines de semana no salgo con nadie.
2. No he consultado a ningún médico acerca de mi tos.
3. Sí, vi a alguien en la biblioteca.
4. Alguien me llama por teléfono.
5. No tengo ningún lápiz que te pueda prestar.

Workout 28 .... p. 56

Exercise 1
1. j
2. e
3. h
4. i
5. b
6. c
7. d
8. a
9. f
10. g

Exercise 2
1. El carro está debajo del puente.
2. El carro está dentro del túnel.
3. El carro está encima del periódico.
4. El carro está delante del bus.
5. El carro está lejos de la ambulancia

Exercise 3
1. b
2. a
3. a
4. b
5. b

Exercise 4
1. Bolivia
2. Colombia

Workout 29 .... p. 58

Exercise 1
1. Correct
2. La mantequilla es para el pan.
3. Correct
4. No fui a ver la película por miedo.
5. Para verano hace demasiado frío.

Exercise 2
1. B
2. B
3. A
4. B
5. A
6. A

Exercise 3
1. Fui / fuimos / fueron a la biblioteca por carro para estudiar.
2. Fui / fuimos / fueron a la playa por dos días para tomar sol.
3. Fui / fuimos / fueron al supermercado para comprar fruta para mi mamá.

Exercise 4
La familia Cobos salió ayer para el Perú. Fueron por avión, aunque piensan viajar en carro por el pais. Van a estar allí por dos meses. Va a ser una experiencia extraordinaria para toda la familia.

Workout 30 .... p. 60

Exercise 1
1. con
2. con
3. sin
4. con
5. sin

Exercise 2
Possible answers:
1. A veces me enojo con mis padres.
2. De noche sueño con Gael García Bernal.
3. Los fines de semana me encuentro con mis amigas.
4. Quiero casarme con un hombre bueno.
5. Generalmente me encariño con bebés.

Exercise 3
—Yesenia, ven con nosotras al parque —dijo Nela—.
Llevamos las bicicletas.
—No sé, chicas. Mi bicicleta está dañada. La tengo que arreglar.
—La puedes arreglar con un destornillador, ¡estoy segura!
—dijo Susana.
—Nos vamos a encontrar con ese chico con el perro.
—Ah, ¡sueño con él! ¡Iré con tal de que él vaya!

Workout 31 .... p. 62

Exercise 1
Possible answers:
1. Voy al Caribe.
2. Estoy a cuatro cuadras.
3. Quisiera aprender a bucear.
4. Ayudo a mi abuela.
5. Veo a mi novia.

Exercise 2
1. a mano
2. A lo mejor
3. a la vez
4. A causa de
5. al menos

Exercise 3

Juan iba de negocios a Cuenca. Se subió al bus y se sentó al lado de una muchacha atractiva. Cuando llegaron a la ciudad, Juan tenía hambre. Le invito a comer a la muchacha. La ayudó a bajarse del bus. Fueron a un restaurante que quedaba a dos cuadras de la estación. Visitaron la ciudad a pie. A las 5 Juan tuvo que regresar a la estación. A causa de una muchacha atractiva, Juan se olvidó de su coloquio!

Workout 32 .... p. 64

Exercise 1
1. A
2. B
3. B
4. A
5. B
6. A

Exercise 2
1. del
2. de
3. en
4. en
5. de
6. en
7. en
8. de

Exercise 3
Possible answers:
1. Dependo mucho de mi familia.
2. Mi almuerzo consiste en dos huesos.
3. Disfruto mucho del sol de la tarde.

Workout 33 .... p. 66

Exercise 1
1. preposition
2. personal
3. preposition
4. personal
5. personal

Exercise 2
1. ¿Viste a alguien en el pasillo?
2. Correct
3. No quiero discutir nada con él.
4. Correct
5. Correct
6. Tengo una amiga peruana.

Exercise 3
1. —
2. a
3. a
4. —
5. a
6. a
7. a
8. —

Workout 34 .... p. 68

Exercise 1
1. d
2. f
3. a
4. e
5. b
6. c

Exercise 2
1. o…o
2. a pesar de
3. No…ni
4. sin embargo / no obstante

Exercise 3
1. ¿Quieres un jugo o una cola?
2. No es doctora sino abogada.
3. Mi mamá hace un postre con helado e higos en almíbar.
4. No había nadie en el baño entonces entré.
5. Me gusta la música cubana porque tiene un buen ritmo.

Workout 35 .... p. 70

Exercise 1

	V			C					
S	E	I	S	I	E	N	T	O	S
	I			E					
	N			N					
	T								
M	I	L							
	U								
U	N	A							
	A								

Exercise 2
1. cien mil doscientas
2. cuarenta y un
3. un millón de
4. trescientas veinticuatro
5. un

Exercise 3
Possible answers:
1. cuarenta mil dólares
2. doscientos cincuenta mil dólares
3. mil quinientos dólares
4. ochocientos dólares
5. un millón de dólares

Workout 36 .... p. 72

Exercise 1
1. La letra A
2. La letra C
3. La letra E
4. La letra G
5. La letra I

Exercise 2
1. décimo
2. segundo
3. tercero
4. cuarto
5. quinto

Exercise 3
—Armando, es el cuarto canal que pones. ¡Por favor no cambies de canal!
—No, es el tercer canal. Primero estaba mirando esa comedia en Univisión, después estaba mirando el programa de Papa Pío el Séptimo.
—Y después estabas mirando el segundo episodio de *Betty la Fea*. Y ahora estas mirando este documentario acerca del rey español Felipe el Cuarto. Son cuatro. Tienes que aprender a sumar!

Workout 37 .... p. 74

Exercise 1

Exercise 2
1. Me despierto a las seis de la mañana.
2. Llego al trabajo a las ocho y media de la mañana.
3. Almuerzo a la una de la tarde.
4. Regreso a casa a las cinco de la tarde.
5. Me voy a la cama a las once de la noche.

Exercise 3
1. son las siete de la mañana
2. son las tres de la tarde
3. es la una de la mañana
4. son las nueve y cuarto de la noche
5. son las tres de la tarde

Workout 38 .... p. 76

Exercise 1
1. El Día de San Valentín es el 14 de febrero.
2. El Día de los Muertos es el 2 de noviembre.
3. El Día de la Raza es el 12 de octubre.
4. La Navidad es el 25 de diciembre.
5. El Año Nuevo es el primero de enero.

Exercise 2
1. c
2. d
3. b
4. e
5. a
6. f

Answer Key

Exercise 3
Possible answers:
1. Mi hermana nació el 26 de febrero de 1979.
2. Mi padre nació el 6 de agosto de 1947.
3. Mi abuelo nació el 2 de enero de 1923.
4. Mi mejor amiga nació el 11 de julio de 1976.
5. Mi primo nació el 28 de junio de 1985.

Workout 39 .... p. 78

Exercise 1

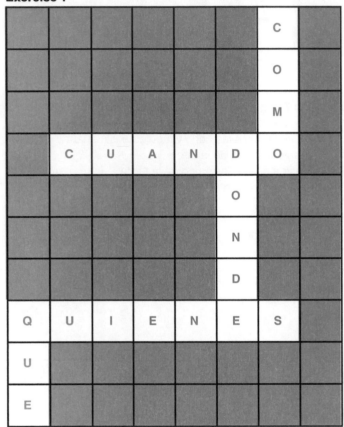

Exercise 2
1. ¿La banda se llama *Obsesión*? / ¿Se llama la banda *Obsesión*? / La banda se llama *Obsesión*, ¿verdad? / Como se llama la banda?
2. ¿Gabriela canta en la banda? / ¿Canta en la banda Gabriela? / Gabriela canta en la banda, ¿no?
3. ¿Rafael toca la guitarra? / ¿Toca la guitarra Rafael? / Rafael toca la guitarra, ¿cierto?
4. ¿A veces Aurelio toca la batería? / ¿Toca a veces la batería Aurelio? / Aurelio toca a veces la batería, ¿no?
5. ¿La banda viaja por todo el país? / ¿Viaja por todo el país la banda? / La banda viaja por todo el país, ¿cierto?

Exercise 3
1. ¿Quién es?
2. ¿Cuántos años tiene?
3. ¿Dónde estudia?

4. ¿Cómo se llama su novio?
5. ¿De dónde es su novio?
6. ¿Cuándo regresa?

Workout 40 .... p. 80

Exercise 1
1. a
2. c
3. b
4. b
5. a
6. c

Exercise 2
1. ¿Cuál de las dos tazas es suya?
2. ¿Qué acaba de pedir, señor?
3. ¿Qué bistec desea?
4. ¿Qué significa Chateaubriand?
5. ¿Cuál desea, el flan o la crema catalana?

Exercise 3
1. Correct
2. ¿Qué tan interesante es su clase? / ¿Es interesante su clase?
3. Correct
4. ¿Qué tan fáciles son las tareas? / ¿Son fáciles las tareas?
5. ¿Cuánto dura la clase? / ¿Es larga la clase?

Workout 41 .... p. 82

Exercise 1
1. tomo
2. espero
3. tomas
4. estudio
5. dibujas
6. miras

Exercise 2
1. venden
2. aprendemos
3. comprendemos
4. cree
5. leo
6. escribe

Exercise 3
1. Yo como el desayuno.
2. Tú miras la televisión.
3. Mi padre, Javier, lee el periódico.
4. Mi madre, Maite, abre las cartas.
5. Hoy nosotros recibimos una carta de tía Roberta.
6. Ella vive en Costa Rica.

222

Workout 42 .... p. 84

Exercise 1
1. yo pienso
2. ella entiende
3. nosotros mentimos
4. tú repites
5. vosotros recordáis
6. ustedes mueven

Exercise 2
1. El señor piensa.
2. Yo encuentro un anillo.
3. Los niños duermen.
4. El bebé sigue a su hermano.
5. Laura juega al baloncesto.

Workout 43 .... p. 86

Exercise 1
1. yo traigo
2. tú traes
3. usted trae
4. él trae
5. ella trae
6. nosotros/as traemos
7. vosotros/as traéis
8. ellos traen
9. ellas traen
10. ustedes traen

Exercise 2
1. traigo
2. pongo
3. doy
4. digo
5. salgo

Exercise 3
Possible answer:

Yo soy estudiante de arquitectura en la Universidad de Salamanca. Hago mis tareas por la tarde, y de noche salgo con mis amigos. Llevo ropa bonita y me mantengo muy bien. ¡Pues estoy siempre en busca de un novio/a! Conozco a mucha gente pero nunca he encontrado a mi «media naranja». Supongo que algún día le encontraré.

Workout 44 .... p. 88

Exercise 1
1. f
2. e
3. d
4. a

5. b
6. c

Exercise 2
Possible answers:
1. Vosotros os graduáis el próximo Mayo.
2. Ella envía una carta de cumpleaños a Mónica.
3. El señor Naula distribuye los folletos políticos.
4. Yo confío en el doctor Espinosa.
5. Tú destruyes los documentos secretos.

Exercise 3
1. te graduas
2. continúas
3. insinúa
4. confío
5. evalúa

Workout 45 .... p. 90

Exercise 1
1. B
2. A
3. A
4. B
5. B
6. A

Exercise 2
1. son
2. son
3. están
4. son
5. están
6. estoy

Exercise 3
1. ¡Hola! ¿Cómo estás?
2. Soy de Uruguay. ¿De dónde eres tú?
3. El restaurante está cerca de la biblioteca.
4. El concierto es en el *Palacio de la Cumbia*.
5. Es medianoche. ¿Estás cansada?

Exercise 4
Possible answer:
Me llamo Eva. *Soy* de Miami. *Soy* estudiante. Amigos, *estoy* en crisis…¡auxilio! Me *estoy* enamorando de mi profesor de biología ¡y no sé qué hacer!

Answer Key

Exercise 1
1. es
2. estás
3. están
4. estáis; sois
5. son

Exercise 2
1. Roberto ganó la lotería. Ahora Roberto es rico.
   Esta sopa de arvejas está muy rica.
2. Martín, tu carro es tan cómodo.
   Me voy a quedar aquí por un tiempo. Estoy cómoda.
3. ¡Estoy tan aburrido! No hay nada que hacer...
   Javiera, tu hermano es tan aburrido. ¿Cómo lo soportas?

Exercise 3
Possible answers:
1. Mi mejor amiga es inteligente. Está cansada por estudiar tanto.
2. Mi abuela es sensible. Está enojada conmigo porque dije una palabra mala.
3. Mi novio es amoroso. Está enamorado de mí.
4. Mi profesor favorito es bueno. Está contento porque hago siempre mis tareas.

Exercise 1
1. se despierta, despierta
2. pongo, me pongo
3. nos bañamos, bañamos

Exercise 2
1. Mamá y papá se levantan a las seis en punto.
2. Romona y yo nos despertamos a las siete.
3. Yo me lavo la cara y me cepillo los dientes.
4. Todos nos sentamos a la mesa para desayunar.
5. Yo me pongo la chaqueta antes de salir.

Exercise 3
Possible answer:
A las 6:30 me levanto. A las 7:00 me cepillo los dientes. A las 7:30 me ducho...

Exercise 1
1. c
2. f
3. a
4. e
5. d
6. b

Exercise 2
1. Mi madre se pone contenta cuando lavo los platos.
2. ¡Nos vuelves locos cuando cantas, Papá!
3. Maite quiere ser doctora.
4. Los perros se ponen deprimidos cuando salimos de casa.
5. ¿Te quieres hacer cura, Miguel? ¿Estás seguro?

Exercise 3
Possible answers:
1. Me arrepiento de no ayudar más a mis abuelos.
2. Los tiburones me asustan.
3. La última vez que me resfrié fue en enero.
4. Me quejo del frío.
5. Me parezco a mi madre.

Exercise 1
1. c
2. e
3. a
4. b
5. d

Exercise 2
1. Se habla Español
2. Se vende terreno
3. Se busca mesero
4. Se prohibe nadar
5. Se entra por la puerta de atrás

Exercise 3
1. Los sábados por la mañana se va de compras al supermercado.
2. Los sábados por la noche se reúne con los amigos.
3. Los domingos por la mañana se descansa.
4. Los domingos por la noche se hace las tareas.
5. Los domingos se acuesta temprano.

Workout 50 . . . . p. 100

Exercise 1
-er: í, iste, ió, imos, isteis, ieron
-ar: é, aste, ó, amos, asteis, aron
-ir: í, iste, ió, imos, isteis, ieron

Exercise 2
1. Max compró un póster de Nirvana.
2. Yo compré una colonia de Armani.
3. Mis hermanos compraron unos discos compactos.
4. Tú compraste un juego de computadora.
5. Tú y Bianca compraron (comprasteis) unas blusas de última moda.

Exercise 3
1. Yo pasé un semestre en Guadalajara, México.
2. Yo viví con una familia muy encantadora.
3. La familia me enseño mucho sobre la vida y la cultura mexicana.
4. Y ellos aprendieron mucho sobre mis costumbres americanas.
5. Mi novio, José, me extrañó mucho, y me escribió muchas cartas.

Exercise 4
Possible answers:
Cristóbal Colón viajó a América, Napoleón Bonaparte nació en Córsica, etc.

Workout 51 . . . . p. 102

Exercise 1
1. yo cerré
2. nosotros encontramos
3. ellos mintieron
4. él siguió
5. vosotros pensásteis
6. ustedes volvieron

Exercise 2

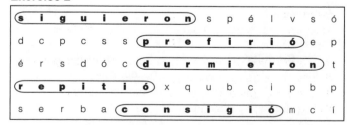

Exercise 3
Hoy me desperté tarde y pensé: «Tengo que conseguir un despertador nuevo. Este ya no sirve». Entonces, cansadísima, me vestí y fui al almacén de electrónicos. El dependiente me dijo «Tenemos dos despertadores. ¿Cuál prefiere, señorita?».

Me mostró los dos, pero sinceramente, no preferí ninguno. El dependiente, impaciente, repitió: «¿Señorita, cuál de los dos prefiere?–». Su tono de voz me molestó, entonces decidí posponer la compra. Pero cuando regresé a casa, me di cuenta de que la pila en mi despertador estaba gastada. Solo tenía que cambiarla. Entonces así conseguí un nuevo despertador.

Workout 52 . . . . p. 104

Exercise 1

Verb	*yo*	*él*	*ellos*
pedir	pedí	pidió	pidieron
caer	caí	cayó	cayeron
alcanzar	alcancé	alcanzó	alcanzaron
pagar	pagué	pagó	pagaron
empezar	empecé	empezó	empezaron

Exercise 2
1. saqué
2. empecé
3. oyó
4. concluí
5. jugué

Exercise 3
Possible answers:
1. Yo leí el periódico.
2. El profesor explicó la equación química.
3. Mi padre apagó las luces.
4. La vecina busco el gato perdido.
5. Ellos oyeron un ruido en el sótano.

Workout 53 . . . . p. 106

Exercise 1
1. ellos/ellas fueron
2. yo di
3. tú viste
4. yo produje
5. ustedes pusieron
6. yo quise

Exercise 2

			Q						
A	N	D	U	V	I	M	O	S	
			I						
			S	U	P	O			
			E		U				
					D	I	S	T	E
					I				
	V	I	S	T	E	I	S		
					R				
					O				
					N				

Exercise 3

1. Todos estuvimos en casa de los abuelos antes de las nueve.
2. Nosotros pusimos muchos regalos debajo del árbol.
3. Yo tuve que ayudar con la comida.
4. Mi tío puso música festiva.
5. Los niños fueron a dormir a las once.
6. A medianoche todos decimos ¡Feliz Navidad!

Workout 54 .... p. 108

Exercise 1

Verb	Present Tense	Preterite Tense
poder	to be able to	succeeded
conocer	to know	met
saber	to know	found out
querer	to want	tried

Exercise 2

1. Conocí al Señor Paez el año pasado en la feria.
2. No pudimos visitar a Iris ayer.
3. Eduardo quiso ir a la fiesta pero tenía demasiado trabajo.
4. Anoche supimos la verdad acerca de Marta.
5. Los niños no quisieron hacer sus tareas.

Exercise 3
Possible answers:

1. Ayer mi mejor amigo supo que su novia le estaba traicionando.
2. Mis padres no quisieron dejarme ir al concierto.
3. Conocí a mi novio/novia en un bar en Madrid.
4. Esta mañana no pude encontrar mi zapato izquierdo.
5. El mes pasado quise estudiar todas las noches.

Workout 55 .... p. 110

Exercise 1

1. nosotros hablábamos
2. él / ella servía
3. vosotros / vosotras metíais
4. tú querías
5. ellos / ellas decidían

Exercise 2

1. había
2. nadaban
3. había
4. podía
5. se preocupaban
6. vivíamos

Exercise 3
Possible answers:

1. Cuando tenías 5 años, me gustaba comer chocolates.
2. Cuando tenías 8 años, jugaba con canicas.
3. Cuando tenías 10 años, me sentía enfermo todos los lunes.
4. Cuando tenías 12 años, discutía con mis padres.

Workout 56 .... p. 112

Exercise 1

Singular	Plural
yo iba	nosotros íbamos nosotras íbamos
tú ibas	vosotros ibais vosotras ibais
él iba ella iba usted iba	ellos iban ellas iban ustedes iban

Singular	Plural
yo era	nosotros éramos
	nosotras éramos
tú eras	vosotros erais
	vosotras erais
él era	ellos eran
ella era	ellas eran
usted era	ustedes eran

Exercise 2
1. eran / era
2. iban
3. veían
4. eran / veían

Exercise 3
Possible answers:

Cuando mis abuelos eran jóvenes, la vida era diferente. Mis abuelos no iban de vacaciones porque no tenían mucho dinero. No veían tantos carros el la calle. Iban siempre en bicicleta. La vida era difícil pero más sencilla.

Workout 57 .... p. 114

Exercise 1
1. True; describes an action completed at a specific time in the past
2. False; describes a habitual or ongoing action in the past
3. False; describes an ongoing action in the past, with no definite start or end
4. True; describes an action completed at a specific time in the past
5. True; describes a series of actions completed in the past

Exercise 2
Possible answers:
1. Llegué a la biblioteca, saqué mis libros, y empecé a estudiar.
2. La película terminó a las nueve menos diez.
3. El bebé nació el once de noviembre.
4. Ayer entramos a la sala y nos sentamos.
5. El año pasado fui a Cataluña.

Exercise 3
El martes pasado me robó un ladrón. Esa mañana salí a las siete, y como siempre, compré un café y me senté a esperar el bus. El bus llegó con solo 5 minutos de retraso. Me subí al bus y le saludé al chofer. En la parada de San Jacinto, se subió un hombre vestido de negro. El señor se sentó junto a mi. Me dio una sonrisa. Yo también le di una sonrisa. El señor se bajó en la próxima parada. Y sin darme cuenta, ¡el bandido se llevó mi mochila!

Workout 58 .... p. 116

Exercise 1
1. éramos
2. vivíamos
3. íbamos
4. nos quedábamos
5. tenía
6. decidió
7. se enfadó
8. Decidimos

Exercise 2
Possible answers:
1. A menudo mi hermano mayor me molestaba.
2. Anoche mi novio me llevó a un nuevo restaurante.
3. De niño, mi primo jugaba conmigo.
4. La semana pasada el profesor nos dio un examen muy difícil.

Exercise 3
Durante mi segundo año en la universidad, conocí a Jaime en una clase de historia latinoamericana. Pronto nos hicimos muy buenos amigos. Jaime era una persona muy simpática. Le gustaba mucho organizar fiestas salvajes en su apartamento. Un sábado, los vecinos se quejaron de la música. Estábamos haciendo mucha bulla. Decidieron llamar a la policía. La policía llegó, pero en vez de arrestarnos, ¡el agente empezó a bailar con una rubia!

Workout 59 .... p. 118

Exercise 1
1. Eran
2. se apagaron
3. Puse
4. leyendo
5. fui
6. tenía
7. llovía
8. sonaban
9. Abrí
10. vi

Exercise 2
Possible answer:
Francisco llevó a María Fernanda a un restaurante muy elegante porque era su cumpleaños. Pidieron una comida de cuatro platos. María Fernanda disfrutó mucho del postre porque estaba lleno de fresas, su fruta favorita. Estaba muy contenta, y besó a su esposo. Cuando Francisco abrió la billetera para pagar la cuenta, vio que no tenía dinero. El restaurante no aceptaba tarjetas de crédito. Por eso Francisco tuvo que lavar los platos. ¡Qué cumpleaños!

Answer Key

Exercise 3
Possible answer:

Era las siete de la mañana, y el sol brillaba en el cielo. Era una mañana perfecta. Pero en el patio de la biblioteca, la bibliotecaria chillaba: ¡alguien entró a la biblioteca! ¡Alguien se robó la primera edición de *Don Quijote*!

Workout 60 .... p. 120

Exercise 1
1. Nosotros hablaremos bien el español.
2. Tú trabajarás en una oficina en el centro.
3. Rosana será una doctora famosa.

Exercise 2
1. En diez años voy a vivir en otra ciudad. / En diez años viviré en otra ciudad.
2. En cinco años tú te vas a casar. / En cinco años tú te casarás.
3. En dos años mi hermana va a tener una casa nueva./ En dos años mi hermana tendrá una casa nueva.

Exercise 3
Possible answers:

En 2100, ya no tendremos carros, sino trenes flotantes.
En 2100, el mundo será mucho más caliente.
En 2100, la comida será toda deshidratada.
En 2100, habrá solo dos partidos políticos en todo el mundo.
En 2100, la gente vivirá en casas de acero.

Workout 61 .... p. 122

Exercise 1
Possible answers:
1. A las cinco de la mañana estoy soñando con los angelitos.
2. A mediodía estoy preparando mi almuerzo.
3. A las ocho de la noche estoy tomando un té.
4. A las diez de la noche estoy estudiando economía.
5. A la una de la mañana me estoy cepillando los dientes.

Exercise 2

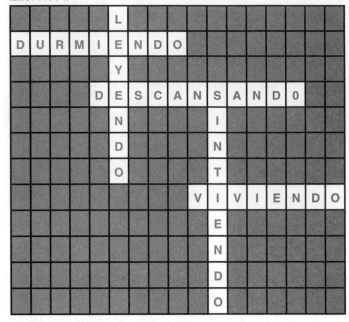

Exercise 3
1. Está quitándose los zapatos.
2. Está preparando la cena.
3. Están jugando con el perro.
4. Está leyendo el periódico.

Workout 62 .... p. 124

Exercise 1
1. hacer
2. pudiendo
3. escuchando
4. hablar
5. riendose

Exercise 2

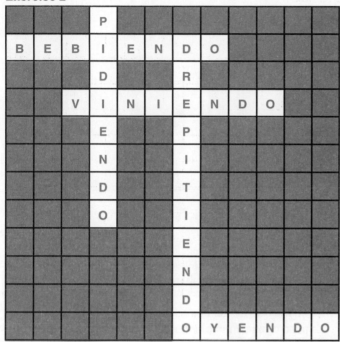

Exercise 3
1. ¡Qué interesante es ella!
2. Necesito comprar papel para escribir.
3. Tiene agua corriente.
4. Estaba parado en la mitad del cuarto.
5. Vi un florero que contenía muchas flores bellas.

Workout 63 .... p. 126

Exercise 1
1. estabas durmiendo / estuviste durmiendo
2. estabais leyendo / estuvisteis leyendo
3. estaba llorando / estuve llorando
4. estaba sintiendo / estuvo sintiendo
5. estábamos mintiendo / estuvimos mintiendo

Exercise 2
1. Los estudiantes se estaban preparando para el examen.
2. El vagabundo estaba cantando una canción de amor.
3. Maite estaba hirviendo el agua.
4. Yo estaba platicando con mi mejor amiga.
5. El gato estaba jugando con el ratón.

Exercise 3
1. estuve desvistiéndome
2. estabas escuchando
3. estaban viviendo
4. estuvo cenando
5. estábamos viendo

Workout 64 .... p. 128

Exercise 1
1. c
2. e
3. d
4. a
5. b

Exercise 2
1. escrito
2. puesto
3. visto
4. resuelto
5. abierto

Exercise 3
Possible answers:
1. He dejado de comer papas fritas.
2. He comenzado a ir al gimnasio.
3. He aprendido a meditar.
4. He hecho una sita con mi doctor.
5. He tomado vitaminas.

Workout 65 .... p. 130

Exercise 1
1. habías ido
2. había visitado
3. Ha sido
4. habías probado
5. había comido

Exercise 2
Possible answers:
1. ...había probado la comida hindú.
2. ...había estudiado todas las noches.
3. ...habían ido a España.
4. ...habías acostado.
5. ...habíamos preparado el almuerzo.

Exercise 3
Possible answers:
1. Antes de graduarme de la escuela secundaria, nunca había ido de *camping*.
2. Antes de graduarme de la escuela secundaria, nunca había buceado en el océano.
3. Antes de graduarme de la escuela secundaria, ya había montado a caballo.
4. Antes de graduarme de la escuela secundaria, había esquiado una vez.
5. Antes de graduarme de la escuela secundaria, había escalado dos montañas.

Answer Key

Exercise 1
1. habremos tomado / habrá corregido
2. habrán viajado / habrán regresado
3. habré dejado / habrás empezado

Exercise 2
1. ¿A dónde se habrán mudado José y Lucía?
2. ¿Cuánto le habrá costado ese mueble a la señora Asunción?
3. ¿Se habrán casado los hijos de Carola?
4. ¿Quién se habrá robado el dinero de la caja?
5. ¿El sobrino de Mario habrá tenido un accidente de carro?

Exercise 3
Possible answers:
1. Habré sacado buenas notas en todas mis clases.
2. Habré dejado de tomar alcohol.
3. Habré encontrado un buen trabajo.
4. Habré encontrado una novia simpática.
5. Habré dejado de decir malas palabras.

Exercise 1
1. nosotros sabríamos
2. tú vendrías
3. vosotros pensaríais
4. yo diría
5. ustedes vivirían

Exercise 2
1. gustaría
2. quisiera
3. encantaría
4. preferiría
5. diría
6. duraría
7. podríais
8. pondríamos

Exercise 3
Possible answers:
1. Yo mandaría mi currículum vitae a muchas empresas.
2. Yo hablaría con todos mis contactos.
3. Yo compraría un terno nuevo.
4. Yo iría a ferias de empleo.
5. Yo buscaría trabajo en los sitios de empleo.

Exercise 1
1. estudie
2. aprendan
3. escribamos
4. leas
5. abra

Exercise 2
1. coman
2. estudies
3. escribáis
4. hable
5. leamos

Exercise 3
1. Es muy importante que laves tus platos todas las noches.
2. Es necesario que ella hable con su madre acerca del accidente.
3. Es bueno que ayudemos a la Abuela.
4. Es malo que no lean mucho.
5. Es importante que Marta abra la ventana mientras cocina.

Exercise 1

			T									
			R									
S	E	P	A	M	O	S				J		
			D			I				U		
			U			N				E		
			Z			T	R	A	I	G	A	N
			C			A				U		
			A			I				E		
						S						

Exercise 2

	estar	ir	ser
yo	esté	vaya	sea
tú	estés	vayas	seas
él	esté	vaya	sea
nosotros	estemos	vayamos	seamos
vosotros	estéis	vayáis	seáis
ellos	estén	vayan	sean

Exercise 3

1. Mi madre dice que es importante que la gente tenga compasión para los demás.
2. Es necesario que haya una reunión de los gerentes ésta tarde.
3. La enfermera de la escuela dice que es urgente que tú vayas al médico.
4. Es mejor que mi hermano conduzca más lento.
5. Es una desventaja que nosotros no sepamos más lenguas.

Workout 70 . . . . p. 140

Exercise 1
Possible answers:

1. ...te acuestes temprano esta noche.
2. ...no hagan mucha bulla.
3. ...ordenen el arroz con pollo.
4. ...tú ganes la lotería.
5. ...el trabajo sea fácil.

Exercise 2

1. escuches
2. pierda
3. ir
4. sean
5. comprar

Exercise 3
Possible answers:

1. Ojalá lleguemos a tiempo.
2. Ojalá haya subtítulos en inglés.
3. Ojalá los cantantes sepan sus papeles.
4. Ojalá el escenario sea hermoso.
5. Ojalá nuestros asientos no estén muy lejos del escenario.

Workout 71 . . . . p. 142

Exercise 1

1. habríamos hecho
2. habrían vivido
3. habría presentado
4. habríais querido
5. habrías viajado

Exercise 2
Possible answers:

1. Yo me habría quedado con el dinero.
2. No me habría subido al tren sin un billete.
3. Yo me habría duchado con agua fría.
4. Yo no habría ido al examen.
5. Yo habría hablado con mi tía.

Exercise 3

1. No creo que hayas salido anoche con Alexandra.
2. Dudo que Jorge y Salvado hayan aprendido a bailar el tango.
3. Me alegro de que mi mejor amigo se haya casado.
4. Que bueno que te hayas ido de vacaciones a Chile.
5. Es imposible que la sopa de pescado me haya dado un tremendo dolor de barriga.

Workout 72 . . . . p. 144

Exercise 1

1. either
2. subjunctive
3. either
4. subjunctive
5. subjunctive

Exercise 2

1. Cuando terminé de estudiar, cerré mi libro.
   Cuando termine de estudiar, cerraré mi libro.
2. En cuanto acabó el concierto, el público empezó a aplaudir.
   En cuanto acabe el concierto, el público empezará a aplaudir.
3. Conduzco despacio para que mamá no se asuste.
   Conducí despacio para que mamá no se asustó.

Exercise 3

1. llegue
2. llamó
3. saluda
4. se baje
5. compre

Answer Key

Workout 73 . . . . p. 146

Exercise 1
1. estudiara
2. hablaras
3. pudiera
4. creyera
5. fueran

Exercise 2
1. Mis maestros me pedían que yo estudiara mucho.
2. Los padres de Orlando no querían que mirara mucho la televisión.
3. Buscaba amigos que fueran aventureros.
4. Esperaba que tu fueras a la fiesta.
5. Queríamos que tú pagaras la cuenta.

Exercise 3
Possible answers:
1. Mis padres querían que yo fuese doctor.
2. Mis padres dudaban que yo pudiera sacar buenas notas.
3. Mis padres recomendaban que yo estudiara todas las noches.
4. Mis padres no querían que yo me mudase a otro país al terminar mis estudios.
5. Mis padres prohibían que yo salgara a discotecas.

Workout 74 . . . . p. 148

Exercise 1
1. ella debiera / ella hubiera debido
2. ustedes estudiaran / ustedes hubieran estudiado
3. nosotros oyéramos / nosotros hubiéramos oído
4. tú durmiéras / tú hubieras dormido
5. yo viera / yo hubiera visto

Exercise 2
1. No habríamos comido el pollo si hubiéramos sabido que era tuyo.
2. No había nadie que hubiera visto el espectáculo.
3. Es posible que ellos hubieran visto la policía y por eso se escaparon.
4. No era cierto que yo hubiera ido con él al concierto.
5. Dudaba que tú hubieras dicho esa mentira.

Exercise 3
Possible answers:
1. Me dio pena que hubiera muerto la abuela de mi amiga.
2. Me alegré de que hubiera ganado la lotería.
3. Me dio mucho placer que mis amigos me hubieran hecho una fiesta.
4. Me deprimió que mi novia hubiera roto conmigo.
5. Me alegré de que hubiera viajado a El Salvador.

Workout 75 . . . . p. 150

Exercise 1
1. ¡Ojalá que puedas ir con nosotros al Museo Central!
2. Correct
3. ¡Ojalá que la entrada no cueste demasiado!
4. Correct
5. ¡Ojalá que todos nos divirtamos!

Exercise 2
1. ¡Ojalá que no llueva esta tarde!
2. ¡Ojalá que no te hubieras caído!
3. ¡Ojalá que no hubiéramos gastado tanto dinero en el centro comercial!
4. ¡Ojalá que hayas recordado de comprar huevos!
5. ¡Ojalá que sea bueno el restaurante!

Exercise 3
1. Ojalá que el avión saliera a tiempo.
2. Ojalá que consiguiera un asiento en la ventanilla.
3. Ojalá que no hubiera tanta gente.
4. Ojalá que yo pudiera llevar la navaja que me regaló mi abuelo.
5. Ojalá que mis padres se quedaran conmigo por un rato.

Workout 76 . . . . p. 152

Exercise 1
1. estará llegando a casa.
2. estará terminando.
3. estarán registrándose en la recepción del hotel.
4. estarán recogiendo sus maletas.
5. estará despertándose.

Exercise 2
Possible answers:
1. El presidente Hugo Chávez estará viajando por el país.
2. Mi profesora de español estará cenando con su familia.
3. Gloria Estefan estará escribiendo una canción.
4. Salma Hayek estará visitando a sus parientes en México.
5. Mi mejor amigo estará estudiando para los exámenes.

Exercise 3
1. Estaría disgustada porque rompí su plato favorito.
2. Se habría enfermado.
3. No habrían practicado suficiente.

4. Habría mucha neblina.

5. Habría sacado malas notas.

Workout 77 .... p. 154

Exercise 1

1. vería, hubiera entradas

2. ganara, compraría

3. pudiera, resolvería

4. dormiría, tuviera

5. nos invitarían, viniéramos

Exercise 2

1. Santiago habría tomado el metro si hubiera trabajado en la ciudad.

2. Santiago habría llevado un traje elegante si se hubiera ganado la vida en una empresa.

3. Santiago habría asistido al teatro si hubiera vivido en la ciudad.

4. Santiago habría comido en un restaurante si no hubiera tenido ganas de cocinar.

5. Santiago habría salido a una discoteca si hubiera conocido a una muchacha bonita.

Exercise 3
Possible answers:

1. ...me compraría un carro nuevo.

2. ...hubiera tenido dos hijos.

3. ...comería tortilla española todos los días.

4. ...cambiaría la política exterior.

5. ...leería muchos libros.

Workout 78 .... p. 156

Exercise 1

1. salga / no salga

2. den / no den

3. saque / no saque

4. vayan / no vayan

5. vuelva / no vuelva

Exercise 2

1. ¡Lleguen a tiempo!

2. ¡Lean la lección!

3. ¡Traigan los libros a clase!

4. ¡Estudien los verbos!

5. ¡No hablen inglés!

Exercise 3

1. Despiértese más temprano.

2. Aféitese cada mañana.

3. Vístase mejor.

4. Báñese con más frecuencia.

5. Busque un trabajo.

Workout 79 .... p. 158

Exercise 1

1. corre / no corras

2. hagamos / no hagamos

3. ven / no vengas

4. temamos / no temamos

5. pide / no pidas

Exercise 2

1. Barre el piso.

2. No planches la ropa.

3. Prepara el desayuno.

4. Pon la radio.

5. No vayas al supermercado.

Exercise 3
Possible answers:

Rompe dos huevos sobre un recipiente.

Bate los huevos con un tenedor.

Agrega sal y pimienta.

Vierte los huevos en una sartén bien caliente.

Mezcla los huevos hasta que estén listos.

Workout 80 .... p. 160

Exercise 1

1. subject of verb

2. object of a preposition

3. direct object of verb

4. subject of verb

5. object of a preposition

Exercise 2

1. No les gusta cantar.

2. Correct

3. El anucio dice: «No fumar».

4. Correct

5. Al salir, no se les olvide llevarse el paraguas.

Exercise 3

1. ...fumar, voy a masticar chicle.

2. ...disfrutar de la juventud.

3. ...ser buen estudiante, hay que estudiar.

4. ...cocinar, tengo que limpiar los platos sucios.

5. ...ser amable con los demás.

Answer Key

Exercise 1
1. Dijo que los muchachos iban al cine.
2. Dijo que Juan siempre llegaba tarde.
3. Dijo que la señora quería un café con leche.
4. Dijo que el policía había capturado al criminal.
5. Dijo que la cena estaba servida.

Exercise 2
1. Dijo que Daniel iría el jueves.
2. Correct
4. Dijo que dudaba que tu vayas.
5. Dijo que la familia había ya regresado a casa.
5. Correct

Exercise 3
Possible answers:
1. Mi hermana me dijo que había subido de peso.
2. Mi amigo me dijo que se iba a casar.
3. Mi profesor me dijo que yo había pasado el examen.
4. Mi doctor me dijo que tenía fiebre.

Exercise 1
1. «No voy al doctor».
2. «Lava los platos».
3. «Dudo que él esté (tú estés) bravo».
4. «Vamos al museo».
5. «Nos ha visto».

Exercise 2
1. e
2. d
3. c
4. a
5. b

Exercise 3
1. José le prometió a María que le vendría a buscar el próximo día a las ocho.
2. Pedro dijo que no creía que la carta llegara hasta el próximo día.
3. El padre dijo que su esposa había dado a luz la semana anterior.
4. Mi padre dijo que entonces iba al banco.
5. El policía explicó que la noche anterior un ladrón había entrado al almacén y se había robado todo el dinero.

Exercise 1
1. c
2. e
3. a
4. b
5. d

Exercise 2
1. El almuerzo para todos los niños fue preparado por mi madre.
2. Todos los paquetes fueron entregados por el cartero.
3. El edificio será construido por los trabajadores.
4. El folleto ha sido preparado por el bibliotecario.
5. El Museo Guggenheim en Bilbao fue diseñado por un arquitecto americano.

Exercise 3
1. Correct
2. Las casas fueron destruidas por el viento.
3. Las comidas fueron preparadas por el cocinero.
4. Correct
5. El hombre fue atacado por dos perros.

Exercise 1
1. sabe
2. conocemos
3. Saben
4. conozco
5. conocen

Exercise 2
Possible answers:
1. Shakira sabe cantar.
2. Penélope Cruz y Antonio Banderas no saben actuar.
3. Jennifer López no conoce a mi abuela.
4. Tú no sabes hablar dos lenguas extranjeras.
5. Yo conozco el lago Titicaca.

Exercise 3
1. c
2. b
3. a
4. c
5. c

Exercise 4
Possible answers:
1. Sé donde vive Juanita.
2. Conozco a tu hermano.
3. Sé como multiplicar.
4. Conozco la Ciudad de México.

5. Sé bailar muy bien.

6. Conozco a la profesora de inglés.

Workout 85 .... p. 170

Exercise 1
1. c
2. a
3. e
4. b
5. d

Exercise 2
1. pedí
2. preguntó
3. preguntaron
4. pidió
5. pidió

Exercise 3
1. No me pidas dinero porque no lo tengo.
2. Si quieres pagar la cuenta tienes que pedirle al camarero que te la traiga.
3. La secretaria me preguntó por qué venía.
4. Le pregunté: «¿De veras tienes diecisiete años?».
5. El empleado le pidió que complete el formulario.

Workout 86 .... p. 172

Exercise 1
1. b
2. c
3. a
4. c
5. a

Exercise 2
1. ¿Qué quisieras tomar?
2. Llevó su plato a la mesa y se sentó.
3. «¿Te podemos llevar a casa?». «No, gracias, tomaré el bus».
4. Mi padre sacó la basura.
5. Aquí está el libro del cual hablabas. Toma.

Exercise 3
1. llevar
2. tomar
3. traigo
4. saco
5. Toma

Exercise 4
Possible answer:
Tomé la basura, la **llevé** hasta la cocina, y la **saqué** al patio.

Workout 87 .... p. 174

Exercise 1
1. d
2. a
3. c
4. b

Exercise 2
1. Raquel y Claudia van a salir esta noche.
2. ¿A qué hora sale tu vuelo?
3. ¿Me puedes dejar en la esquina, por favor?
4. Dejó su maleta con el recepcionista del hotel.
5. Luis se enfadó y se fue.

Exercise 3
1. salieron
2. ir
3. salía
4. irse
5. habían ido
6. habían salido
7. dejó

Workout 88 .... p. 176

Exercise 1
1. b
2. c
3. a
4. c
5. b

Exercise 2
1. Metió la mano en el bolsillo.
2. Correct
3. Correct
4. Daniela, ¿puedes poner la televisión?
5. Ponte las botas antes de salir.

Answer Key

Exercise 3

```
. . . . . . P .
P . M . . . O .
O . E . . . N .
N . T . . . E .
G U A R D A R .
A . S . . . T .
S . . P O N E R
```

4. b
5. d

Exercise 2

1. ¿Qué piensas de la novela que leímos en clase?
2. ¿Crees en Dios?
3. Creo que está enfadado conmigo. / Pienso que está enfadado conmigo.
4. Siempre pienso en ti.
5. Magdalena no piensa que luzca bien. / Magdalena no cree que luzca bien.

Exercise 3
Possible answers:
1. Pienso viajar a América Latina.
2. Pienso que es una persona muy amable.
3. Todos los días pienso en mi mascota.
4. Pienso que es un idiota.
5. Creo en tu bondad.

Workout 89 .... p. 178

Exercise 1
1. A
2. B
3. B
4. A
5. B

Exercise 2
1. No podemos escuchar la radio porque está descompuesta.
2. Correct
3. La bandeja de vidrio está rota.
4. Se descompuso el despertador de Consuelo.
5. Correct

Exercise 3
Possible answers:
1. Rompió la muñeca de Marilú.
2. Quiso romper la taza de té de mi tía.
3. Se rompió los pantaloncitos.
4. Quiso romper la cola del gato con tijeras (¡pero no tuvo éxito!).
5. Tiró la cámara de Josefina al piso, y la cámara se descompuso.

Workout 90 .... p. 180

Exercise 1
1. c
2. e
3. a

Workout 91 .... p. 182

Exercise 1
1. gustaron
2. gustará
3. gustaría
4. gusta
5. guste

Exercise 2
1. Te gusta el vino.
2. No me gusta la música clásica
3. (A los estudiantes) no les gusta el invierno.
4. (A los chicos) les gustan los parques de atracciones.
5. (A María Fernanda) le gusta bailar en discoteca.

Exercise 3
1. A ti te gustan las películas románticas.
2. A tu hermano le gustan las películas cómicas.
3. A todos nosotros nos gustan las películas de ciencia ficción.
4. A vosotros os gustan las películas de aventura.

Exercise 4
Possible answer:
¡Hola! Me llamo Nela y soy neoyorquina. ¿Qué me gusta? Me gusta mucho bailar. También me gusta salir con mis amigos. Me gustan los muchachos respetuosos y honestos. ¿Qué no me gusta? No me gusta que me mientan. Tampoco me gusta el frío.

Workout 92 .... p. 184

Exercise 1
1. I'm very sleepy: I'm thinking about taking a nap.
2. How old is Tomás?
3. You're always in a hurry, Daniel.
4. Catalina has to clean the floor.
5. What are you afraid of, Grandpa?

Exercise 2
1. b
2. d
3. e
4. c
5. a

Exercise 3
1. tiene 99 años.
2. tienes mucho sueño
3. tienes prisa
4. Tienes sed
5. tengo que

Exercise 4

		T			T					
		I			E					
		E			N					
		N			E					
	T	E	N	G	O	M	I	E	D	O
		H			O					
		A			S					
		M			S					
		B			U					
		R			E					
T	I	E	N	E	A	Ñ	O	S		
					O					

Workout 93 .... p. 186

Exercise 1
1. Mi suegra me vuelve loca.
2. Me puse triste cuando oí las malas noticias.
3. La semilla se convirtió en un árbol hermoso.
4. Juan Romero se hizo médico.
5. No te pongas bravo, papá.

Exercise 2
1. physical change
2. change from one state to another
3. sudden change
4. change due to personal effort
5. physical change

Exercise 3
Possible answers:
1. ...oigo esta canción.
2. ...un pájaro.
3. ...mi padres pelean.
4. ...me avergüenzo.
5. ...abogado.

Workout 94 .... p. 188

Exercise 1
1. d
2. c
3. a
4. b

Exercise 2
1. Arturo faltó a clase porque perdió el bus.
2. Corroot
3. Me perdí el show de comedia de Carlos Mencía.
4. Correct
5. Correct

Exercise 3
1. se perdió
2. pierdas
3. faltan
4. extrañar
5. faltaban

Exercise 4
Possible answer:
Extraño mucho a mi mejor amiga, Cristina. El año pasado decidió mudarse a Madrid. Siempre ha querido vivir en un país extranjero, y por fin pudo alcanzar esta meta. Me hace falta su sentido del humor. También extraño su ánimo. Cristina siempre estaba de buen humor. ¡Ojalá regrese pronto!

Workout 95 .... p. 190

Exercise 1
1. d
2. e
3. b
4. a
5. c

Answer Key

Exercise 2
1. equivocado / incorrecto
2. apropiado / adecuado
3. mal
4. malo
5. Qué le pasa

Exercise 3
1. Julio, no le pegues a tu hermana. Eso es muy malo.
2. ¡Esta sopa tiene demasiada sal! La receta está incorrecta.
3. Correct
4. Jaime, yo tengo razón, y tú estás equivocado.
5. Correct

Exercise 4
Possible answers:
1. No tenía razón cuando le mentí a mi madre.
2. Me equivoqué cuando te dije que tenía la respuesta correcta.
3. Fue muy malo pegarle a mi hermanita.

Workout 96 .... p. 192

Exercise 1
1. d
2. e
3. a
4. b
5. c

Exercise 2
1. Quédate con mi chaqueta.
2. ¿Dónde queda la parada de bus más cercana?
3. Sólo nos quedan cinco días en Santo Domingo.
4. El señor quedó cojo a causa del accidente.
5. Cuando visitamos a Quito, nos quedamos con Doña Elisa y Don Fernando.

Exercise 3
Possible answers:
1. Anoche me quedé con el paraguas de Enrique.
2. Hoy me quedé con la pluma de Margarita.
3. Hace tres días qué me quedé con el libro de Susana.
4. Ayer me quedé sin dinero.
5. Anteayer nos quedamos sin leche.
6. La semana pasada nos quedamos sin jabón.

Workout 97 .... p. 194

Exercise 1
1. Hay
2. están
3. están
4. hay
5. haber
6. esté

Exercise 2
1. Correct
2. No hay suficientes fondos para cubrir su cheque, señora.
3. Correct
4. El libro que usted busca está en la Biblioteca Nacional.
5. Hay un problema grave con el programa.

Exercise 3
—Hay un problema con tu computadora portátil?
—Sí. Temo que esté descompuesta.
—Qué pena. Mira, hay un taller de reparación de computadoras cerca de mi casa. Te doy la dirección... Aquí está.
—Gracias. Está el técnico ahora?
—Creo que sí. Y si no está hoy, hay dos otros que te pueden ayudar.
—¡Qué desastre! ¡Mi ensayo es para mañana a las 8:30!

Workout 98 .... p. 196

Exercise 1
1. A
2. B
3. B
4. A
5. A

Exercise 2
1. funciona
2. andaba
3. apagó
4. se nos acabó
5. comienza

Exercise 3
1. Los niños corrían en el parque.
2. El motor dejó de funcionar.
3. Voy a arrancar el coche para que se caliente.
4. ¿Cuándo empezó la película?
5. Apaga las luces.
6. Salimos a las ocho.

Exercise 4
Possible answers:
1. Todas las tardes corro en la pista del gimnasio.
   Ando mal cuando hace mucho frío.
2. Salí a bailar con mis amigas.
   Cuando la familia me apaga, el cuarto se oscurece.
3. Trabajo 40 horas a la semana.
   Mi motor está dañado; por eso no funciono bien.

Workout 99 .... p. 198

Exercise 1
1. d
2. e
3. a
4. b
5. c

Exercise 2
1. mistreat
2. review
3. subsoil
4. antibody
5. interchange

Exercise 3
1. The automobile crashed against the motorcycle.
2. I hope we get to the championship semifinals.
3. The monkey removes the lice from her baby.
4. The psychic predicted an earthquake.
5. You need to remove the bones from the fish before eating it.

Workout 100 .... p. 200

Exercise 1
1. e
2. c
3. a
4. b
5. d

Exercise 2

Exercise 3
Possible answers:
1. gatito (gatillo), gatón (gatote)
2. mesita (mesilla), mesona (mesota)
3. librito (librillo), librote (librón)
4. cocinita (cocinilla), cocinota (cocinona)
5. arbolito (arbolcillo), arbolote (arbolón)